a second
Quilter's
companion

DOLORES A. HINSON

Author of *A Quilter's Companion*

ARCO PUBLISHING, INC.
NEW YORK

To My Mother,
the best critic a quilter and writer
ever had.

Published by Arco Publishing, Inc.
219 Park Avenue South, New York, N.Y. 10003

Library of Congress Cataloging in Publication Data

Hinson, Dolores A

  A second quilter's companion.

  Includes index.
  I. Quilting — Patterns.   2. Appliqué — Patterns.
I. Title.
TT835.H52   746.46 ′041   80-17912

ISBN 0-668-04924-3 (Library Edition)

Printed in the United States of America

Contents

To THE READER

The pattern for the quilt shown on the cover — Shoo Fly, #121 — can be ordered by mail. Send $1.50 in check or money order, postage included, with your order to:

The Stearns & Foster Company
Quilt Center
P.O. Box 15380
Cincinnati, Ohio 45215

CHAPTER ONE

General Information

Important General Information

The art of quilting is to choose a pattern for the blocks, a color combination, a method of setting the blocks together, and a border and quilting pattern that will all blend together to make a lovely and decorative quilt when finished.

Here are some general directions that will help you make just such a quilt. Remember that each pattern is the actual size you will need and can, therefore, be traced on the material you choose.

1. Choosing a pattern

If you have never made a quilt before, choose an easy pattern. I know of many hundreds of unfinished quilt tops gathering dust in attics because the quilters were too inexperienced to finish the patterns they chose. Each quilt you make will increase your expertise.

Color variations can be made by rearranging placement of light and dark shades within a block. However, if you change the placement of these blocks, you will change the pattern. I have seen quilts made with variations on a basic pattern and they are almost never successful. If you wish to experiment with variations of a pattern, place each variation in its own quilt top and study the effect before going ahead.

2. Choosing the material

After the color scheme has been determined, it is time to choose your materials. The cloth should be nearly as pure a cotton as you can find, because it is the easiest to sew by hand. Some of the new blends have stiff fibers that will not give when a needle is forced through them. This can cause the needle to break. Test the cloth by inserting the needle through two thicknesses of the material as if you were sewing. All of the cloth should be of the same weight. It should be as close to the thickness of gingham or percale fabrics as possible.

Each quilt in each size takes a different amount of cloth. Appliqué quilts take the most cloth because the background color covers the whole top and the other colors are applied to it. If the background material is cut into blocks, estimate the size of each block as ½-inch longer and wider than the pattern to provide for seam allowances. The pattern pieces are actual size and each has to have the seam allowance added when estimating the amount of cloth for each color to be used. Then using the chart in section No. 4 giving quilt sizes, estimate the amount of cloth of each color needed for the quilt top. Remember it is always better to have too much cloth than too little.

Note—A pieced quilt only needs the amount of material for the number of blocks used to make the top, adding the ½-inch of material for each seam in the block, without the background material needed for the appliqué quilt.

Choose a Dacron batt for your quilt. Dacron batts are much easier to work with than cotton batts. They allow smaller quilting stitches and do not require that the lines of quilting be as close together as the cotton batting does. Since Dacron batts wash without matting, your quilt will retain its puffiness. These batts come in crib size, single quilt size, or double quilt size. Queen and king size batts are more difficult to find, but each batt wrapper lists its exact size in inches. Two batts equaling the size of your quilt top may be used for the queen or king size quilt top.

To back your quilt you will need a length of cloth thinner than the cloth used in the top. Measure the length and width of the quilt top and get one yard more of fabric than is called for. This extra yard is needed to fasten the backing to the quilt frame. A cheap cotton sheet of the next size larger than your quilt top makes a fine quilt backing. For instance, a double bed quilt will need a queen size sheet.

3. Putting the quilt blocks together

There are four ways of putting a top together. I have shown them on Plate No. 1. In the first drawing, top left, is the simple Windmill pattern in an all-over design. In the second drawing the same basic block was turned to make a diamond. A plain block was placed between each pieced block. In the third drawing a lattice strip was placed between each pieced block. The fourth drawing shows the plain block placed between each pieced block and a border added around the outside of the top.

Study these four ways of putting a top together before you start your own quilt top. In the first drawing, the top is a simple multiple of the length and width of the single block. In the second drawing, the block must be measured across the diagonal from corner to corner and half squares will be needed to fill in the outside edge of the quilt top. Lattice strips may be two, three, or four inches wide and each lattice strip in the top must be added to the size of the single blocks when determining the size of the top. In the fourth drawing, the size of the border multiplied by two must be added to the overall size of the quilt top.

4. Determining the size of the top

Do not make your quilt too small. With today's central heating we usually do not need quilts for warmth. They are used as beautiful bedspreads. Since mattress sizes are standard, quilt sizes can also be standardized.

crib size	—3 ft by 4 ft
throw size	—4 ft by 6 ft
twin bed size	—6 ft by 8 ft
double bed size	—7 ft by 8 ft
	8 ft by 8 ft
queen bed size	—9 ft by 8 ft
king bed size	—10 ft by 9 ft

1.

2.

3.

4.

Note that in the king and queen bed sizes the quilts are wider than they are long. Your quilts can be smaller or larger (by six inches or less) than these measurements.

5. Cutting your patterns

To begin work on your quilt, you will need cutting patterns. The patterns in this book are all made in finished-size — this means that the patterns do *not* have the seam allowance included.

> a. Trace off the patterns on tissue paper
> b. Cut out the tissue paper patterns
> c. Trace the tissue paper patterns onto cardboard
> d. Mark the name of the pattern and piece number on each pattern piece

Note — Cardboard wears down with use. Cut at least three sets of patterns so the size will remain the same.

6. Cutting the cloth

Lay the pattern on the correct color of cloth. Place it in one corner, one-quarter of an inch from each edge, excluding the selvage edge. Draw a firm pencil line around the edge of the pattern. On light colored cloth use a No. 2 soft pencil. For dark colors, use a white china marker pencil, which may be bought at a stationery store. Move the pattern ½-inch and trace the outline of the pattern again. Continue until all of the patterns needing that particular material have been traced at ½-inch intervals. *Cut the cloth between the traced lines so ¼-inch is left on the edge of each piece of cloth to allow for the seam.*

Do not try to sew the cloth pieces together by sewing inside the penciled lines. The pieces will not fit nor will they make a square. Sew the pieces together *along the penciled lines.*

For appliqué patterns mark the pencil lines on the face of the cloth. For pieced patterns mark the pencil lines on the reverse side of the cloth. This is so the pencil lines will be on the correct side of the cloth to serve as a guide for sewing. Be very sure to add ¼-inch seam allowance when cutting the quilt blocks. A 12-inch-square, finished-size quilt block should be cut 12½ inches square or with ¼-inch seam allowance on all four sizes.

In making patterns it is often impossible to print the full size of a very large pattern piece. This is true of all patterns whether meant for dressmaking, furniture, quilts, or whatever. To indicate that a piece with two identical sides can be cut from half of the pattern, a dotted line indicates the center of the piece. To use this type of pattern on cloth, fold the unused cloth in half. Place the dotted line of the pattern along the fold and cut out the pattern as if the cloth were not folded. When the cut-out cloth is opened the piece will be complete. If two sides of the pattern have dotted lines, the cloth must be folded in half lengthwise and then across the width, with the pattern placed in the corner so the dotted lines are on the

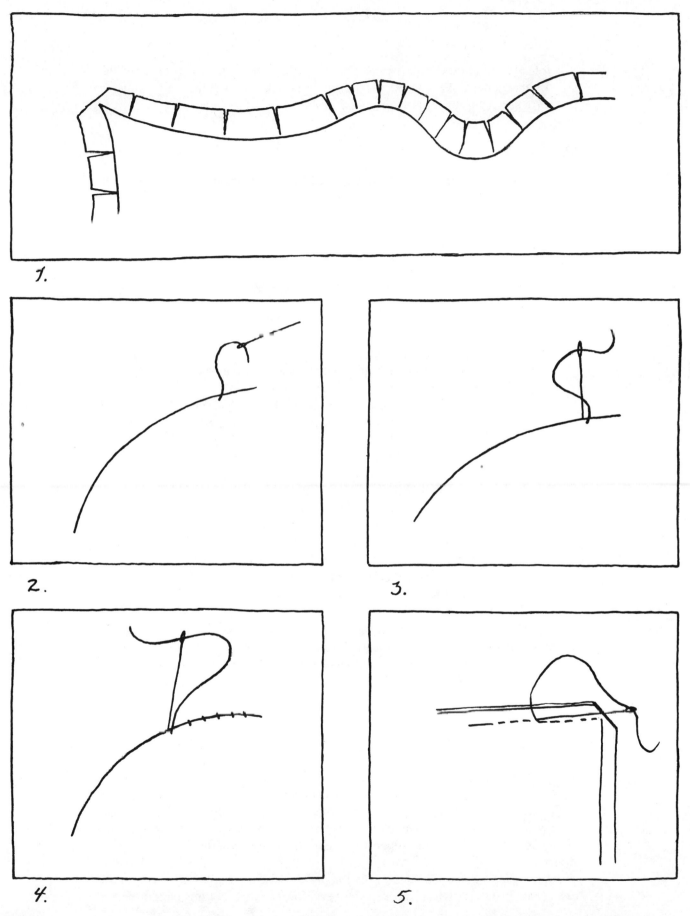

1.

2.

3.

4.

5.

two folds. Cut. This will give a piece with four identical corners, four times the size of the pattern. Follow all the other directions for marking and cutting a pattern when using patterns with dotted lines.

7.   Making an appliqué quilt block

Assemble all of the cut cloth pieces needed to make one complete block.
Lay the background square to one side.
Ready the appliqué pieces by clipping excess material in the seam allowance away from all points. Clip the seam allowance nearly to the penciled line on all curves (see Plate No. 2). This will allow you to turn the seam allowance under smoothly all the way around.
Baste the seam allowance under on all of the pieces.

> a.   Pin all of the appliqué pieces to the background cloth and make sure they are in the correct place, ready for sewing. Pieces that must touch should touch all along the side seams.
>
> b.   Start the needle from the back and make a blind stitch (see Plate No. 2). To make a blind stitch, put your needle through both the background cloth and the exact edge of the appliqué piece as near to being in the fold as you can manage. Put the needle back down through the background material right beside the place where your needle came out through the appliqué piece. The next stitch should be ¼-inch or less from the first stitch. When done correctly and neatly a blind stitch hardly shows at all.

Note—Do not sew the appliqué to the background cloth with embroidery stitches without first sewing the edges down with the blind stitch. This is very important because embroidery floss is no longer made with a tight twist, so it is not as strong as thread. It will wear out very fast and leave your appliqué pieces loose to ravel or tear away from the quilting stitches or background material.

8.   Making a pieced quilt block

Assemble all of the cut cloth pieces needed to make one block of your quilt.
Sew the pieces together along the pencil lines.
Clip the cloth of the seam allowance almost to the pencil line on all curves and cut away some of the excess cloth in the seam allowance from all the points, nearly to the penciled line. Open the seam allowance and flatten it with your fingers.
Even the most complicated patterns can be broken down into small, easily sewn units. For instance, I have broken the very complicated-looking pattern called

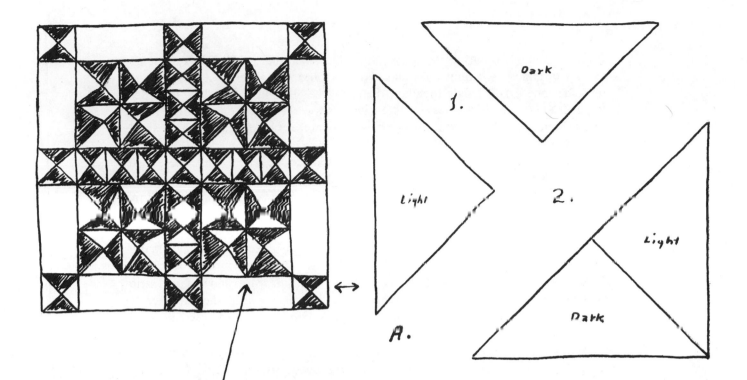

A.

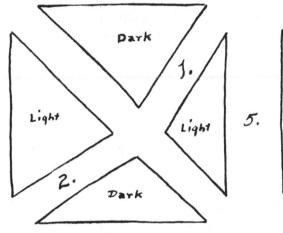

B.

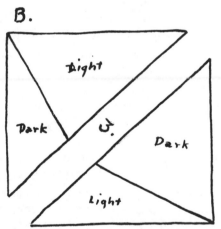

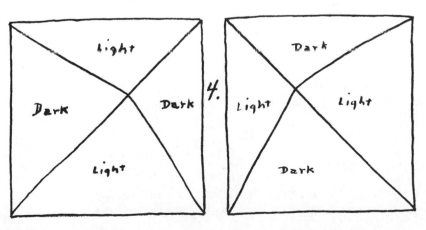

Constellation down into its two basic units. The small unit marked *A* is made up of four triangles, two light ones and two dark ones (see Plate No. 3). Sew one light and one dark triangle together, then sew the other light and dark triangles together (1); then sew the two double triangles together along one straight seam (2), completing the unit. Make 19 of these units for one block and set them aside (see Plate No. 3).

Next, make four of the *B* units. There are 16 pieces in each *B* unit; these also can be broken down into four smaller units with two light and two dark pieces in each. *Always make a straight seam without a bend in it when possible.* To follow this last rule, put the dark and the light pieces together (1) and then the dark and light pieces marked (2) together. Sew the seam marked (3). Do this four times. Sew the two small units together on the seam marked (4) and then (5) and finally sew the whole unit on the long seam marked (6).

Assemble the units in order. Sew three of the *A* units in a strip and sew this strip between two of the *B* units. Place this aside and repeat, sewing another three *A* units between two *B* units. Sew seven *A* units into a strip and sew this strip between the two sections you have already completed. You now have the center of the block finished. Sew two strips of an *A* unit and two No. 4 white strips from the pattern. Sew these strips to the top and the bottom of the center. Make two more strips of three of the *A* units and two No. 4 white strips and sew these to the two sides of the center, finishing your block.

Finish all the blocks for the quilt top first before sewing them together. In this way the colors in a scrap quilt may be arranged so they are pleasing. I have seen quilts where a person did not have quite enough material to finish a quilt top with the same colors and made a few blocks with a different color combination. The last row of the top was finished with these blocks and a quilt that could have been beautiful was made ugly. However, if these different color blocks had been carefully arranged to form a balanced pattern, the quilt could still have been lovely.

To sew a pieced quilt, take two adjoining sections of a block and place them face to face. Stick a pin through the left corner on the pencil line and test whether or not the two pencil lines are together. If they are not, adjust them until they are exactly together. Sew along the line using a running stitch and make the smallest stitches you can manage (see 5, Plate No. 2). Use No. 40 or 50 mercerized cotton thread and size No. 7 or 8 "quilting" or "betweens" needles for your work. Keep practicing until you can make small, even stitches. A stitch and the interval between stitches should be of exactly the same length.

9. Making a half-pieced, half-appliquéd quilt

Reread sections 7 and 8 very carefully. The description with the pattern will tell you which section of the block is pieced and which section is appliquéd. Work the pieced section first.

10. Putting your top together

When all of the blocks (plain and either pieced or appliquéd) are finished, lay them out in order on a large surface or floor. Place each block, lattice strip, and border in its position. Now stand back and look at the results. If you do not like something, now is the time to change it, especially in scrap quilts. Now is the time to check whether several blocks of the same color are too close together. Study the arrangement carefully until you are satisfied with the quilt top.

Starting with the top left-hand corner, take up each row of blocks with the left block on top. Pin a paper with the number of the row on each row of blocks. Carefully sew each block of the first row together. When you have sewn each of the blocks together into rows, sew each of the rows together in numerical order. Be sure each corner is exactly together with the corners of the next row.

11. Marking your quilt

There are two ways of marking a quilt. Most patterns can be traced onto the cloth with a No. 2 (soft) pencil. For hard or complicated patterns you may obtain an iron-on pencil from most needlework supply houses.

To mark the entire quilt top with one pattern in the old-fashioned way where fans, shells, diamonds, or squares are used in an all-over design, reverse the quilt in the frame and mark the pattern on the backing of the quilt so the pattern on the top does not confuse you.

If you decide to use one of the fancy patterns in the clear areas of the quilt, you must outline the appliqué or all the pieces in the pieced sections. Fit your fancy patterns into the exact center of the clear spaces and make sure they are the correct size to fill the space without crowding it.

Read section 5 on making a pattern before you make your quilting patterns. A quilting pattern is made exactly like a quilt top pattern.

To use the iron-on pencil, trace the pattern onto tissue paper with a regular pencil and then retrace the pattern with the iron-on pencil. Reverse your paper pattern and, using a slightly hot iron, transfer the pattern to the cloth. After you have finished quilting the quilt and have bound the edges, you will have to wash the quilt to remove the water-soluble, iron-on pencil markings. If you have used Dacron as your quilt filler, washing the quilt will not hurt its looks. It will still look brand-new after washing.

12. Putting your quilt in the frame

There are three basic types of frames for quilting.

1. The large room-size frame is made with four 1 × 2-inch boards about ten feet long (12 feet long for king-size quilts). They may be held in position by four "C" clamps, one for each corner of the frame. The frame may be held up by four chairs, four stands, small wooden horses, or by fastening it to four pulleys attached to the ceiling. However your frame is set up, two of the boards must be two feet longer than the side measurement of your quilt and the other two boards must be two feet longer than the length of your quilt. (See Plate No. 4.)

2. A table-size frame is made with two ten foot long dowels and two side stands which hold the dowels about two feet apart. If you do not have an entire large room to devote to a quilting frame, this table frame is the next best solution.

3. A lap frame is a large, oval, wooden hoop much like a very large embroidery hoop. If you wish to carry your quilting with you from room to room

or even away from your home, a lap frame is the solution.

To fix a regular frame or a table frame for quilting, there is some work to be done. Take an old, worn out sheet and tear it across the center width. Wrap one piece of the cloth around each of the two end boards of the regular frame or around each dowel of the table frame. One edge of the cloth can be fastened to the board by thumb tacks. Then wrap the material loosely around the board and sew the outer edge down. This is so that the quilt can be attached to the frame. If you use tacks to attach the quilt, it could tear.

To place the quilt in the regular or table frames, baste one end of the backing to one of the end boards wrapped with the sheet. Place the filler smoothly on this backing. Spread the top of the quilt over the filler smoothly and stretch all three layers tautly. On the regular frame, pin holding strips to the quilt, loop them around the board, and pin again to the quilt (see 2, Plate No. 4). This will hold the quilt stretched along the two sides. On the table frame, roll the dowel and quilt smoothly. When just enough of the end of the quilt is left to stretch the width of the table, baste the other end to the front dowel.

After basting the end of the quilt to the front of the regular frame, make sure the four boards are stretched tautly and all four corners are fastened securely. Baste the top and filler around the edge to the backing.

To fix a quilt for quilting in a lap frame, lay the backing on the floor or a very large table and spread the filler and top smoothly over it. Baste all the way around the outside of the top, through all three layers. Then baste the width and length of the quilt with lines of stitches about six inches apart. Be sure to baste the entire quilt so the three layers cannot slide out of position. Then place the hoop in the center of the quilt and begin quilting. When the area of the hoop has been filled, move the hoop to an adjoining area and continue.

13.   Binding your quilt

Cut strips of cloth 1½-inches wide and sew them to the front edge of your quilt ¼-inch from the edge. If your quilt has rounded or projecting edges, such as those on the Double Wedding Ring quilt, cut these strips on the bias. Fold the strip over the raw edge of the quilt and fold ¼-inch of the strip under. Sew this to the back edge of the quilt with a blind stitch (see Section 7).

Do not use a sewing machine to sew the quilt binding. It is the first place that wears on a quilt and you will need to replace this binding about every fifteen years if your quilt is in regular use.

14.   Washing your quilt

Do not dry-clean any but the oldest and most fragile quilts. Wash the quilt in warm water and mild detergent in the washing machine. It will not hurt the quilt. Tumble dry in a dryer with the setting on warm. Remove the quilt just before it is entirely dry. The greatest danger to the life of a quilt is overdrying the cloth, which weakens it.

If you do not have access to a dryer, hang the quilt between two lines so it forms a U. *Never use an iron on a quilt.* The beauty of a quilt is in the puffiness, which ironing can completely destroy.

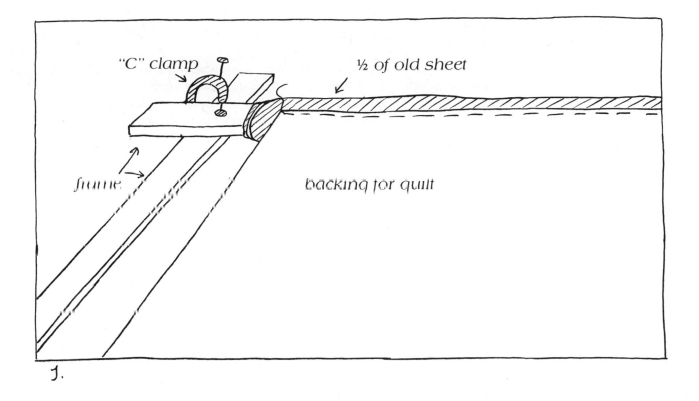

"C" clamp

½ of old sheet

frame

backing for quilt

1.

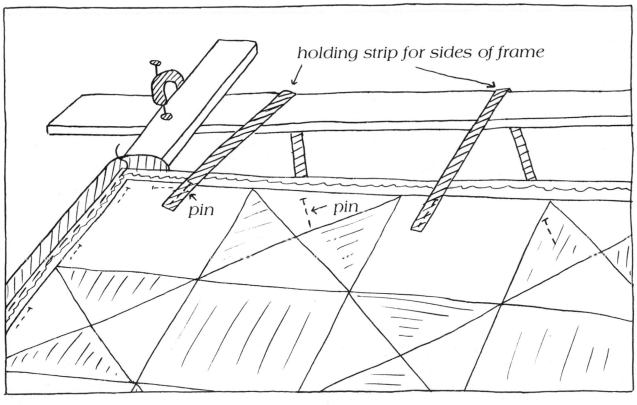

holding strip for sides of frame

pin

pin

2.

11

15. Maintaining your quilt

Quilts should be treated just like any fine linens. Wash them when they become soiled or dusty. A most important point is never to fold a quilt twice on the same fold marks. A quilt can wear badly along fold marks. If the quilt is folded in fourths the first time, it should be folded in thirds the next time. Remember, a quilt should last anywhere from twenty-five to three hundred years, according to the care taken of it.

CHAPTER TWO

Appliqué Quilts

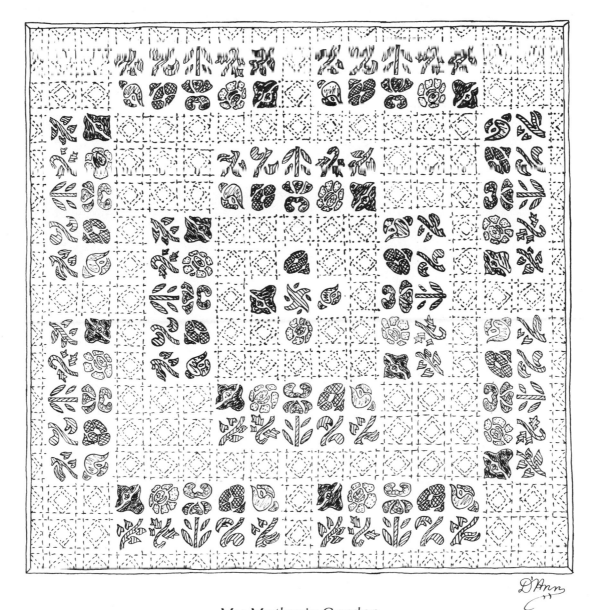

My Mother's Garden

My Mother's Garden

One of the nearly lost arts of quilting is reverse appliqué. I have designed an easy pattern which makes a pretty quilt.

Cut out 125 six-inch square blocks, finished-sized. Take two blocks and draw the pattern for one of the flowers on one and the matching leaves on the other. Cut the inside of the patterns out, leaving a ¼-inch seam allowance inside each line. Clip this seam allowance on all curves almost to the pencil line so it will turn under smoothly. Place a light green square of exactly six inches under the leaf and stem block and a light, plain-colored square under the flower; baste them in place. Appliqué the white to the colored square on the pencil lines. Make each of the flowers in the quilt a different color. The lilies should be pink or rose, the daisies a yellow, the irises a lavender, the morning glories a shade of blue, and the calla lilies a pale orange or melon color. After the appliquéing on a block is finished, cut the excess material away from the colored background square about ¼-inch from the appliqué stitches. For the white background of the quilt cut more six-inch, finished-size white blocks and mark them with the quilting pattern shown on the last pattern. The drawing of the finished quilt top design is for a double bed quilt. A beginner could make this quilt if she is careful.

Please read Section 7 in Chapter One on General Information before starting any work on this pattern. Always add one-quarter inch seam allowance to all patterns before cutting them from the cloth. Finished-size means tracing the block, adding the additional one-quarter inch seam allowance.

LILY

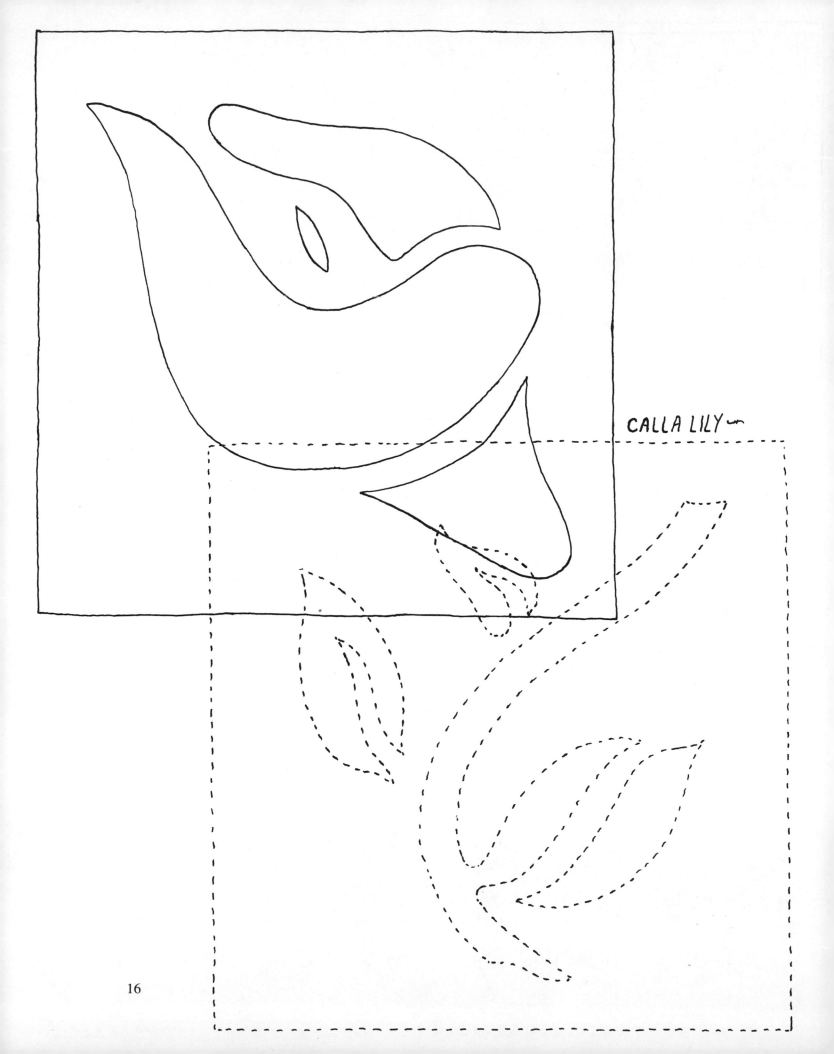

CALLA LILY

16

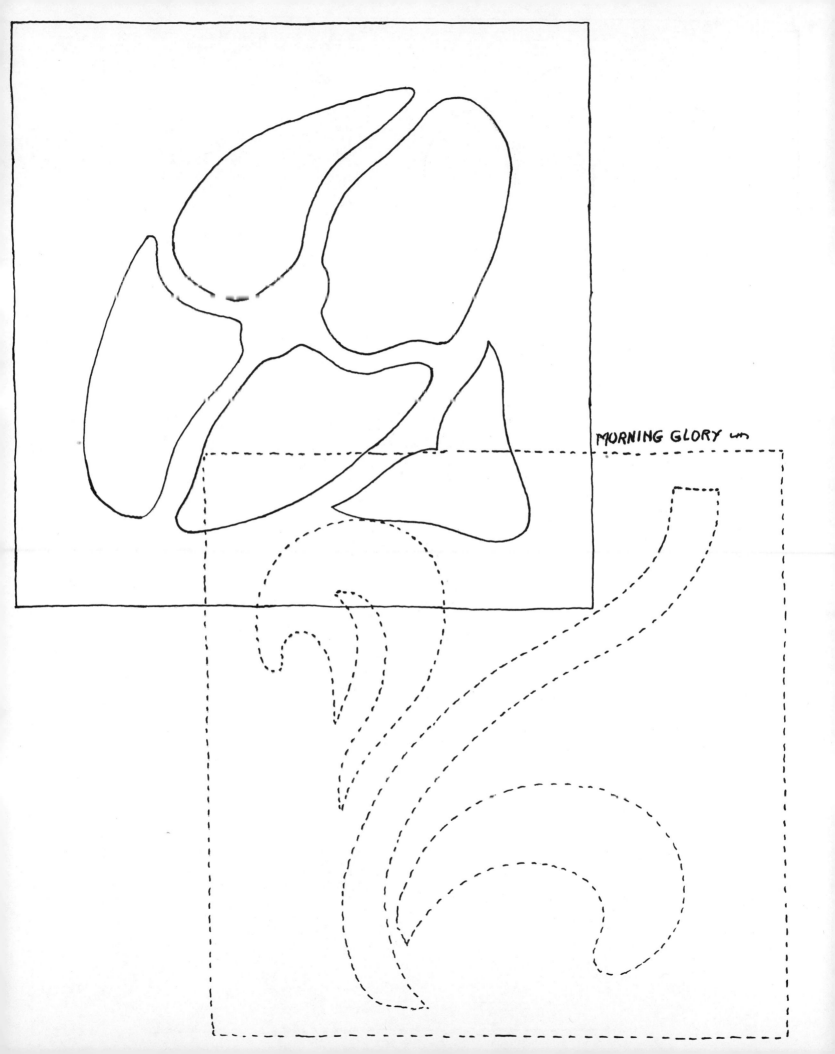

MORNING GLORY um

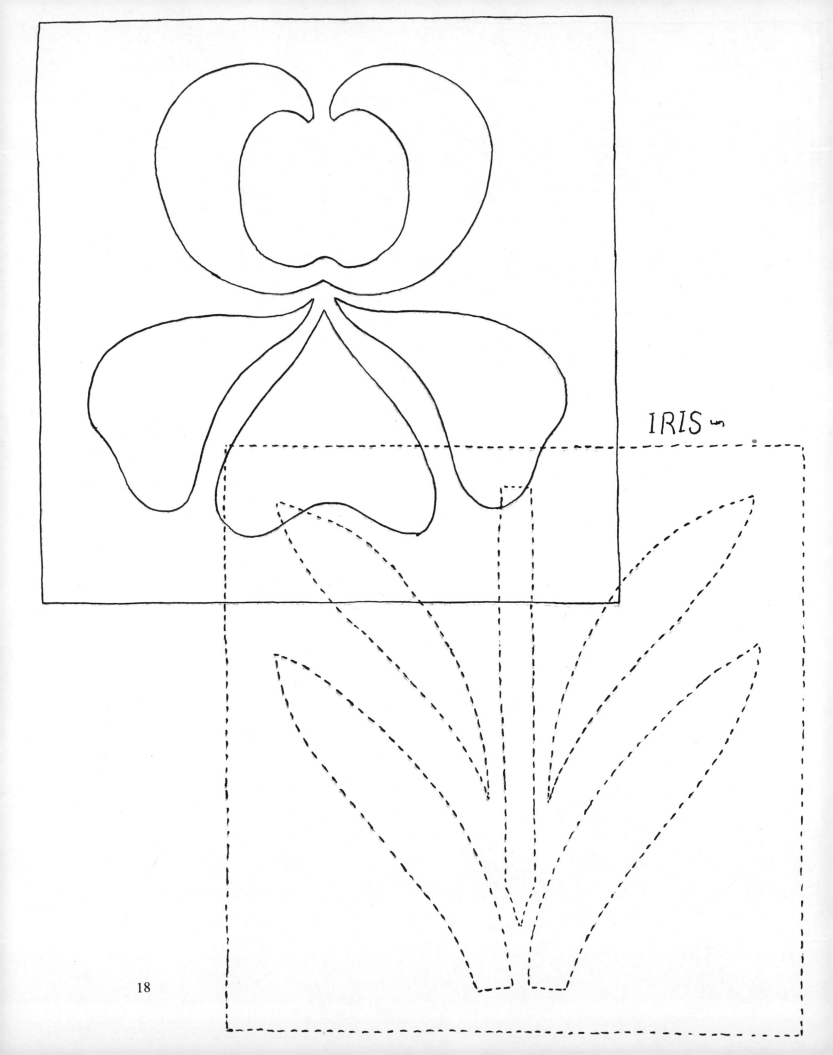

IRIS

18

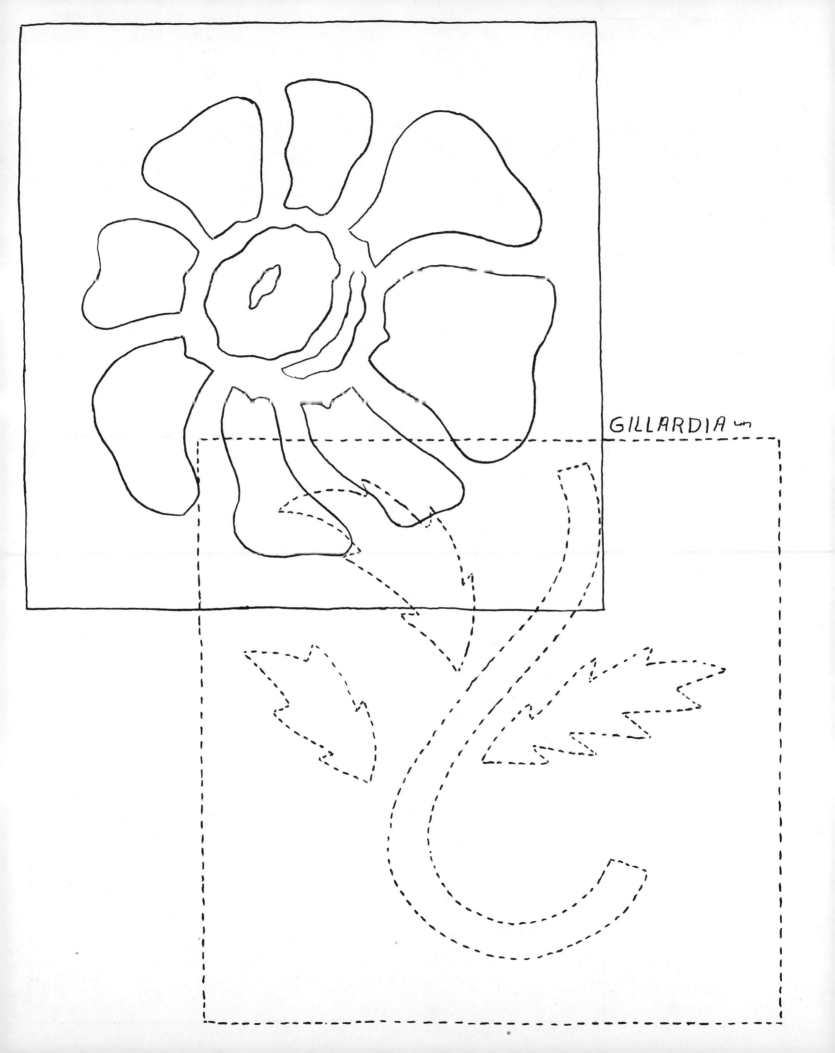

GILLARDIA

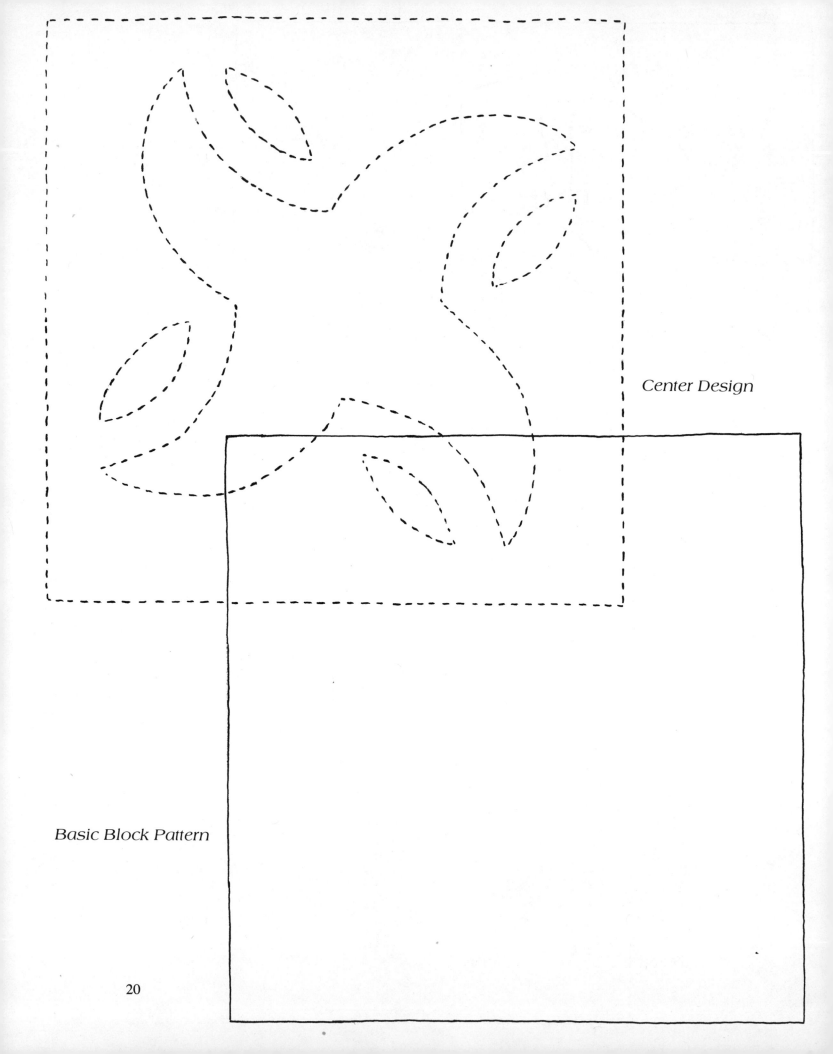

Center Design

Basic Block Pattern

20

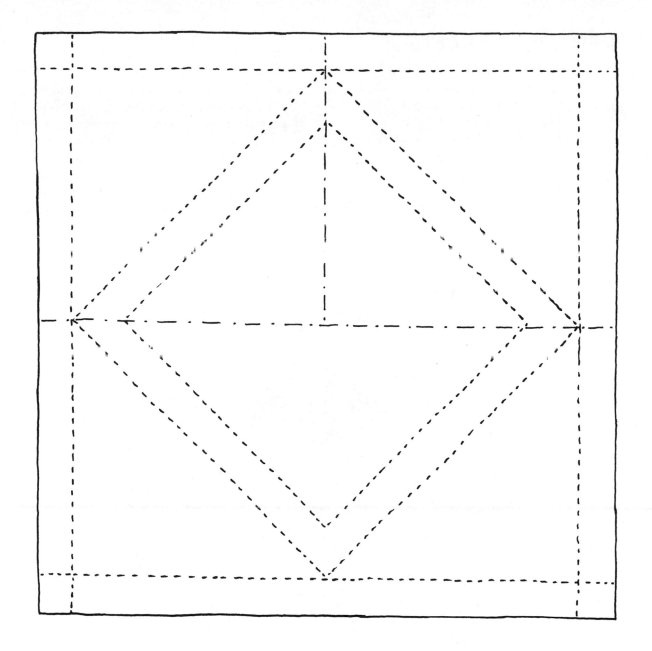

Basic Quilting Pattern (for plain blocks)

Rainbow Flowers

This is an original pattern which was designed just for the beginning quilter. The pattern has only three pieces. Number 1 is the background square which should be some shade of white or ecru. The flower (No. 2) should be a scrap of either a small print or a plain color, and each flower may be different. All the leaf and stem patterns (No. 3) should be the same shade of green. Appliqué a flower to one six-inch square, finished-size block and a stem to another. Leave some squares without appliqué.

I have shown one way to put this pattern together but you might lay the squares out on a large surface before sewing them together and see if you cannot devise some other way of putting the top together. If you leave large white areas in your quilt, you could use the flower and stem patterns for quilting patterns. Otherwise, quilt around each appliqué and around each square, then quilt an X across each plain square.

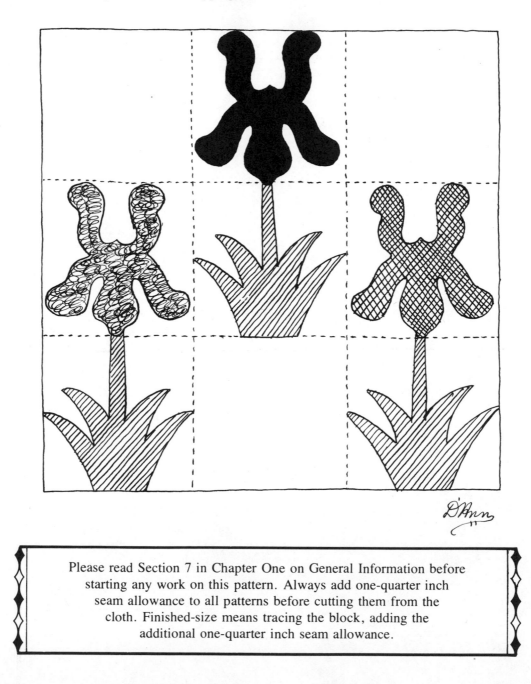

Please read Section 7 in Chapter One on General Information before starting any work on this pattern. Always add one-quarter inch seam allowance to all patterns before cutting them from the cloth. Finished-size means tracing the block, adding the additional one-quarter inch seam allowance.

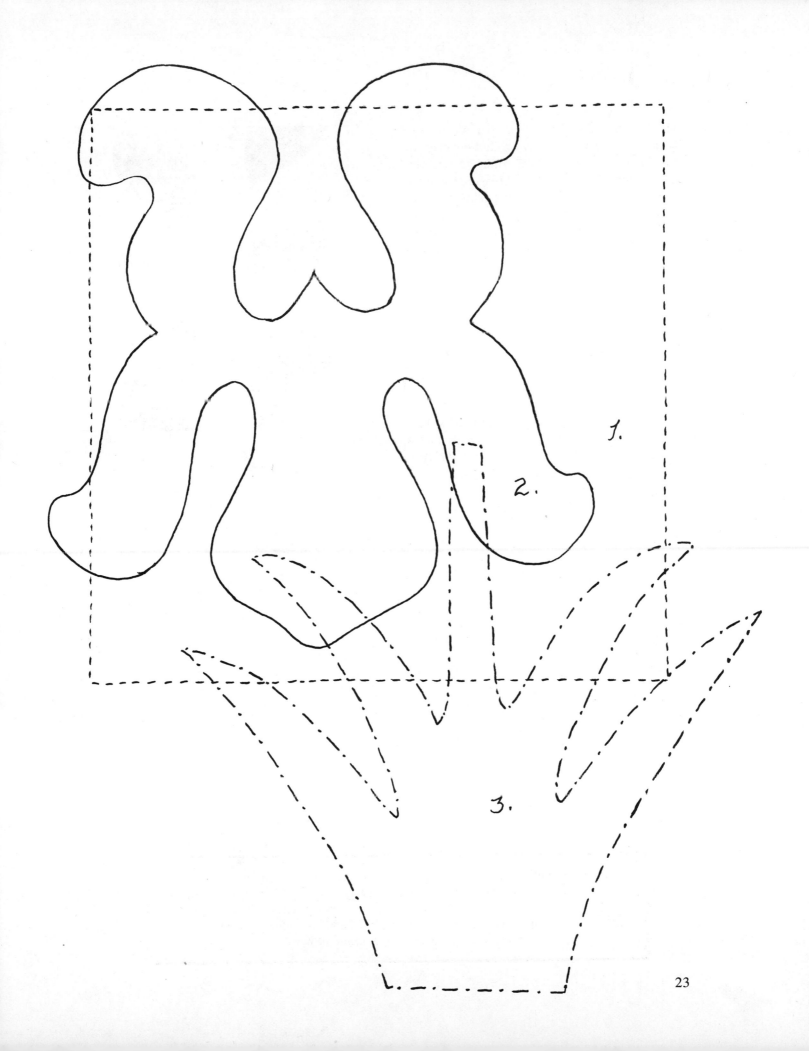

1.

2.

3.

23

Cloister Walk

This is an original quilt pattern which is a little unusual. The pattern is worked on strips of white cloth, two feet wide, finished-size, by eight feet long, finished-size. Measure the cloth and make a pencil line the length of the strip four inches from each finish edge. Then mark two more lines six inches inside those first lines. This will give you two strips six inches wide and three strips four inches wide. The appliqué is worked down the two six-inch strips. Tip the piece of appliqué so the two edges touch the penciled lines of the six-inch strip. Appliqué the pieces one at a time until you have the two six-inch wide strips completely filled.

The colors for this quilt should be a plain color and a matching print on each double strip. I have a twin pair of quilts with a green, yellow, and orange flowered print which is matched with a plain yellow for the four outside strips and a plain orange for the two middle strips. For twin beds each quilt takes three double strips; a double bed will need four double strips. This is not a hard pattern but it does take patience to work.

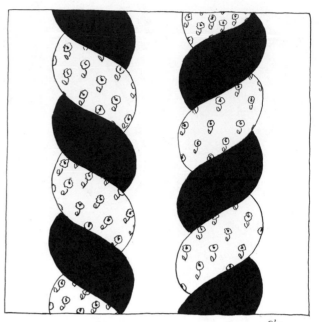

My Stars!!!

This pattern is an original one made for appliqué and embroidery. Notice that the diamonds do not touch in the center but are about ¼-inch apart around the center point of the block. The embroidered lines or rays *do* cross the center point between the separated diamonds. You may make this pattern with plain blue diamonds, but it is prettier done in a small blue print or checked material. When laying the cut diamonds on the block, mark the block with a tiny dot in the exact center. Place the diamonds in a ring around this

dot ⅛-inch from the dot. Measure the distance between the side points of the diamonds and make sure the interval between the diamonds is exactly the same size all the way around the circle. A dark gold embroidery floss shows up best for this pattern. Use a light pencil stroke and a ruler to draw the lines or rays. The same kind of quilting pattern that is used for a Dresden Plate quilt looks attractive with this pattern. This is a very easy pattern. It was drawn for a 12-inch square block, finished size.

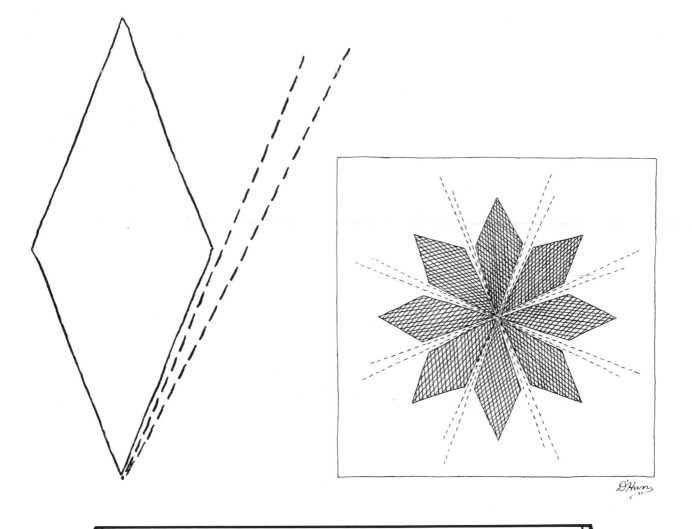

Please read Section 7 in Chapter One on General Information before starting any work on this pattern. Always add one-quarter inch seam allowance to all patterns before cutting them from the cloth. Finished-size means tracing the block, adding the additional one-quarter inch seam allowance.

The Aquatic Gardens

Have you ever seen a water garden with water lilies and their leaves floating on the blue water, sunlight glancing off the waves? It is a lovely sight and so is this quilt. Cut a medium blue block 14 inches square, finished-size. Appliqué the rest of the motifs in place on it. The water lilies may be pale orchid, white, pink, or rose. The leaves and stems should be pastel green, and the rays in the corners yellow. Form a square in the center of the block with No. 6 placed as shown by the dotted lines. Use four No. 6 pieces for the sides of the square. The stems, four No. 5 pieces, are arranged in the four corners of the center square. Place a No. 3 circle of yellow at the top of each No. 5 stem. Make a water lily from one No. 1 center petal and two No. 2 petals (one No. 2 petal is cut with the pattern reversed). These flowers are appliquéd at the top of the circle with the point of the center petal in the center of the side of the block. One No. 4 leaf should be placed on either side of the center circle. One leaf should be cut reversed. Appliqué the yellow corner diamonds in each corner so the leaf tips touch the end of the diamond. It would be best to baste all the elements of this block in place before appliquéing them. The quilt top should be put together with 14- by 3-inch medium blue lattice strips and three-inch yellow corner squares between each block. This pattern is not too hard if you are very careful in your work.

Please read Section 7 in Chapter One on General Information before starting any work on this pattern. Always add one-quarter inch seam allowance to all patterns before cutting them from the cloth. Finished-size means tracing the block, adding the additional one-quarter inch seam allowance.

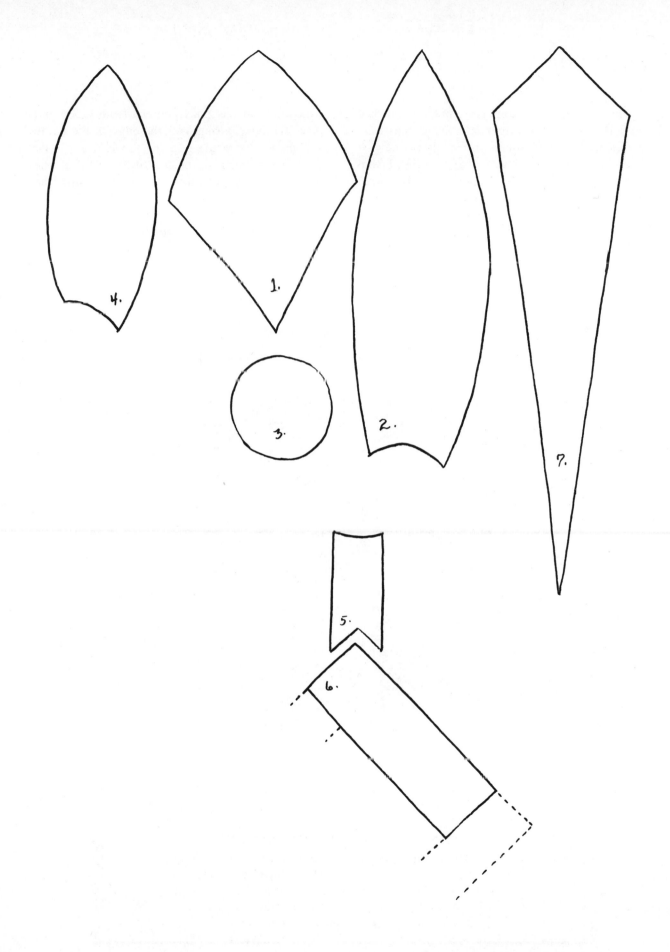

Charlotte's Rose

This is a difficult appliqué, but the finished quilt is worth the extra effort. The patterns are drawn for 12-inch square, finished-size blocks. The rose is in three shades of rose, pink, lavender, or blue. The leaves are green and the corner diamonds are yellow. Choose only one color for all the roses in a single quilt.

To assemble the design on a block, first baste the four yellow diamonds in the four corners. Baste the outside curved edges of the eight No. 2 petals and No. 4 leaves in place, touching the point of the corner diamonds. Place the No. 5 dark circle in the exact center of the block and place the No. 3a ring over the edge of the circle and under the inside edge of the No. 2 petals. Baste everything in place. Stuff each of the No. 2 petals lightly with filler before basting the inside edge.

Finish the block by appliquéing everything in place. The pattern marked No. 3 is the quilting pattern for ring No. 3a. Draw the lines lightly with a pencil. A small pieced border may be used with this pattern.

Please read Section 7 in Chapter One on General Information before starting any work on this pattern. Always add one-quarter inch seam allowance to all patterns before cutting them from the cloth. Finished-size means tracing the block, adding the additional one-quarter inch seam allowance.

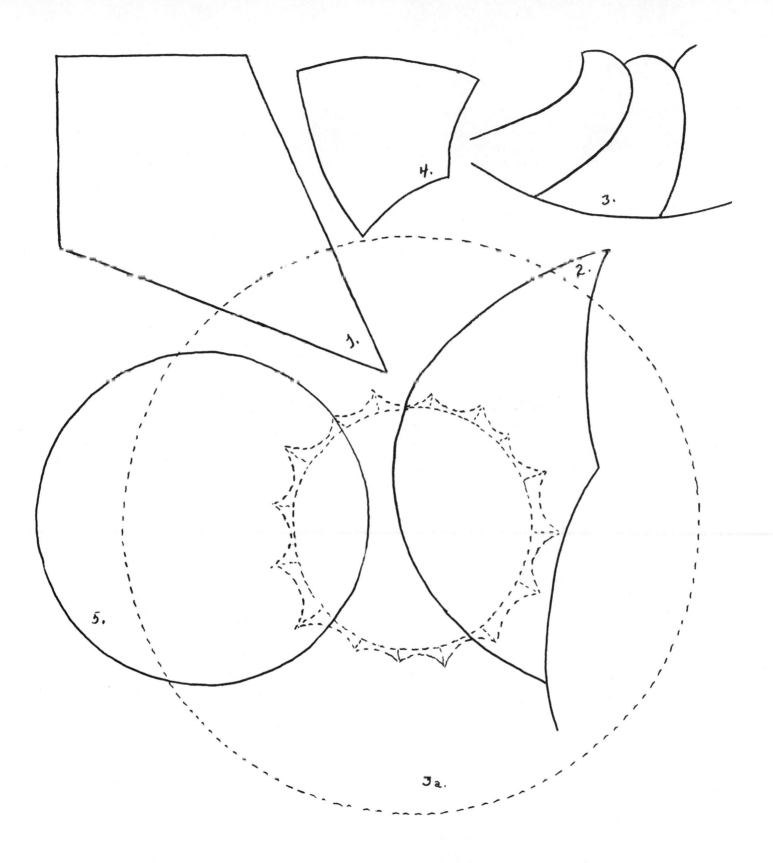

Lily of the Day

Find a pretty, soft orange or melon print to make the lilies for this quilt. With green leaves on a white background it makes a striking quilt. I placed four 12-inch square, finished-size blocks together with the flowers pointing to the center and the leaves in the outer corners, forming a wreath. Then I placed a four-inch wide white lattice strip between the wreaths to set them off. This would also be pretty with plain blocks set between single appliquéd blocks. Use a plain white border for the quilt. This could be a beginner's first quilt.

Please read Section 7 in Chapter One on General Information before starting any work on this pattern. Always add one-quarter inch seam allowance to all patterns before cutting them from the cloth. Finished-size means tracing the block, adding the additional one-quarter inch seam allowance.

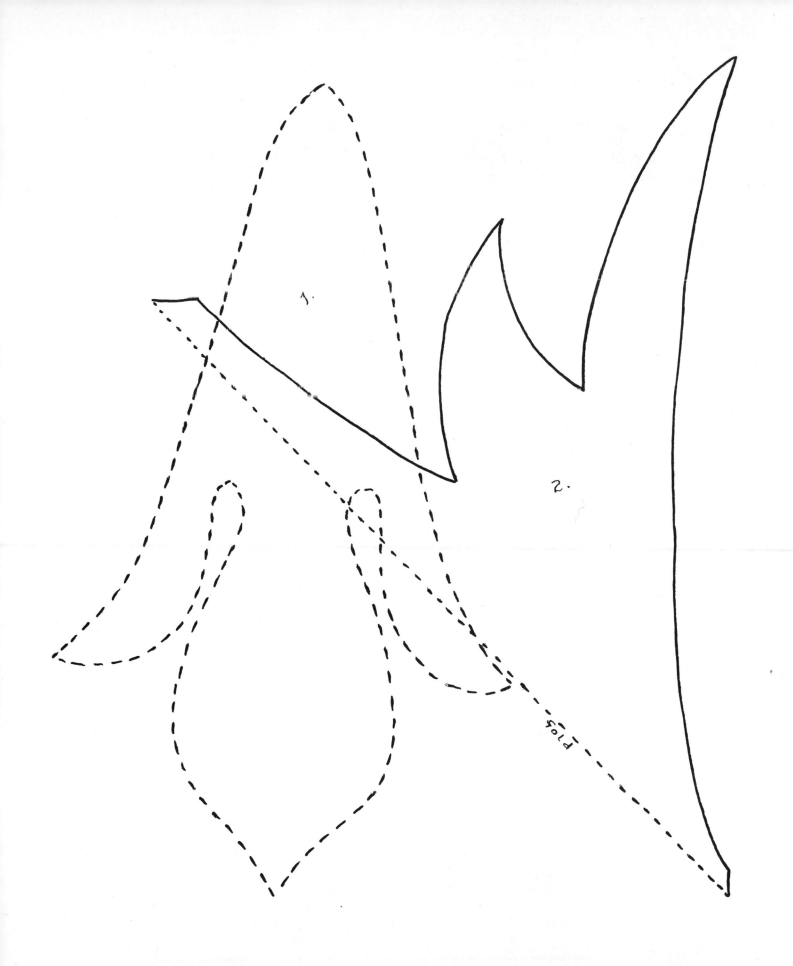

1.

2.

fold

31

Window Garden

The white background blocks are 15 inches square, finished-size. Place the flower pots as shown in the drawing and baste them first before appliquéing them in place. Place one or two leaves in the pots as shown in the drawing. This quilt should be made with a plain square between the appliquéd ones, and it may have a border if you wish. In the drawing two of the flowers are pink, two are rose, two are blue, and the last two are yellow. This would make a lovely scrap quilt. The pots should be a light shade of brown or brownish-red. Cut the leaves along the dotted lines, as shown. This is a fairly easy pattern.

Please read Section 7 in Chapter One on General Information before starting any work on this pattern. Always add one-quarter inch seam allowance to all patterns before cutting them from the cloth. Finished-size means tracing the block, adding the additional one-quarter inch seam allowance.

1.

2.

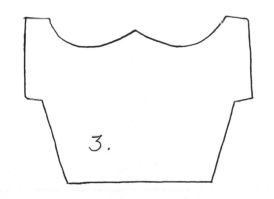

3.

Tennessee Iris

Tennessee's state flower is the iris. This pattern is for a 16-inch square, finished-size block. Arrange the flowers in the corners with the top pointing toward the side so that the top of the flower is two inches from the edge of the block, and the center depression of the top is three inches from the other edge. Leaf No. 2 goes to the right of the flower and curves over the top. Leaves No. 3 and No. 4 with stem No. 5 (which is for the next flower) are arranged from the center of the left side of the flower to the bottom of the next flower. The No. 5 stem should be approximately three inches from the side of the block. The background square should be white, the leaves green, and the flowers a medium shade or print of almost any color.

Put the blocks together in six rows of seven blocks each. You may place a plain block between each of the appliquéd ones. This pattern, which is fairly easy, does not need a border. Baste the elements in place before appliquéing them.

Please read Section 7 in Chapter One on General Information before starting any work on this pattern. Always add one-quarter inch seam allowance to all patterns before cutting them from the cloth. Finished-size means tracing the block, adding the additional one-quarter inch seam allowance.

35

Art Nouveau

Try this modern pattern. The colors are maroon, orange, yellow, and white. Be careful to use shades of colors that go well together for this is an extremely colorful quilt. Try the blocks in several arrangements before you sew them into a top. The half-flowers can form stripes and flowerettes as well as several other motifs. Measure the block to find the exact center of the left side. Baste pattern No. 6 so that its center is in the center of the left side of the block. Add patterns No. 5 and No. 4. Piece together five petals, each made of one No. 1, one No. 2, and one No. 3 pattern. Baste these petals around the outside of the No. 4 pattern. Appliqué the entire flower. This is a very easy pattern to make.

Please read Section 7 in Chapter One on General Information before starting any work on this pattern. Always add one-quarter inch seam allowance to all patterns before cutting them from the cloth. Finished-size means tracing the block, adding the additional one-quarter inch seam allowance.

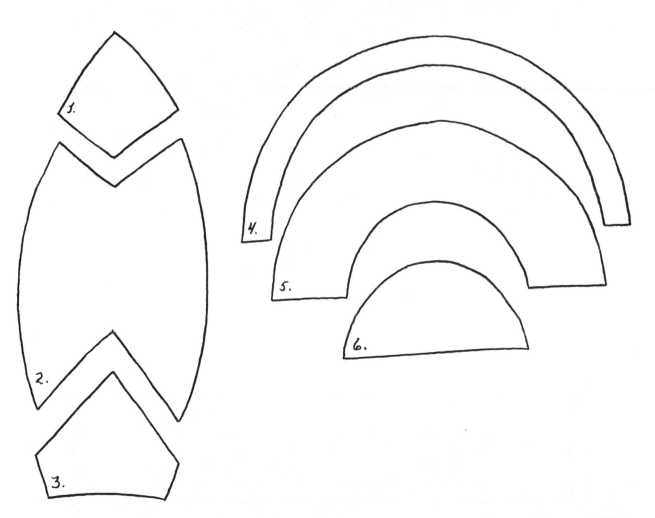

1.

2.

3.

4.

5.

6.

Dolores' Fancy

I designed this abstract design and liked it so much I gave it my own name. Sew the quilt top in an all-over pattern so the green flower shapes make strips that cover the whole quilt. Make each six-petaled flowerette with a different flower-patterned cloth to make this a scrap quilt. The background blocks are 14 inches square, finished-size. For the border use a 3½-inch-wide white strip and appliqué No. 3 patterns in a line down the center of the strip. This pattern is for an experienced quilt maker.

Please read Section 7 in Chapter One on General Information before starting any work on this pattern. Always add one-quarter inch seam allowance to all patterns before cutting them from the cloth. Finished-size means tracing the block, adding the additional one-quarter inch seam allowance.

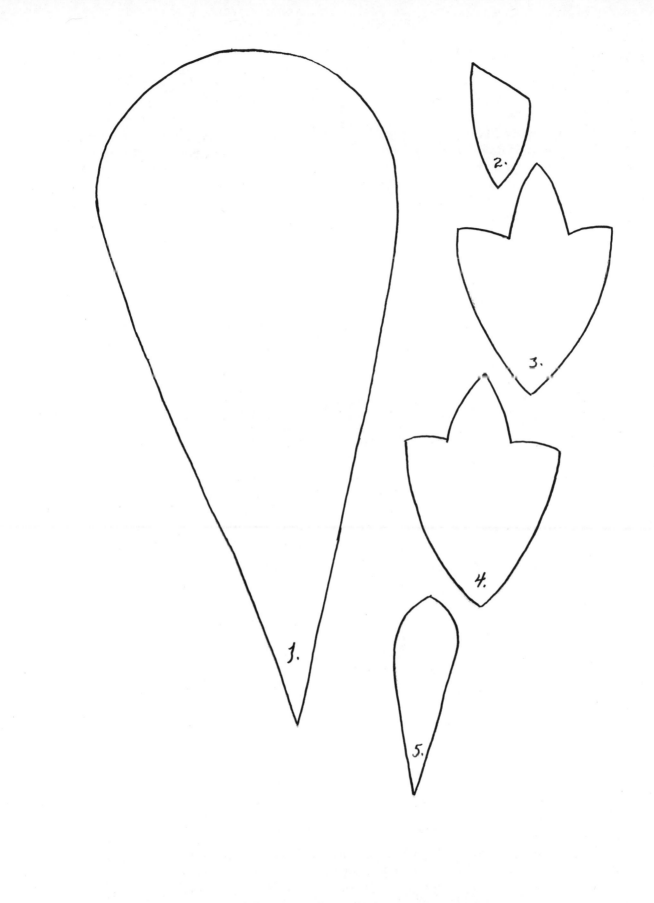

The Twelve Days of Christmas

This design features twelve motifs and two holly wreaths. This original design is a versatile one because the patterns may be appliquéd, embroidered, or fabric-painted onto the blocks. Work the motifs on white blocks 12 inches square, finished-size. Use two shades of green throughout the entire quilt top, or try red and green for a really bright Christmas quilt. The light green blocks between the motifs are 18 inches square, finished-size. This is a series quilt and is truly beautiful when finished. Only an expert quilt maker should attempt this pattern.

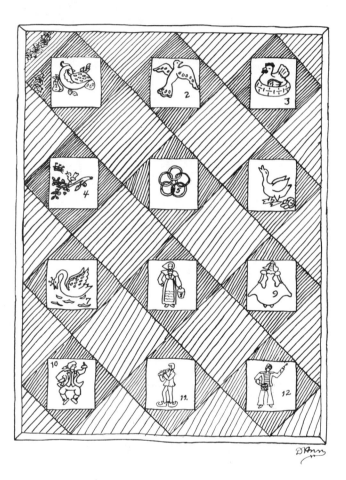

Please read Sections, 5, 6, 7, and 8 in Chapter One on General Information before starting any work on this pattern. Always add one-quarter inch seam allowance to all patterns before cutting them from the cloth. Finished-size means tracing the block, adding the additional one-quarter inch seam allowance.

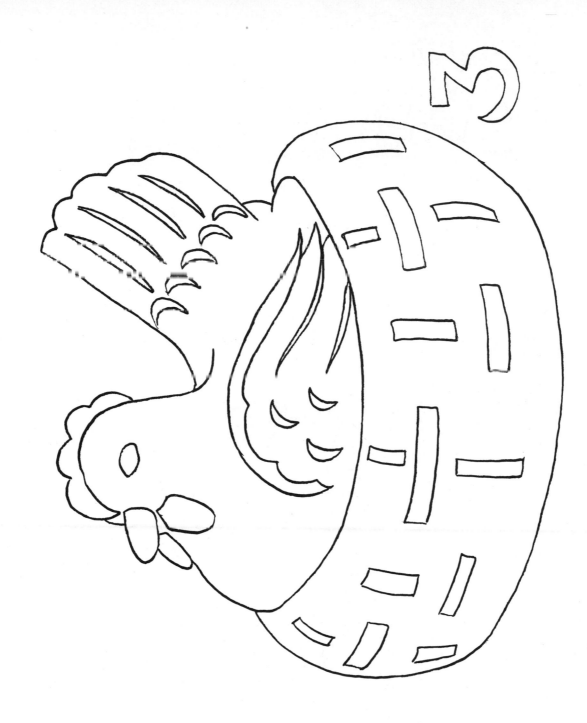

43

44

45

48

11

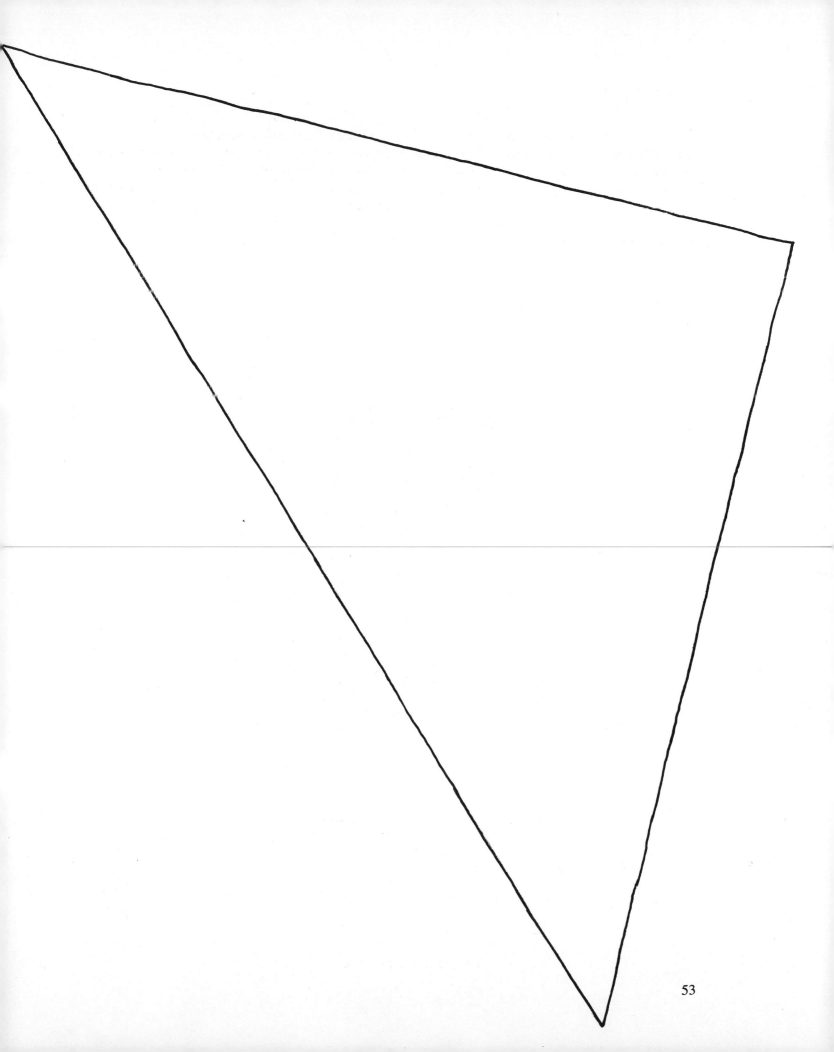

53

Holly Wreaths

Holly No. 1 is quilted on four plain triangles which surround each motif square. The No. 2 holly pattern is one-fourth of a circle and four of these should be quilted on each plain square to form a quilted holly wreath. A semicircle (two holly No. 2 patterns) should be quilted on the large plain triangles on the four sides of the quilt.

One holly No. 2 pattern should be quilted to each of the small triangles in the four corners of the quilt. Remember to quilt around each of the theme motifs. You may add a simple background quilting pattern to fill the spaces between the elaborate quilting patterns if you wish.

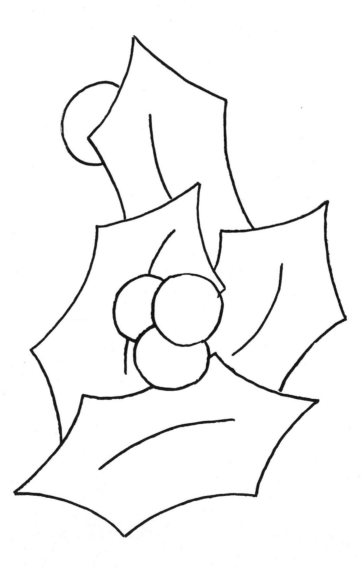

Quilting Pattern No. 1

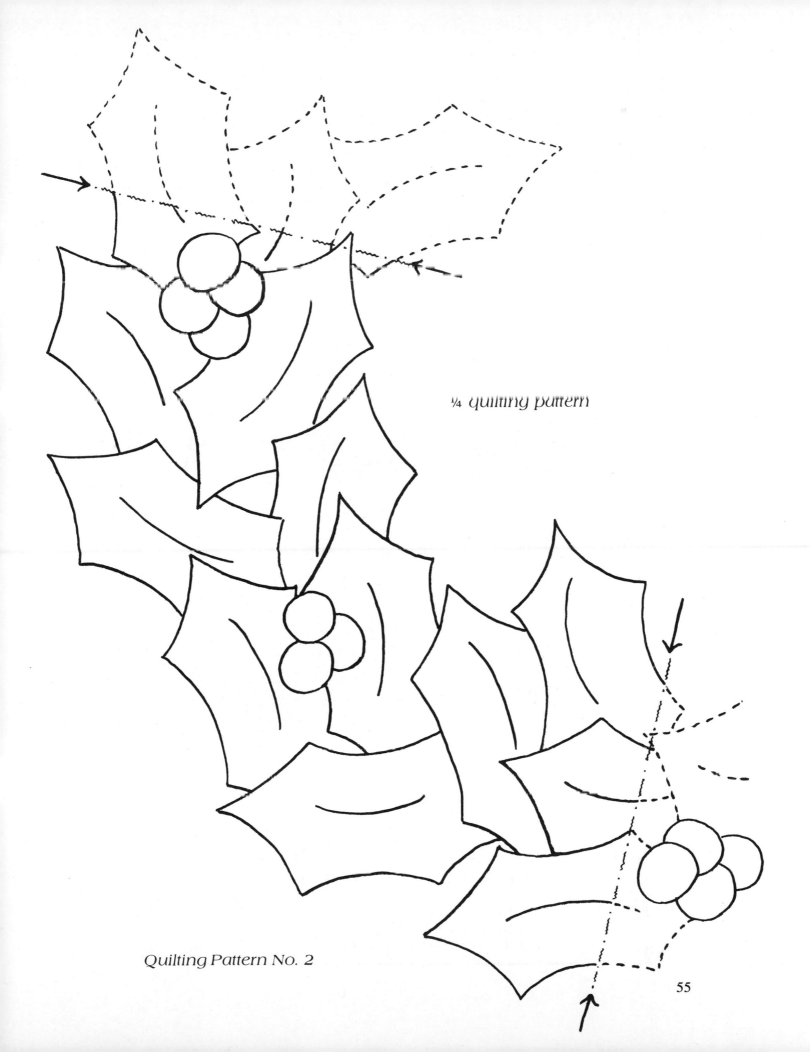

¼ quilting pattern

Quilting Pattern No. 2

55

Daffodil Bouquet

Grandmother loved the colors yellow, blue, and green. Here is a new pattern that uses this old color combination. The flowers may be cut out in one piece and embroidery or fabric paints used to mark the petals and the center, or the petals may each be cut out and appliquéd sepa-rately. This quilt needs a plain block between the appliquéd ones. The blocks are 14 inches square, finished-size. A border of 1½-inch-wide yellow, blue, and green strips will finish the edges for a very pretty quilt top. This is a simple pattern and could be made by a beginner.

Please read Section 7 in Chapter One on General Information before starting any work on this pattern. Always add one-quarter inch seam allowance to all patterns before cutting them from the cloth. Finished-size means tracing the block, adding the additional one-quarter inch seam allowance.

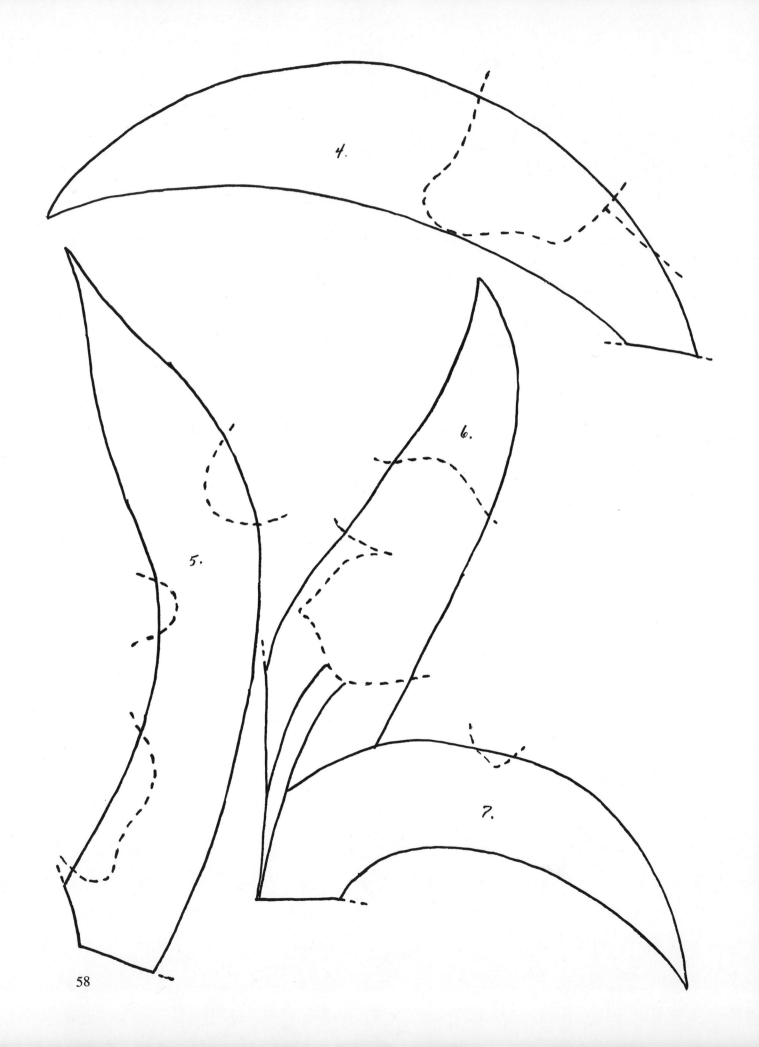

58

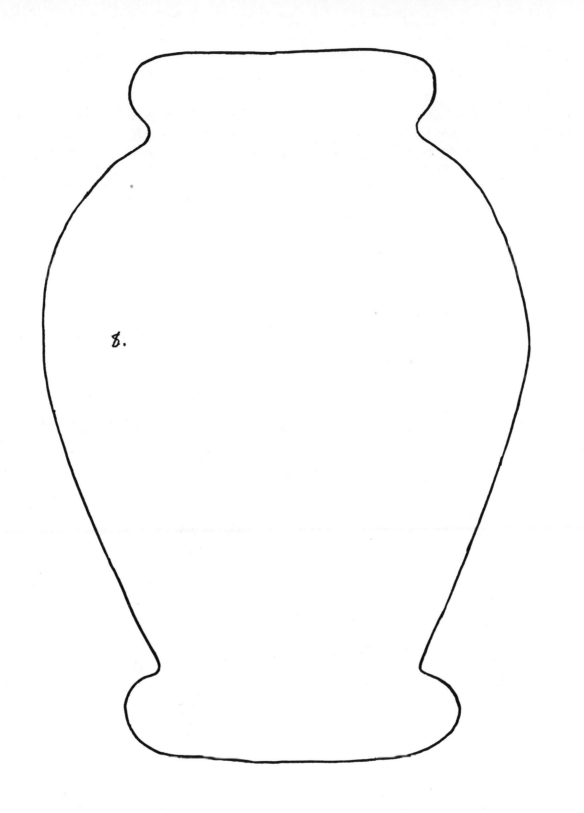

8.

The Strawberry Patch

This quilt should be made with strawberry-red and green on a white background. Arrange four of the motifs as shown in the drawing on a 12-inch square, finished-size block. Set the blocks together with plain blocks of white or a pastel shade between the appliquéd blocks. The No. 4 and No. 5 patterns should be alternated on an eight-inch-wide border strip. Trace the appliqué pattern onto the plain blocks between the appliqué blocks and use it as the quilting pattern. Only an experienced quilt maker should try making this quilt.

Please read Section 7 in Chapter One on General Information before starting any work on this pattern. Always add one-quarter inch seam allowance to all patterns before cutting them from the cloth. Finished-size means tracing the block, adding the additional one-quarter inch seam allowance.

1.

2.

3.

center

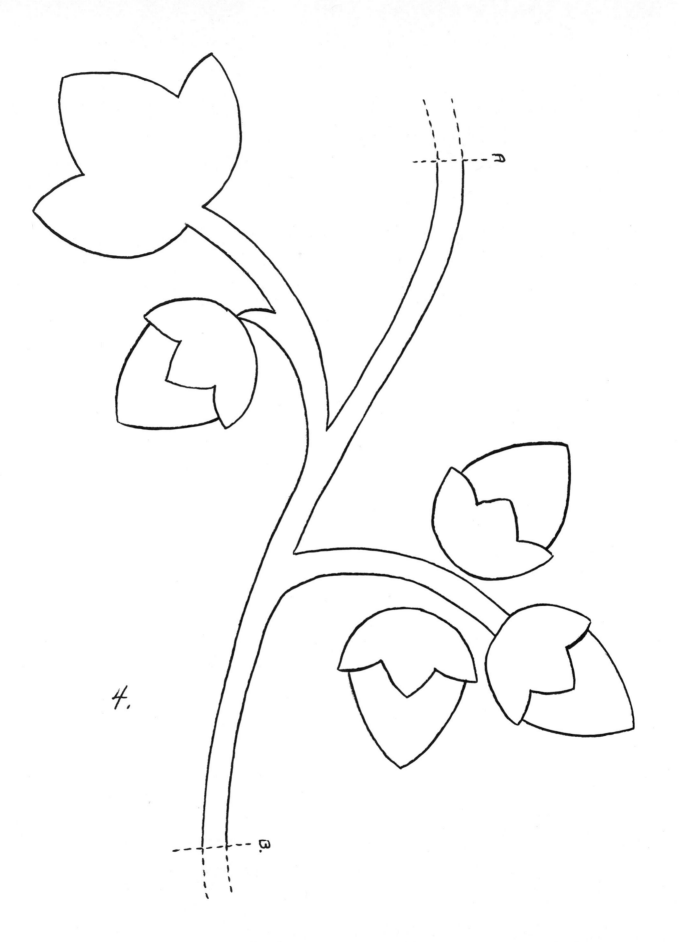

A

4.

B.

5.

Tulip Tile

This pattern is for a 14-inch square, finished-size block. Place the short No. 4 stem in the exact center of the block. Place a tulip at each end of the stem, making sure that the center points of the tulips are on the center line of the block. Place a No. 5 stem under the side points of the tulips and place a tulip in each corner of the block with the center points toward the cor-ners. Add the No. 2 and No. 3 leaves and center them. Use pastel colors for the flowers and light green for the leaves. This is not a difficult pattern if care is taken in placing the elements of the design. This pattern would look attractive with either plain blocks or lattice strips used between the appliquéd blocks.

Please read Section 7 in Chapter One on General Information before starting any work on this pattern. Always add one-quarter inch seam allowance to all patterns before cutting them from the cloth. Finished-size means tracing the block, adding the additional one-quarter inch seam allowance.

65

Basket Appliqué

This pattern comes from the Alice Brooks collection of designs made in the 1930s. It was published in the Pittsburgh, Pa. *Press*. The basket should be a brown print or solid color, remaining the same throughout the quilt. The flowers, however, may either remain the same color or print or may be different, to make this a scrap quilt. The stems of the flowers should be embroidered in an outline stitch. This is a fairly easy pattern. Be careful in the placement of the elements in each block you make. The patterns are drawn for a 12-inch square, finished-size block.

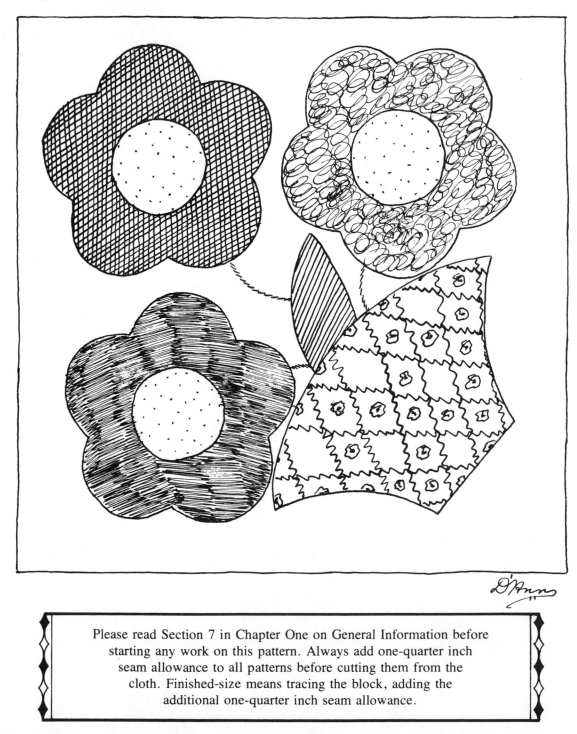

Please read Section 7 in Chapter One on General Information before starting any work on this pattern. Always add one-quarter inch seam allowance to all patterns before cutting them from the cloth. Finished-size means tracing the block, adding the additional one-quarter inch seam allowance.

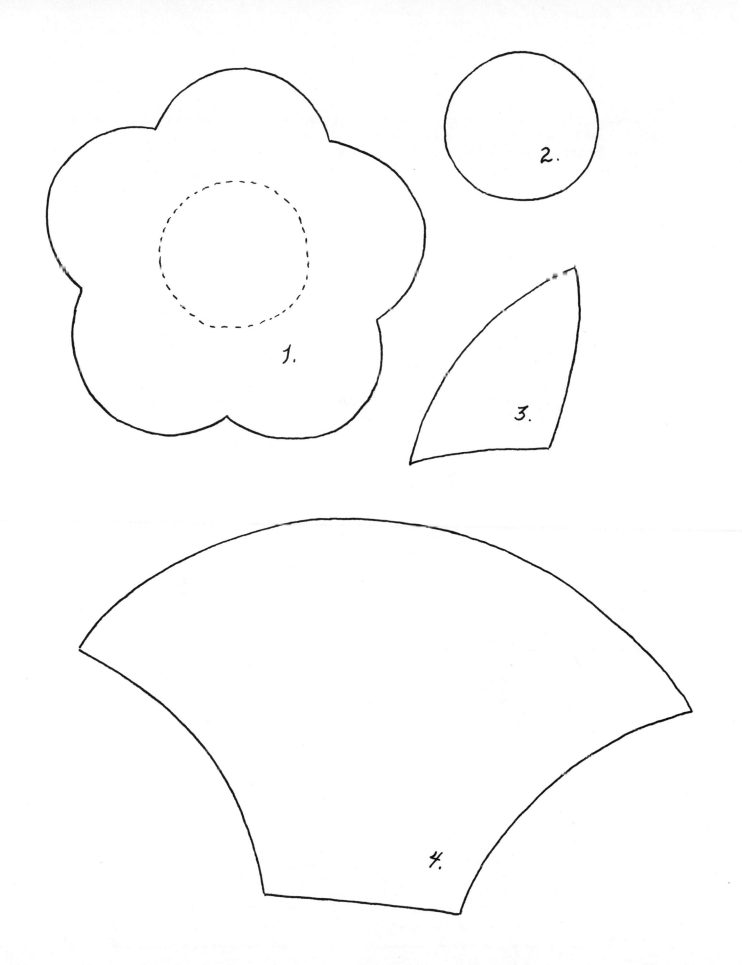

1.

2.

3.

4.

Tile Flower

This is one of the harder appliqués. However, with slow and careful work, even a beginner can master it. Pin the pieces in place on your block. Cut No. 5 with one straight and one reversed piece for each block. I have shown each of the flowers made from a different print to make a scrap quilt. You may make the entire quilt with one print if you wish. This pattern has been drawn for a 12-inch square block.

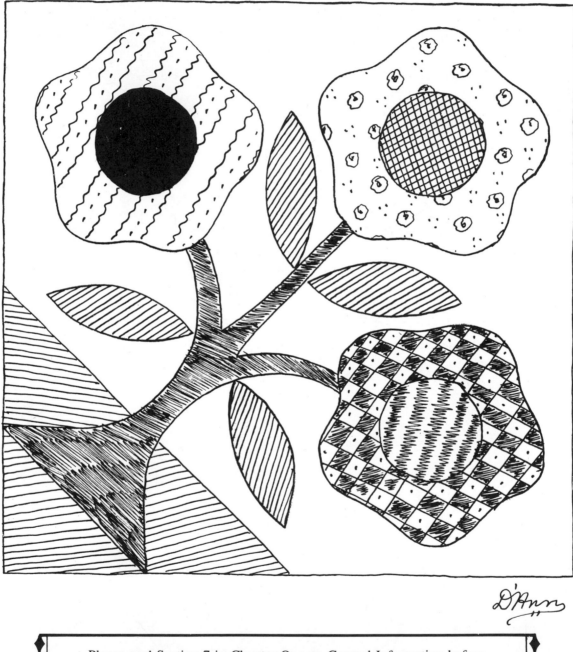

Please read Section 7 in Chapter One on General Information before starting any work on this pattern. Always add one-quarter inch seam allowance to all patterns before cutting them from the cloth. Finished-size means tracing the block, adding the additional one-quarter inch seam allowance.

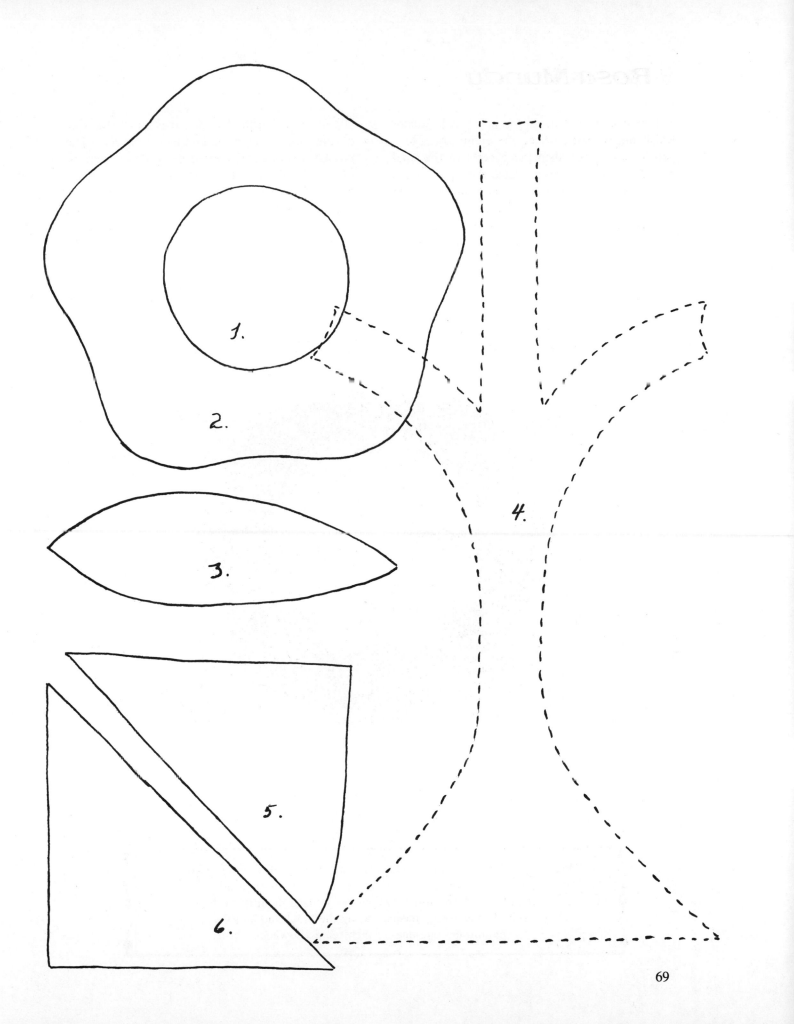

1.

2.

3.

4.

5.

6.

69

Rosa Mundy

This pattern is made for a 14-inch square, finished-size block. Piece the eight large No. 3 petals into a ring, then piece eight of the small No. 2 petals into a ring. Place the two rings on the block so the center of the hole in the smaller ring is in the exact center of the block. Appliqué both rings to the block and then place the center of the No. 1 flower over the hole in the center of the petal ring and appliqué it to the block. Before appliquéing the larger ring to the block, slip the edges of the No. 4 leaves under the edge of the ring and appliqué them in place. The points of the leaves should be in the corners of the block one inch from the corner point of the block. The leaves should be a medium green and the petals should be two shades of a pastel color. The darker shade may be a print. Use your own judgment of which ring should be the darker on any block. This is an easy pattern to make.

Please read Section 7 in Chapter One on General Information before starting any work on this pattern. Always add one-quarter inch seam allowance to all patterns before cutting them from the cloth. Finished-size means tracing the block, adding the additional one-quarter inch seam allowance.

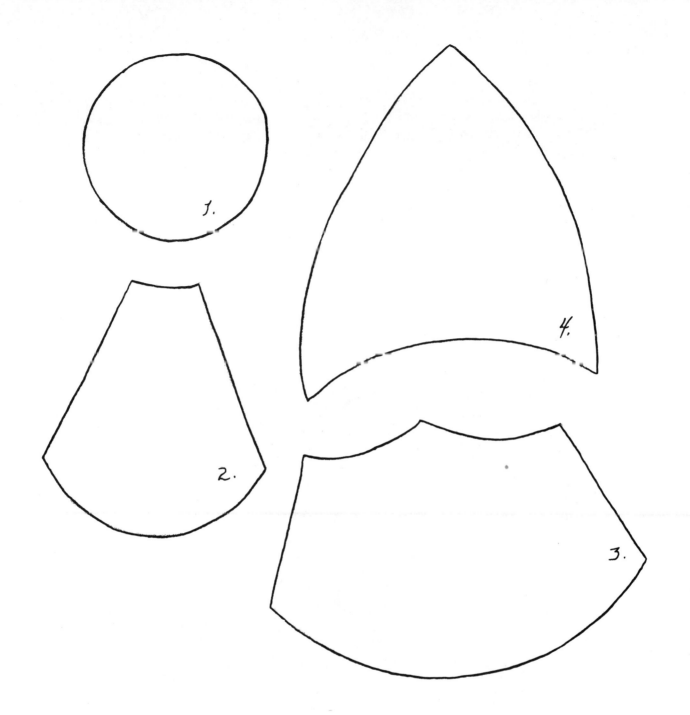

1.

2.

4.

3.

71

Old Spice Pink

A Jacobean pattern is something a little different from what you have been used to in quilt patterns. This design was taken from a Jacobean needlework pattern. Try it with an elaborate appliqué border and quilting pattern (see the 18th Century border on page 000). Use two shades of rose and pink, plus green and yellow. Do not try this as a scrap quilt. It should be put together with a plain block between the appliquéd ones. Appliqué the pattern to a 12-inch square, finished-size block. Cut out each pattern and arrange them according to the drawing of the finished block. Pin and then baste the elements in place. Take care to put the design on each block in the same place each time. Leaf No. 5 has reverse appliqué for the vein. Place a small piece of yellow under this leaf to show through the V-shaped opening. The leaf and stem sections are green and yellow; they are not two shades of green. This is a pattern only for an experienced needlewoman.

Please read Section 7 in Chapter One on General Information before starting any work on this pattern. Always add one-quarter inch seam allowance to all patterns before cutting them from the cloth. Finished-size means tracing the block, adding the additional one-quarter inch seam allowance.

CHAPTER THREE

Half-Pieced
and Half-Appliquéd
Patterns

Ring Around Rosie

Ring Around Rosie

Pink, rose, and two shades of green make this a very pretty quilt pattern, but any two shades of a color may be used instead of the pink and rose. Piece the center of the rose together (patterns No. 1, No. 2, and No. 3). Baste it and the other motifs in place on a 12-inch square, finished-size block. Be sure leaf No. 6 has its top point in the exact center of the sides of the square. In the drawing of the finished quilt top I have shown four-inch lattice strips with windmill corner blocks; the patterns for these can be found in the chapter on Borders. Use white and the dark color used for the flower motif or the darker green used in the leaves for the windmill corner block. This makes a lovely formal quilt top. The top should be finished with the lattice strip and a 1½-inch colored strip used as a border. Although this is a new pattern it resembles some of the patterns beloved by our nineteenth century grandmothers. This pattern should not be a beginner's first quilt.

Please read Sections 7 and 8 in Chapter One on General Information before starting any work on this pattern. Always add one-quarter inch seam allowance to all patterns before cutting them from the cloth. Finished-size means tracing the block, adding the additional one-quarter inch seam allowance.

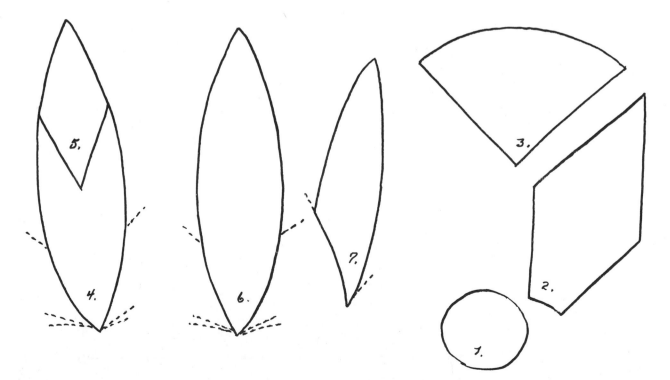

Rambling Rose

This is a lovely all-over design for a quilt. The center star of this design (No. 1) should be pieced and then basted in the exact center of the 16-inch square, finished block. Next baste the four leaf clusters (patterns No. 2 and No. 3) from the star center to the exact center of each side of the block. Baste the No. 7 stems, a light-colored No. 4 flower (embroider its center in yellow), a No. 5 leaf, a dark No. 4 flower, and a No. 6 leaf in a straight line to the corner of the block. Add the two No. 6 leaves from the dark flower to the edge of the blocks as shown in the drawing of the finished block. When all of the elements are basted in place, appliqué them to the block.

If the blocks are sewn together with every other one a plain block, the diamond pattern formed is a large one that covers the quilt top. The pattern will form smaller diamonds if done in an all-over design. You will need 30 blocks for a double-bed sized quilt. This design is of medium difficulty.

Please read Sections 7 and 8 in Chapter One on General Information before starting any work on this pattern. Always add one-quarter inch seam allowance to all patterns before cutting them from the cloth. Finished-size means tracing the block, adding the additional one-quarter inch seam allowance.

79

Faceted Diamonds

If you would like a different and brand-new pattern, try this pattern that looks like an expanding or exploding star. I designed it several years ago and worked it in two shades of green and yellow on a white square. It could be done in almost any color combination, and each block in a quilt top could be different, making this a scrap quilt. It may be done with plain blocks or lattice strips between the pieced ones, but the blocks are large enough so that an all-over pattern would look attractive. The patterns are drawn for 16-inch square blocks. A double bed-size quilt will need four rows of five blocks each with a 12-inch-wide border on each side.

Sew together a dark and light diamond from pattern No. 4. Make three more of these units. Then sew the units together into two units of four diamonds each. Sew these together to form the center star. Sew two dark No. 2 triangles (one reversed) on each side of a light diamond No. 1 and add a very light No. 3 diamond on the right side of this unit. Make eight of these units. Sew these units to the center star between its points. The first seam should start at the bottom point between the points of the star and go to the point of the star. Return to the bottom point and sew that seam to the adjoining point of the star. Look very carefully at the drawing of the finished block. Place each of the other seven units around the star in this same manner and then sew the side seam between the units. When the entire pattern is finished, place it in the center of a 16-inch white square. Mark the center of each side so that the points of the pattern can be appliquéd in the exact center of the block.

Please read Sections 5, 6, and 8 in Chapter One on General Information before starting any work on this pattern. Always add one-quarter inch seam allowance to all patterns before cutting them from the cloth. Finished-size means tracing the block, adding the additional one-quarter inch seam allowance.

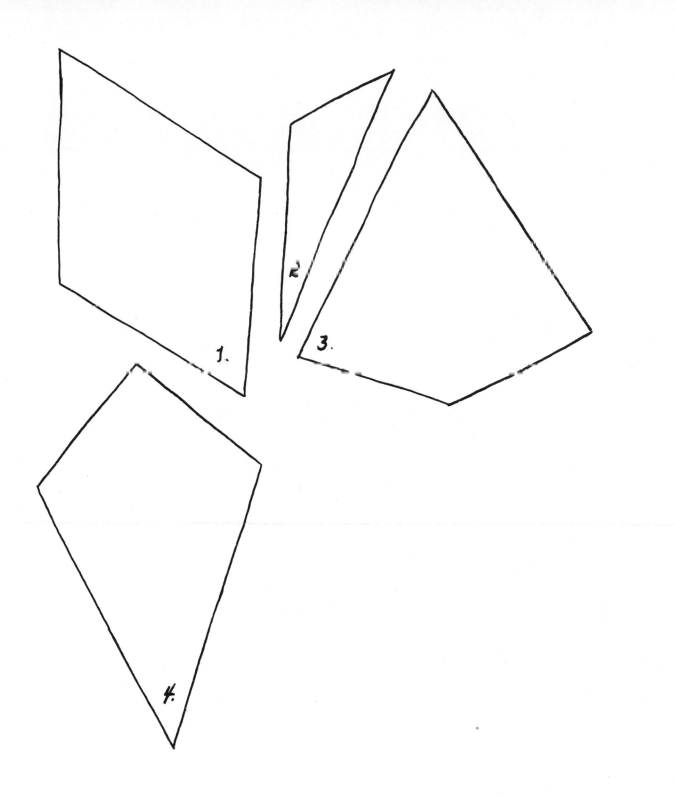

Spiderwort

Another favorite flower from my garden that I decided to make into a quilt pattern is the old-fashioned spiderwort, also called Job's Tears or Widow's Tears. The grass-like, dancing leaves and tiny bluish-purple flowers should make a lovely, dainty quilt. Make the background squares by piecing patterns Nos. 1, 2, and 3 (see the drawing for the finished block). Appliqué the four flowers and stems Nos. 4, 5, and 6 to the center of each square. Do not use plain blocks or lattice strips with this pattern. Six rows of eight blocks will make a twin bed quilt. This quilt will not need a border. This pattern is much too hard for a beginning quilter.

Please read Sections 7 and 8 in Chapter One on General Information before starting any work on this pattern. Always add one-quarter inch seam allowance to all patterns before cutting them from the cloth. Finished-size means tracing the block, adding the additional one-quarter inch seam allowance.

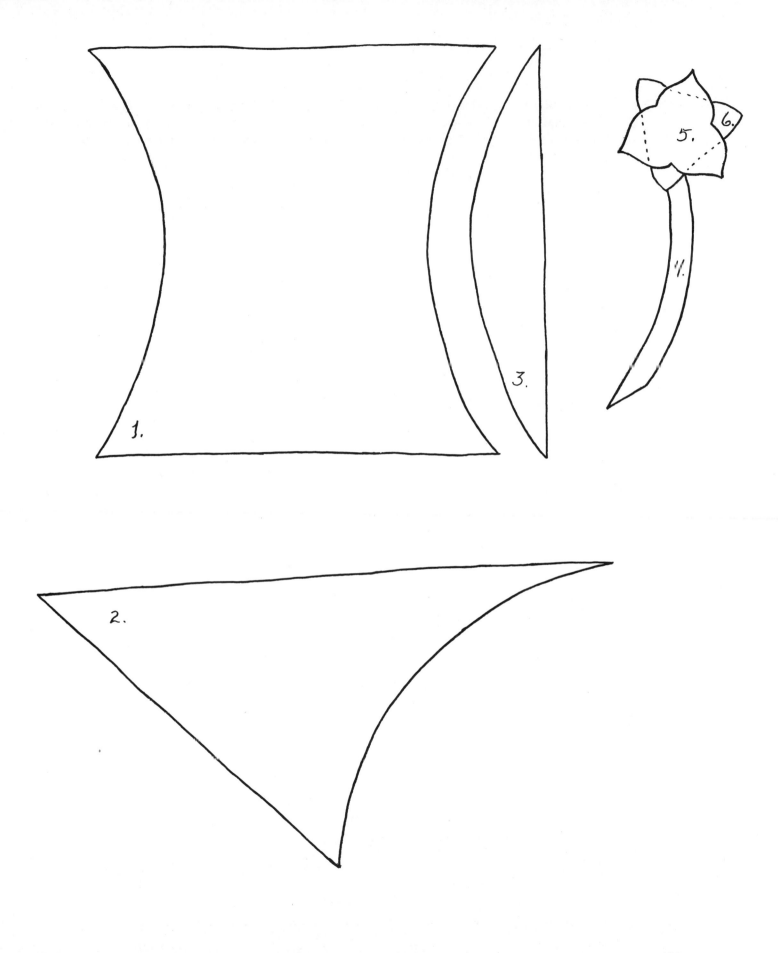

1.

2.

3.

5.

6.

Mountain Laurel

One of my favorite flowers is the lovely mountain laurel. I tried many ways to show the sunlight through dark leaves and the clusters of pinkish-white flowers. I think this pattern solves the problem best. Make half of the blocks without the appliquéd flower clusters. The flowers are two shades of pink with the darker shade in the center. On each flower center make a double X of yellow with embroidery floss or embroidery paints. The hexagons are 16 inches, finished-size, across the center point. There should be five rows of six blocks each for a double bed quilt top and four rows of five blocks each for a twin bed quilt top. If you are very careful with the placement of the flowers, this pattern should be easy enough for a beginner.

Please read Sections 7 and 8 in Chapter One on General Information before starting any work on this pattern. Always add one-quarter inch seam allowance to all patterns before cutting them from the cloth. Finished-size means tracing the block, adding the additional one-quarter inch seam allowance.

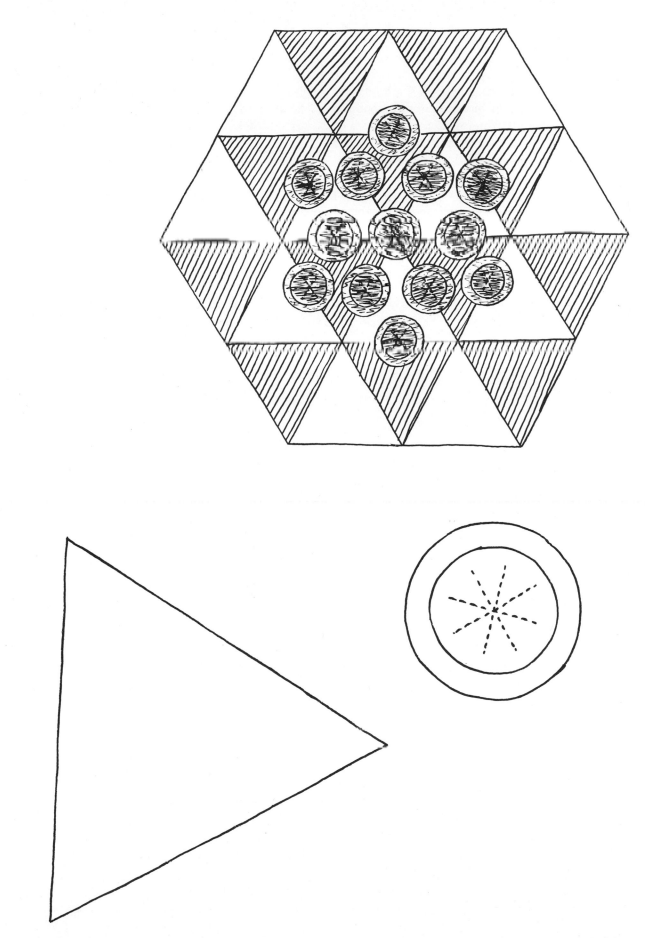

Flowery Night

A summer night when the stars are out and the flowers are all in bloom sets the mood for this romantic quilt pattern. Cut four pieces of pattern No. 5, and then reverse the pattern and cut four more for each block. Sew pattern No. 6 (*A* side) to *A* of pattern No. 5. Repeat for the reverse patterns. Now sew pattern No. 7 (*B* side) to pattern No. 6 (*B* side) and add the reversed section. Make three more of these corners and sew them into a block. Piecc four No. 3 petals into a circle and baste them along with four No. 4 leaves to the background block. Sew four No. 2 petals into a circle and baste this to the center of the block. Finish the flower with the center (No. 1). When all of the flower sections are in place, appliqué them to the block and to each other. This quilt is not nearly as hard to make as it looks. Put the blocks together in an all-over pattern without lattice strips or plain blocks. It does not need a border. The finished blocks are 12 inches square, finished-size.

Please read Sections 7 and 8 in Chapter One on General Information before starting any work on this pattern. Always add one-quarter inch seam allowance to all patterns before cutting them from the cloth. Finished-size means tracing the block, adding the additional one-quarter inch seam allowance.

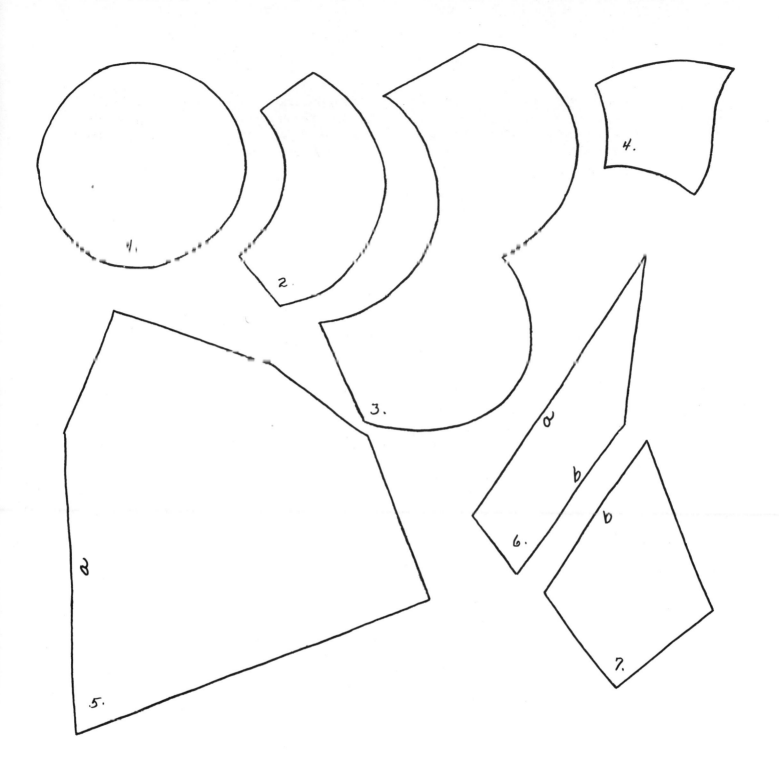

Susan's Wreath

The gay black-eyed Susan of the fields makes a lovely quilt design in medium brown, yellow, green, and white. This pattern looks more difficult than it really is. Cut a yellow 14-inch square, finished-size block for the background. Appliqué a brown No. 2 circle in the exact center of this block. Piece together a circle of eight No. 1 white petals and appliqué them to the background square, measuring carefully before sewing them in place. (See drawing of the finished block.) Appliqué the wreath in place on the center of the circle of petals. The square is now finished.

There is a trick to this pattern. The outline of the white flower edges forms the yellow corners and center flower. This is a simple form of reverse appliqué and one of my original designs.

Put this quilt top together in an all-over pattern or with plain blocks between the appliquéd squares. Make a plain border using two or three strips of the colors used in the blocks. A twin bed quilt will need five rows of seven blocks each and a two-inch-wide border.

Please read Sections 7 and 8 in Chapter One on General Information
before starting any work on this pattern. Always add one-quarter
inch seam allowance to all patterns before cutting them from
the cloth. Finished-size means tracing the block, adding
the additional one-quarter inch seam allowance.

1.

2.

3.

4.

5.

6.

Janie's Garter

This is another original pattern that is a variation on the traditional Dresden Plate pattern. This design has 16 short petals and leaves. Eight different prints or solid materials are needed for each circle, which makes this a very nice scrap pattern. If prints are used, be sure that they are small prints.

Cut two No. 1 petals for each circle from the same material, so that you can make one half of the finished circle duplicate the other half. Piece the ring of petals and baste it to the background square, measuring carefully so that the circle is placed evenly. Before appliquéing the section between each petal point, insert a green leaf, pattern No. 2, and appliqué it in place.

There is a large area in the center for a fancy quilting pattern which you can draw by first making a circle ¼-inch from the inside edge of the appliqué. Then draw lines vertically and horizontally ½-inch apart to fill this circle. This is not a hard pattern to make and could easily be worked by a beginner.

Please read Sections 7 and 8 in Chapter One on General Information before starting any work on this pattern. Always add one-quarter inch seam allowance to all patterns before cutting them from the cloth. Finished-size means tracing the block, adding the additional one-quarter inch seam allowance.

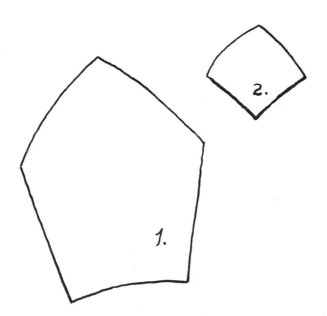

Climentus

This original pattern features the showy climentus vine in a lattice strip. I have designed the block in pink, blue, green, and white. Climentus flowers come in many pretty colors, so you should be able to choose an attractive color combination that will complement any bedroom. Cut a colored background square 14 inches square, finished-size. Appliqué the flower patterns No. 1 and No. 2, vine patterns *A* through *D*, leaves No. 3 and No. 4, and the buds No. 5 and No. 6 on the square. Carefully follow the letters on the vine patterns and the drawing of the finished quilt block. Use embroidery thread or embroidery paint on the dotted lines on the flower center and petals, the buds, and the leaf veins.

When making the cutting patterns for the lattice strips, place the ends of the two strips (marked 1a) together on the dotted lines and cut them as one pattern strip. Do the same for the strips marked 2a. Piece together two No. 1a strips with a No. 2a strip between them; make four of these. Piece four corner nine patches by sewing two No. 3a squares on opposite sides of a No. 4a oblong; make two of these strips. Then make another strip of two No. 4a oblongs on opposite sides of a No. 5a square. Sew this last strip between the first two strips. Piece the lattice strips and corner blocks to the finished block. The block and lattice strips will make a finished square, 24 inches on a side. A double bed-size quilt will need three rows of four blocks each. This quilt does not need a border.

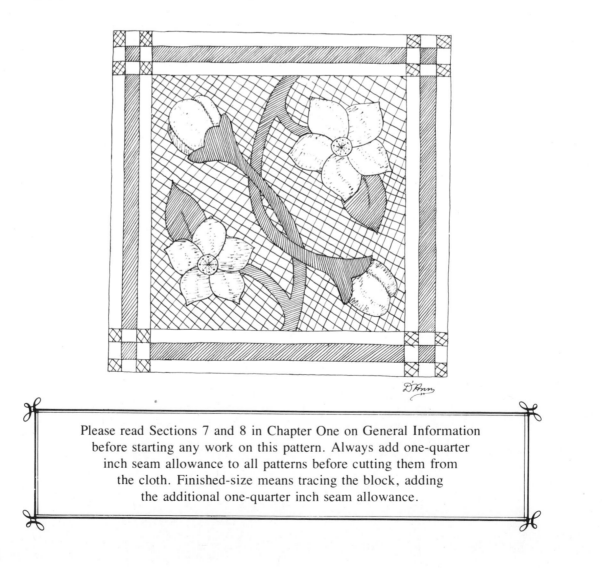

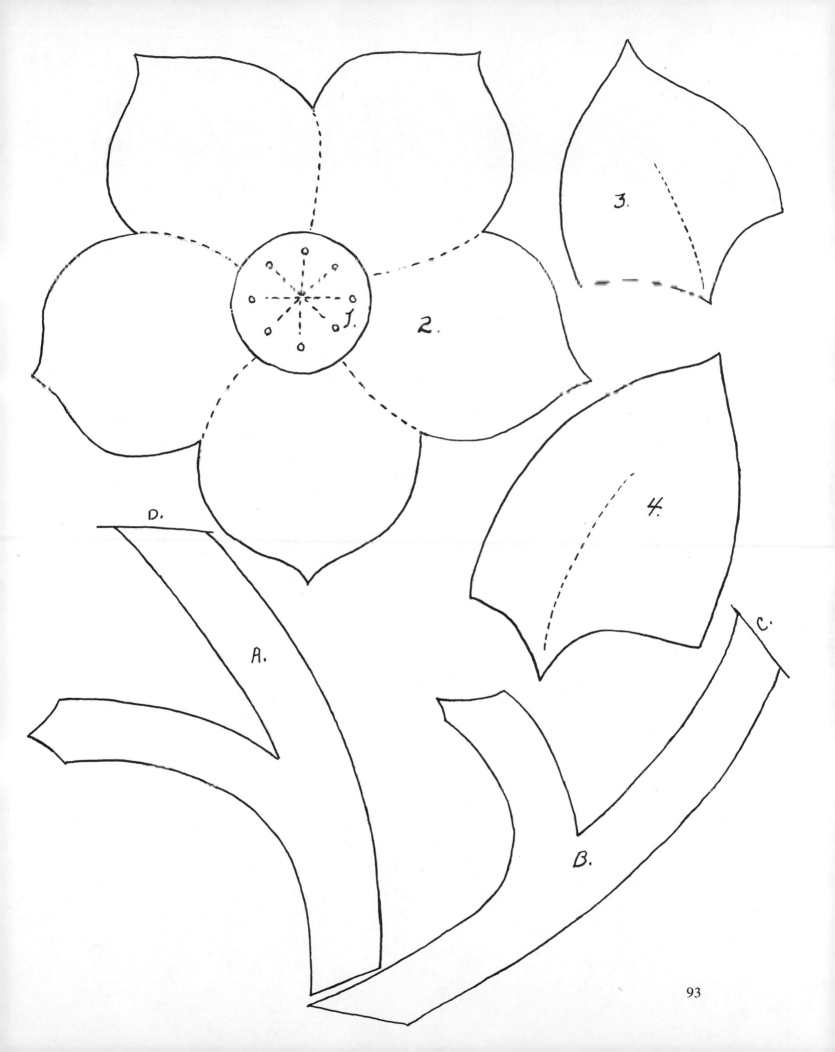

1.

2.

3.

4.

A.

B.

C.

D.

93

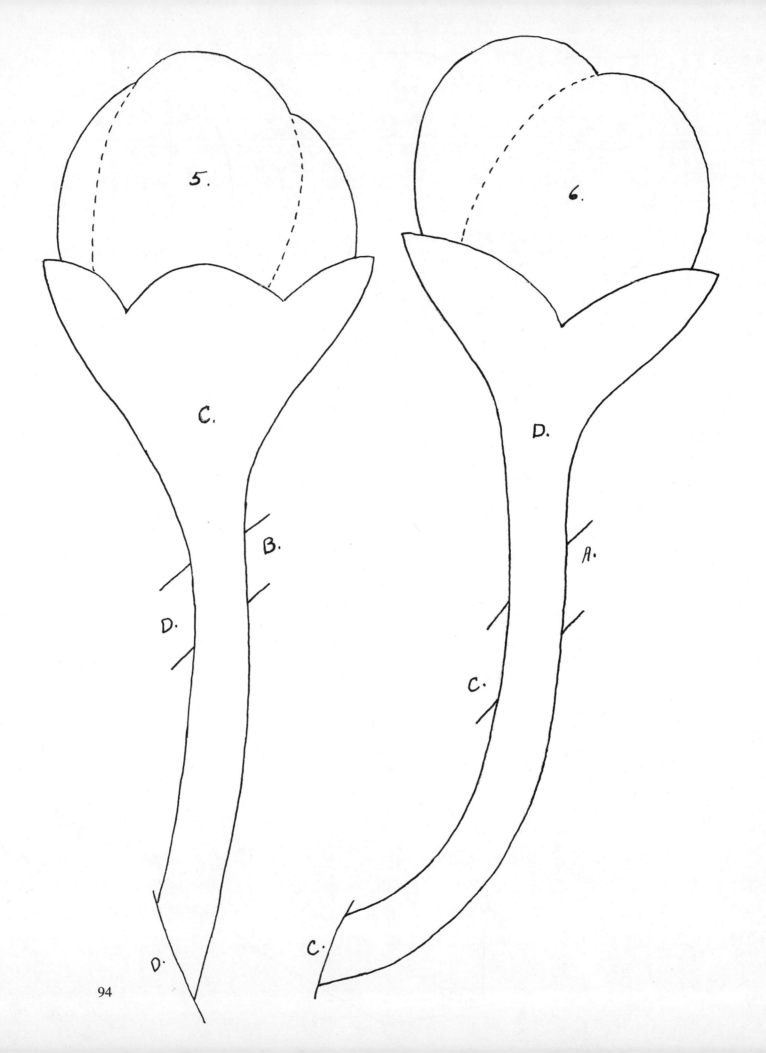

5.

C.

D.

B.

D.

6.

D.

A.

C.

C.

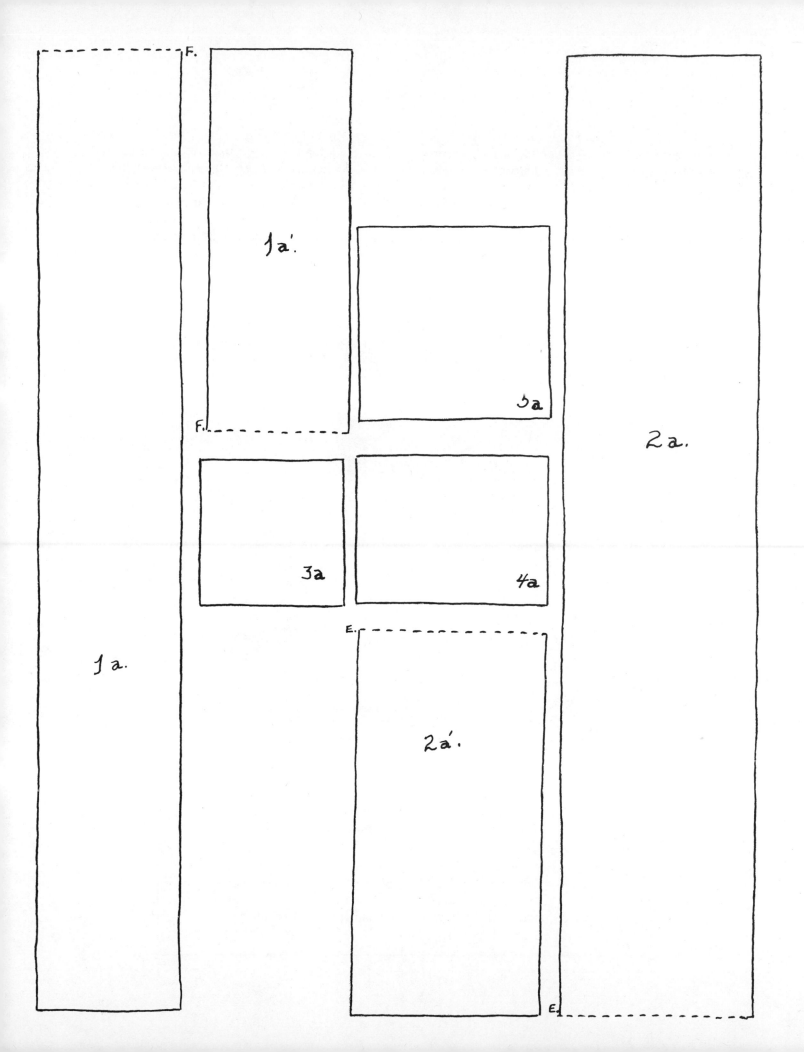

Rose and Fly Foot

I designed this original pattern to solve the problem of bulkiness in appliqué. The rose has two rows of pieced petals and a center, yet it has only one layer of fabric.

Piece the green and white diamonds and triangles into a background square that will have a large triangle missing on each side. Fold three green leaf squares, No. 6, on the dotted lines. Sew together four dark rose petals, No. 5, and place them over the missing triangle. Appliqué this row of petals down and catch the pointed corners of the leaves (not the two folded sides) in the seam indentations of the petals. See the drawing of the finished block. The leaves are not fastened down on their folded sides. Sew the row of four light-colored petals together into a half circle and appliqué them to the inside of the dark half ring. Sew two completed blocks together. There will be a small circle missing in the center of the seam. Cover this with the No. 3 circle and appliqué it to the center of both the half roses. This completes the flower. When finishing the top, sew a white border on the pieced blocks and appliqué half roses and their center over the seam onto the border.

This is a lovely, dainty design which can even be used to make a crib quilt. Although this is a very easy pattern to sew, it is not easy to assemble, and a beginner should not try it.

Please read Sections 7 and 8 in Chapter One on General Information before starting any work on this pattern. Always add one-quarter inch seam allowance to all patterns before cutting them from the cloth. Finished-size means tracing the block, adding the additional one-quarter inch seam allowance.

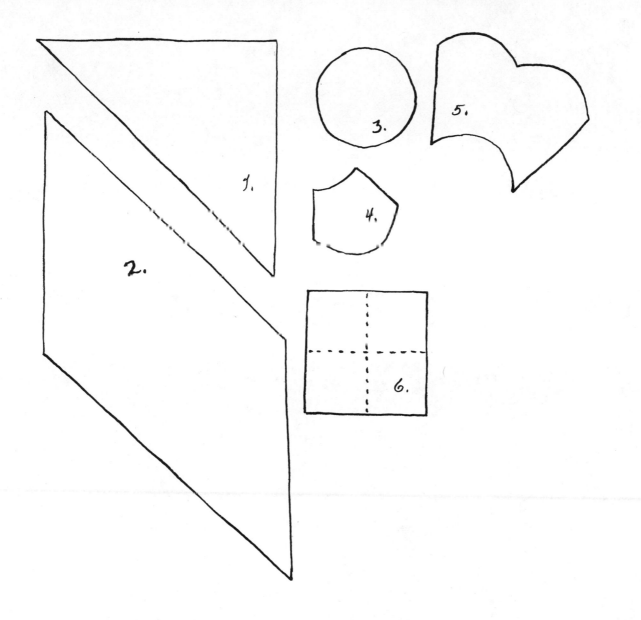

1.

2.

3.

4.

5.

6.

CHAPTER FOUR

Two, Three, and Five Patch Patterns

Maryland Beauty

Maryland Beauty

The Maryland Beauty pattern comes from a quilt made in the first decade of the nineteenth century. It was originally made in a soft, tiny print, using red material and homespun white. A triangular feather was worked into each white triangle in the quilting. I found this quilt displayed in the Star Spangled Banner House Museum in Baltimore, Maryland.

The finished-size patterns were drawn for a 9½-inch square block. Piece a strip of four white and three dark triangles from pattern No. 2. Sew this strip to one of the two short sides of the No. 3 triangle pattern. Sew four white and three dark No. 2 triangles into a second strip and add a dark square, pattern No. 1, to the left end of this strip; sew the strip to the second short side of triangle No. 3. This makes a large pieced

triangle that should be exactly the same size as the No. 4 triangle. (Before cutting pattern No. 4 from the cloth, join triangle 4a to section 4 along the dotted line.) Sew these two triangles together to form a square.

In the original quilt, the top was made from all pieced blocks. However, it would look attractive with every other block plain white and with a square or round feather in the quilting. This quilt may have a simple small border or will look just as nice with the edges bound simply. A single bed quilt will need eight rows of eleven blocks, and a double bed quilt will need at least eleven rows of eleven blocks. This patch is easy enough for a beginner who can follow directions carefully.

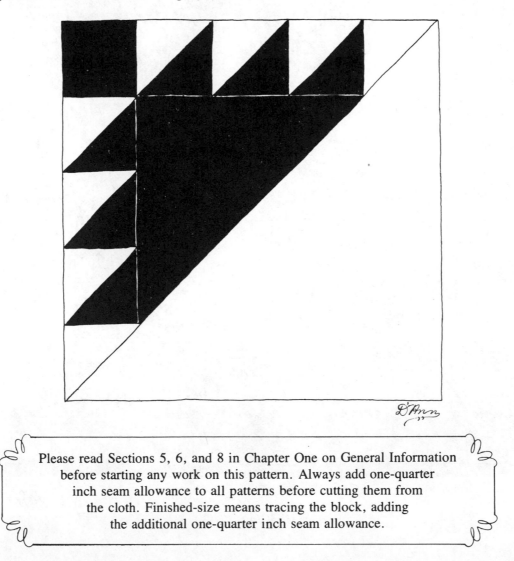

Please read Sections 5, 6, and 8 in Chapter One on General Information before starting any work on this pattern. Always add one-quarter inch seam allowance to all patterns before cutting them from the cloth. Finished-size means tracing the block, adding the additional one-quarter inch seam allowance.

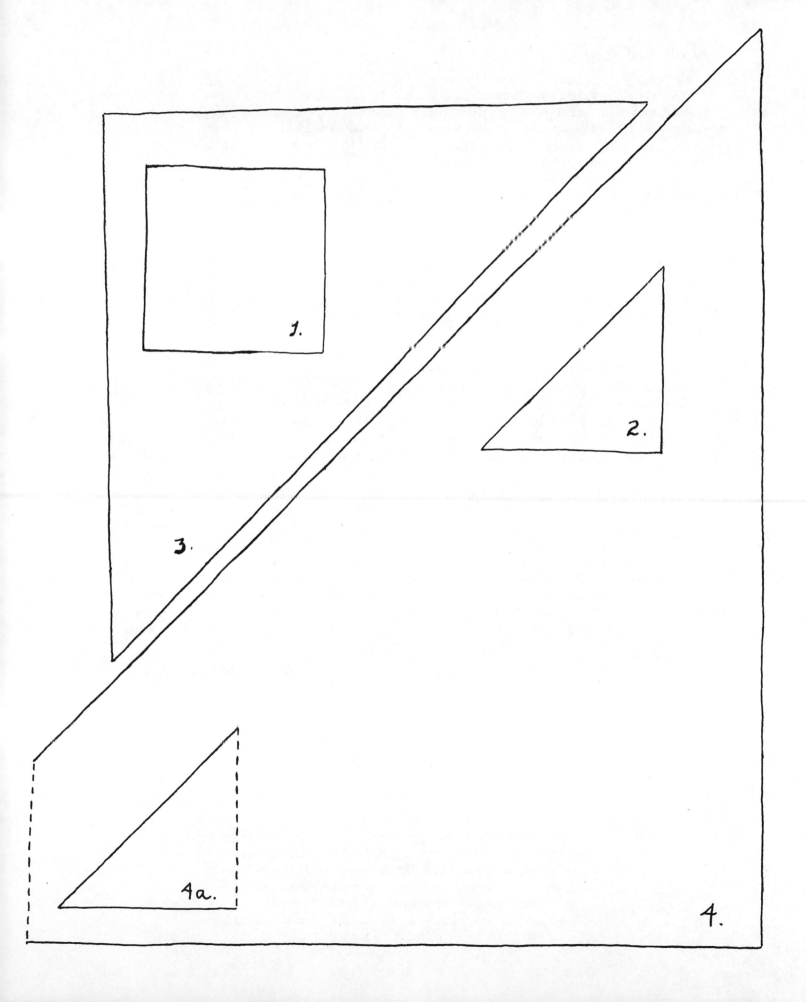

The Basket

This simple pattern comes from a 1930 Virginia Snow quilt pattern book. As the drawing illustrates, the original pattern called for two prints and a dark colored material. The background was white or brown domestic, also called unbleached muslin. The only parts which might be hard for a beginner are the two corner strips formed from patterns No. 1 and No. 2. These form the handle of the basket and the upper corner of the block. The diagonal seams leading to the corner are a little harder than straight seams; make sure that you sew exactly on the seam lines. If you are very careful with these two seams, even if you are a beginner you can make this quilt.

Sew a white No. 5 block to the longest side of a light print, patterned No. 4. Repeat, reversing pattern No. 4, to form the other side of the basket. Sew two dark print No. 7 triangles to two sides of a dark No. 6 square to form a larger triangle. Sew a large white triangle, pattern No. 8, to the pieced triangle so that they form a square as shown in the lower right corner of the drawing. Add the two light print basket parts finished first. A dark No. 7 triangle will fill in between the two sections of the basket, finishing this section of the block. Sew a dark strip, pattern No. 2, to a white strip, pattern No. 1, and repeat, reversing the colors for the other side of the handle. Sew the two dark strips to each of the short sides of the No. 3 triangle. Sew the diagonal corner seam. Add this section to the basket and your block is finished.

The finished-size patterns are drawn for an 11-inch square block. A finished twin bed quilt top will need six rows of eight blocks with a border three or six inches wide. A double bed quilt will take either seven or eight rows of eight blocks with a border three to six inches wide. This pattern is quite plain, and the border should be made of strips of the same colors used in the blocks. It would look attractive with all blocks done in the same colors or as a scrap quilt. The true beauty of a quilt done in this pattern is in the stitches. If the stitches are small, neat, and even, this will be a quilt that will please the owner for many years to come.

Please read Sections 5, 6, and 8 in Chapter One on General Information before starting any work on this pattern. Always add one-quarter inch seam allowance to all patterns before cutting them from the cloth. Finished-size means tracing the block, adding the additional one-quarter inch seam allowance.

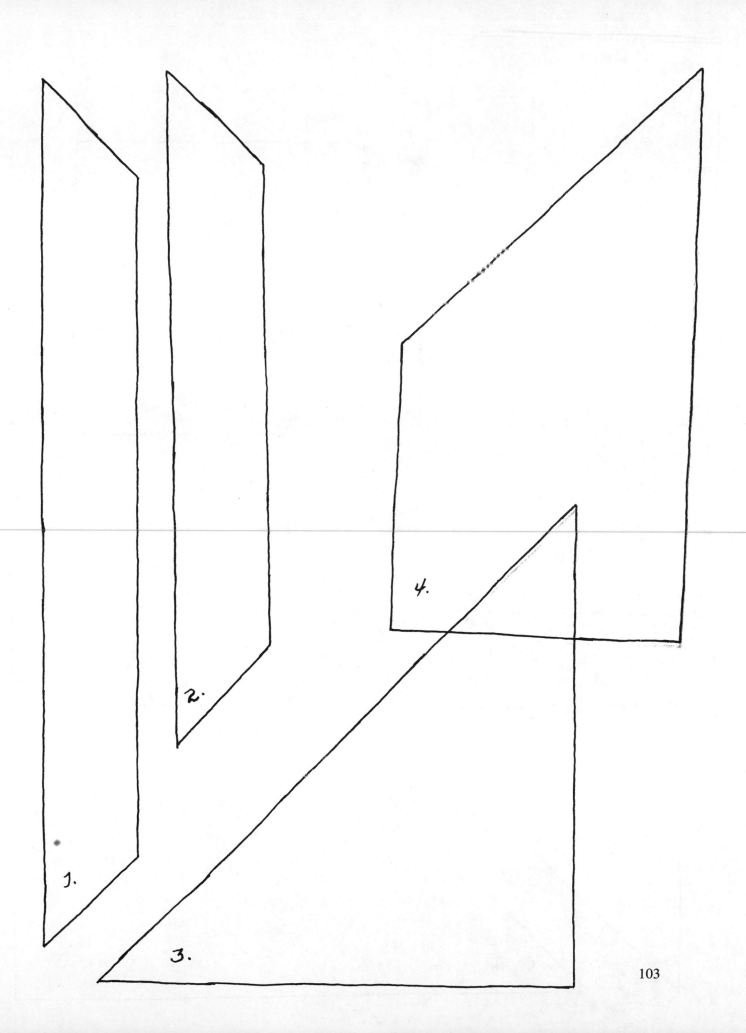

1.

2.

3.

4.

103

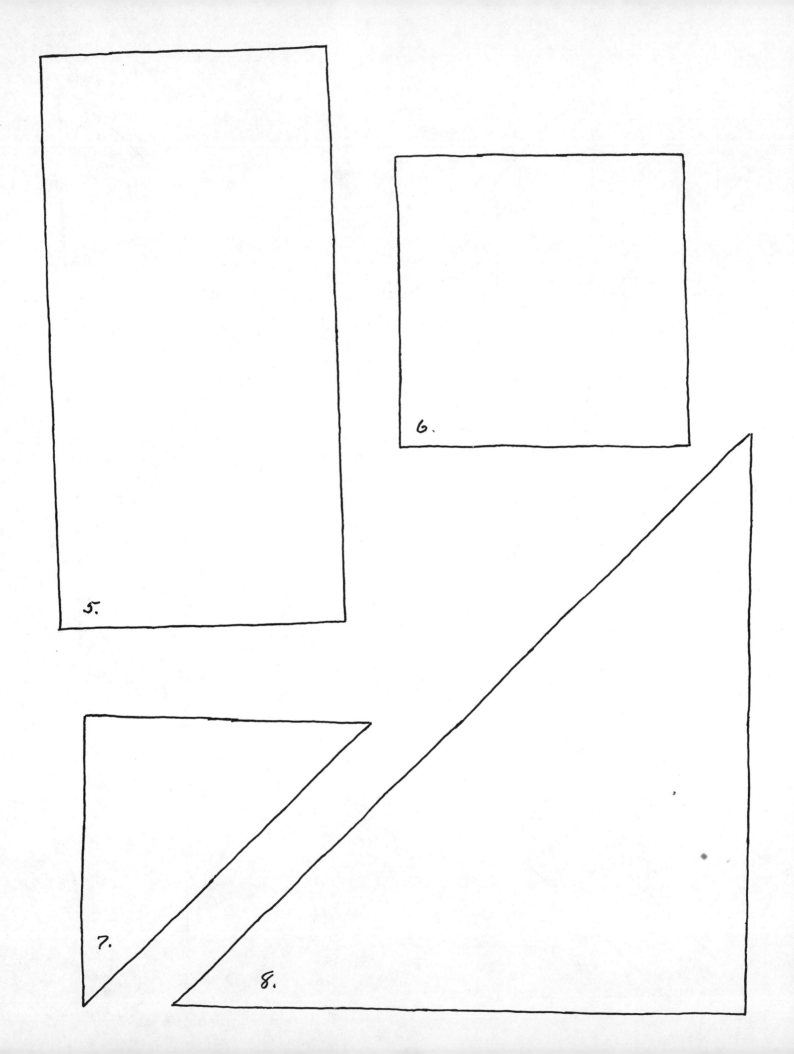

Honeymoon Cottage

I have been able to collect a few quaint folk patterns with pieced houses as a motif. These patterns seem to fascinate most quilters, so I am including one of the more unusual designs.

Sew together a white and an orange No. 7 strip. Then sew the No. 3 chimney between two white No. 8 pieces, reversing one No. 8 piece. Sew the two No. 7 pieces to the left side of the chimney pieces. Next sew a green No. 6 strip to a white No. 1 piece and add this to the left corner of the chimney piece. Sew, in order, strips of orange No. 7, white No. 9, orange No. 7, white No. 9, orange No. 7, and white No. 7. Sew together a green No. 4 piece and a white No. 5 piece; sew this piece to the top of the previous strip. Add a white No. 2 strip to the top.

Sew the entire piece to the right side of the chimney. This completes two-thirds of the finished block — the house and sky. To finish the block, make a strip of a green No. 10, a white No. 11, and a green No. 12 piece, and sew this strip to the bottom of the house.

The block is 12 inches square, finished-size. This kind of pattern looks best with either lattice strips or plain blocks between the squares. It may be made either on a quilt with blocks of the same colors or as a scrap quilt. If you make this a scrap quilt, use the same background color for all the squares. The placement of the patterns is rather complicated, but the sewing should not be too hard. If careful, even a beginner can make this quilt.

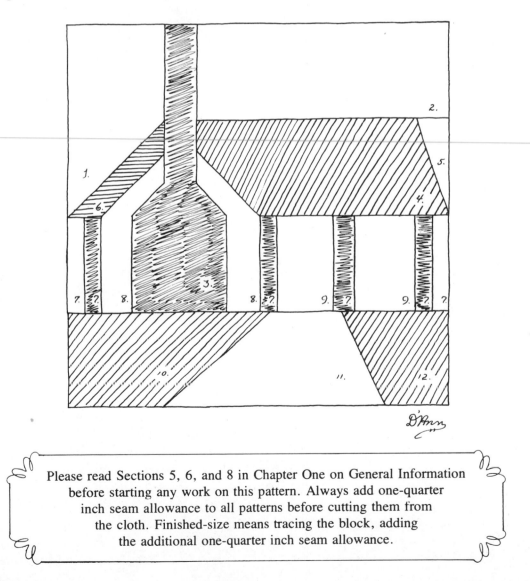

Please read Sections 5, 6, and 8 in Chapter One on General Information before starting any work on this pattern. Always add one-quarter inch seam allowance to all patterns before cutting them from the cloth. Finished-size means tracing the block, adding the additional one-quarter inch seam allowance.

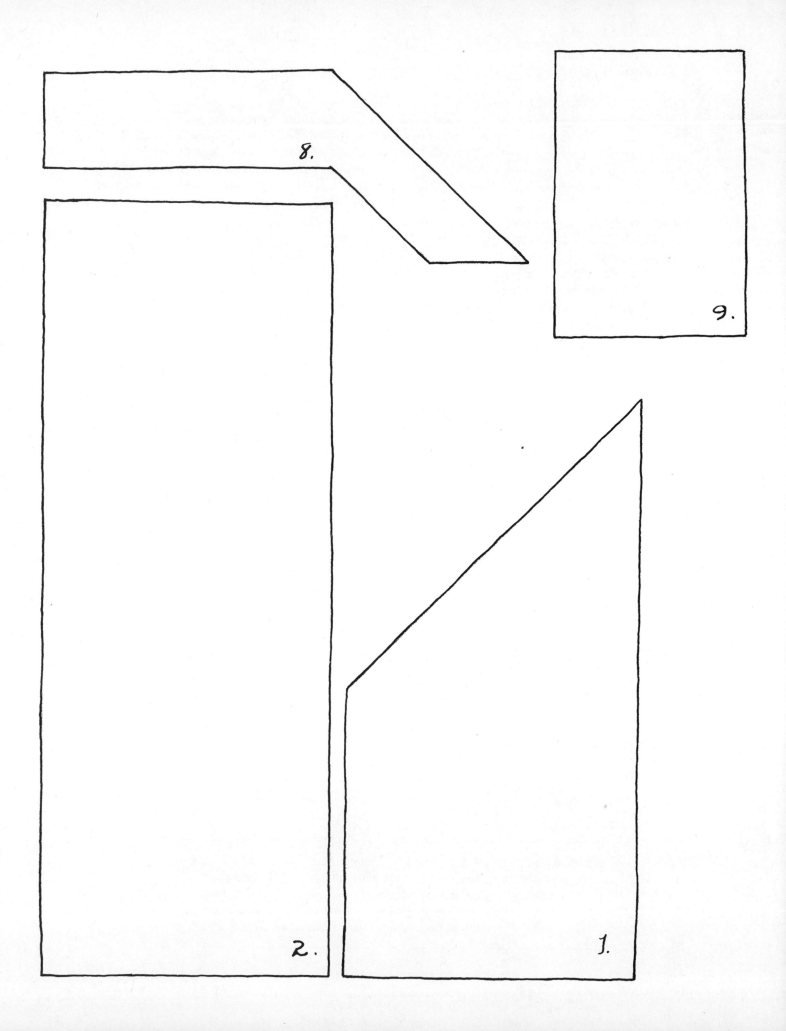

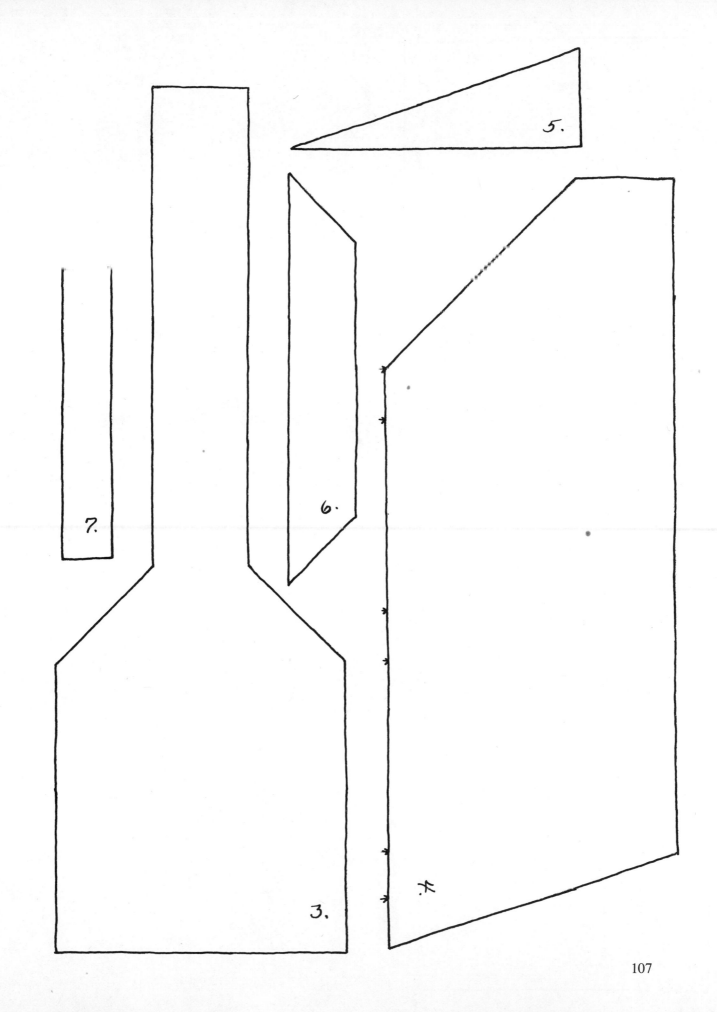

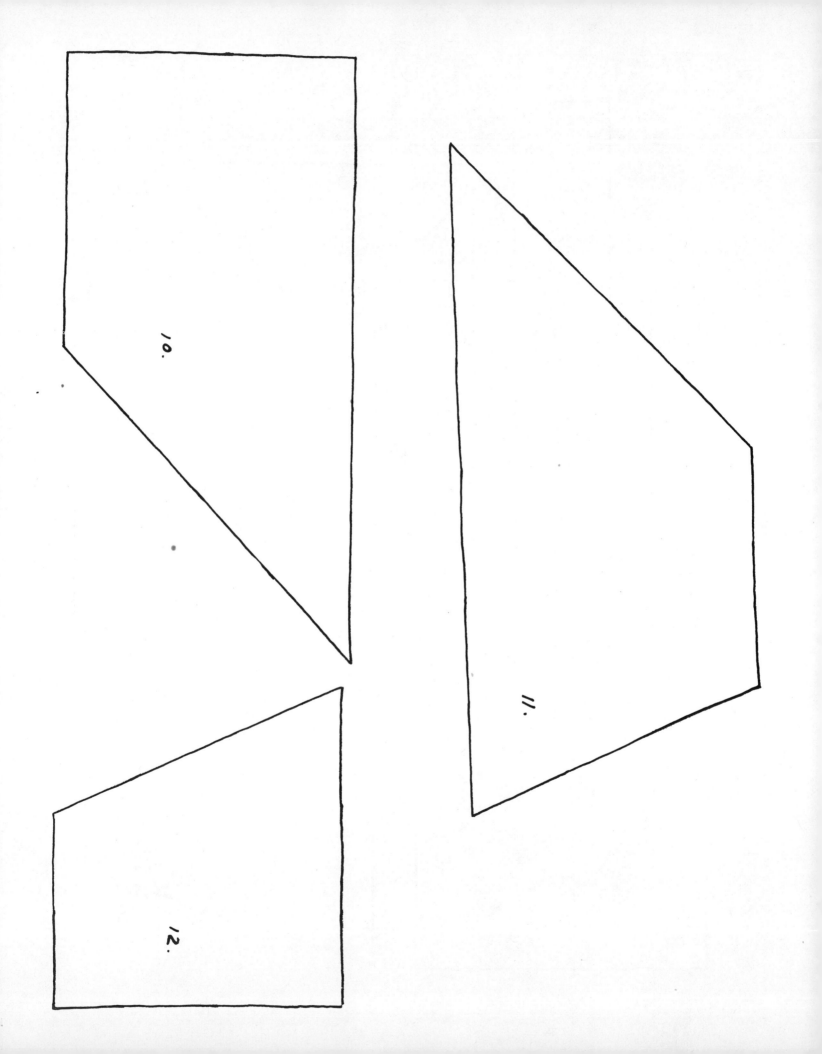

Tennessee Pine Tree

This is a pattern from the eighteenth century. It was found in a lovely old green calico and white quilt from middle Tennessee. These colors make a clean, crisp-looking quilt that will look beautiful in any decor.

The block is an old two patch pattern. The easiest method of piecing a block would be to piece it in strips. Consult the drawing carefully when following these instructions. Sew two white strips, pattern No. 1, on each side of a green No. 2 trunk. Add a white No. 4 triangle at one end. Make the next strip by sewing two white No. 5 triangles to the short sides of a No. 4 green triangle. Make three of these blocks and sew them together, as shown in the drawing. Add a green No. 4 triangle to the left end. Sew these first two pieces together and you will have the diagonal center strip of the blocks, which includes the trunk of the tree. Now make two large triangles in the following manner: sew together five pairs of one green and one white No. 5 triangle so as to form five squares. Sew three of the squares together with the green triangles at the right. Finish this strip with a green No. 5 triangle on the left. Make a second strip from two squares and a green triangle; sew the two strips together with the shorter strip on the bottom. Add a white No. 4 triangle to make the corner of the large triangle, and add a large white No. 3 triangle to the other corner. Make the second triangle reversed to the first. Sew these triangles to either side of the first strip.

This pattern looks best when made with lattice strips or plain blocks between the blocks. The finished block is 12 inches square.

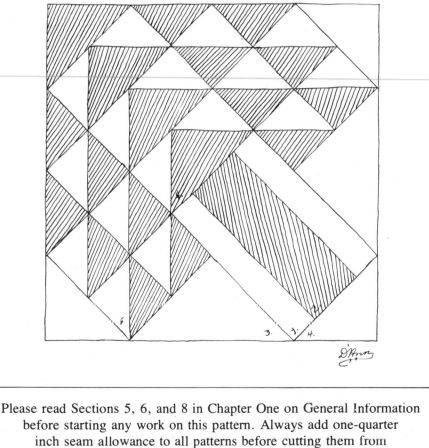

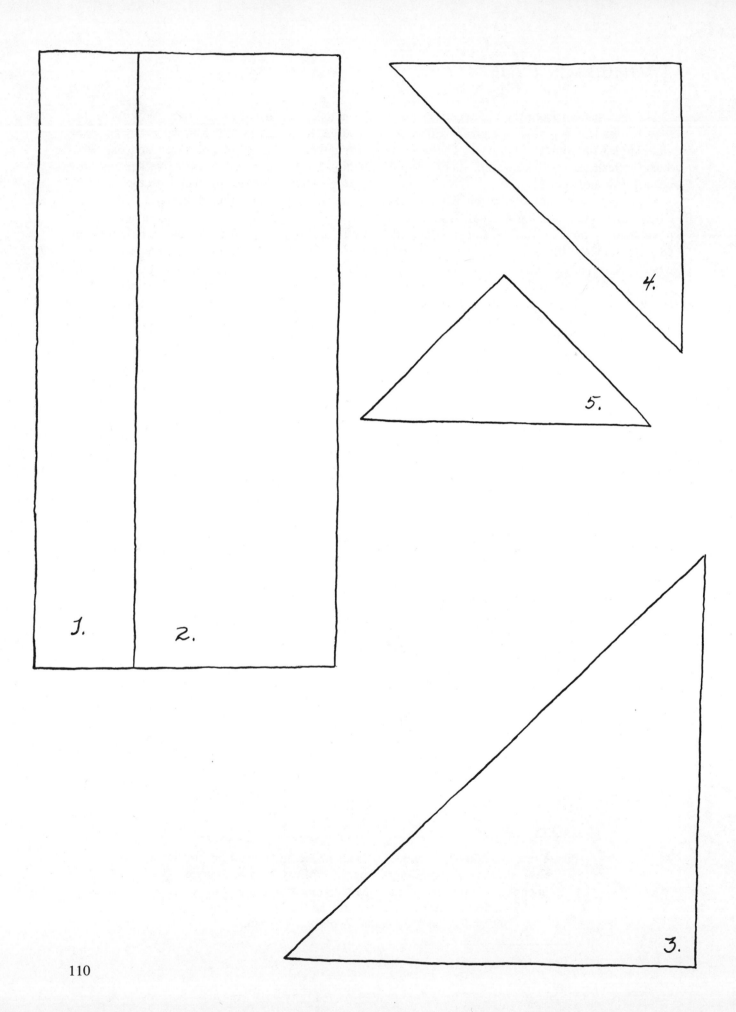

1.

2.

4.

5.

3.

110

The Fan

Fan patterns were at the height of their popularity during the last two decades of the nineteenth century and the first two decades of the twentieth. I have received many requests for fan patterns because quilters wish to make quilts just like the ones their grandmothers made. All fan patterns are scrap quilts. If you can obtain sufficient materials, many of the original fan pattern quilts were made in silks, velvets, and satins, or else in brightly colored prints set off with black. Fancy embroidery outlined each seam.

To begin this pattern, sew a No. 1 triangle to a print No. 2 section and add a No. 3 triangle to the other end. Make six of these three-piece sections. The seams will be more even if two of these sections are sewn together, making three double sections. Finally, sew the double sections together to form the fan.

Sew one No. 4 section to the right half of the fan by starting in the center of the seam and pulling the two curves together as the seam is stitched. Return to the middle and stitch the other end of the seam on the other side. Repeat with the left side of the fan, using the reverse of pattern No. 4. Sew the corner seam between the two sections of pattern No. 4.

This method of sewing a curved seam may seem more complicated than necessary, but it will insure a perfect seam, one more easily made than by any other method. This fan pattern is not for a beginner because of the curved seam.

The finished block is 12 inches square. This pattern does not need a border, but would look attractive with a plain dark border six inches wide.

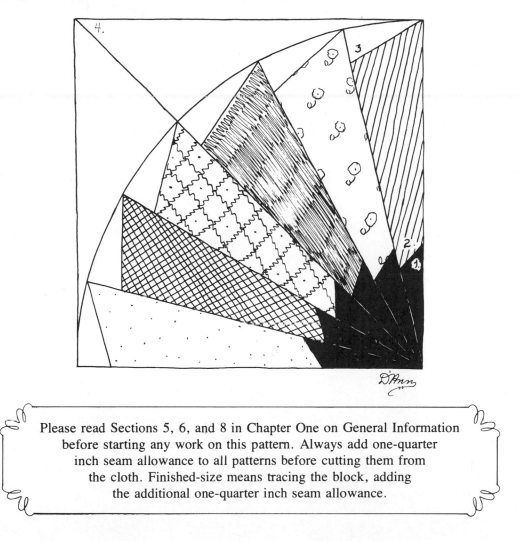

Please read Sections 5, 6, and 8 in Chapter One on General Information before starting any work on this pattern. Always add one-quarter inch seam allowance to all patterns before cutting them from the cloth. Finished-size means tracing the block, adding the additional one-quarter inch seam allowance.

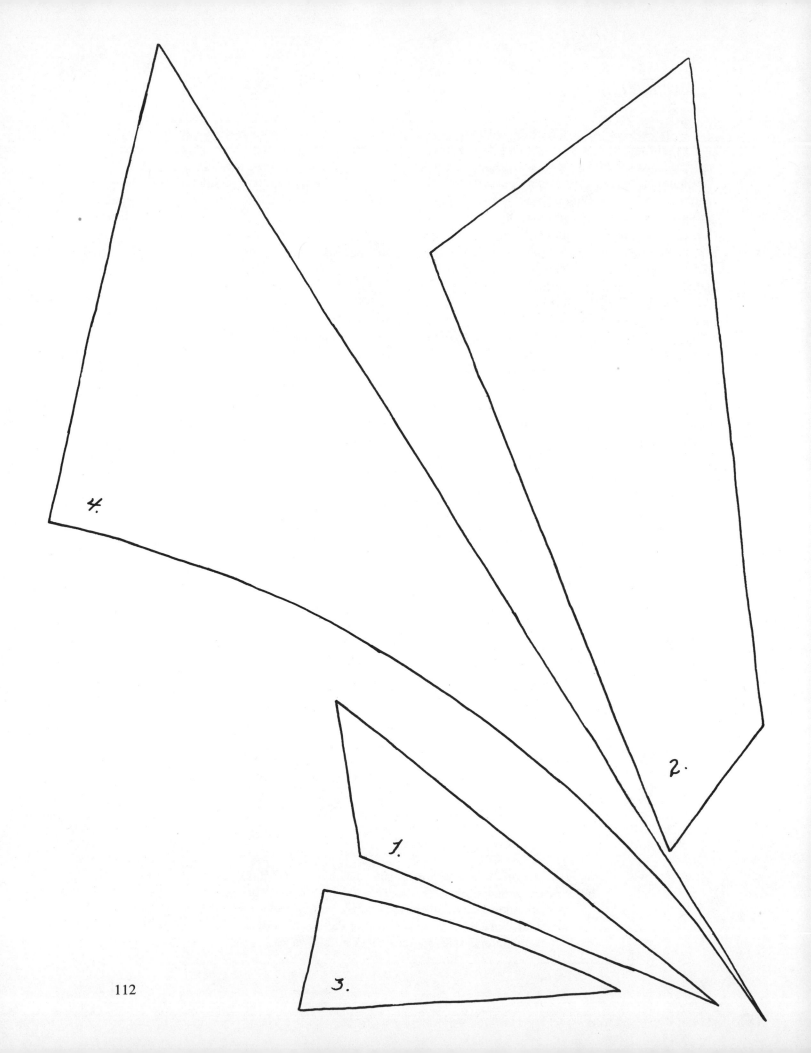

Flower of Autumn

This is probably a pattern from the 1930s. It is a lovely variation of the fan pattern and is also a scrap quilt pattern. The patterns are cut to make a 9½-inch square block, finished-size. The top will look attractive with either a lattice strip or a plain block between the pieced blocks.

Piece together two sets of patterns Nos. 2, 3, and 4, with the second set reversed. Sew them together into the fan like petals of the flower. Add the flower base, pattern No. 5, and the top corner, pattern No. 1, to form a square. Sew a leaf pattern No. 8 to pattern No. 7. Sew a second set of patterns Nos. 7 and 8 reversed. Fill in between the two sections of pattern No. 7 with a stem, pattern No. 6, and sew the two leaves, pattern No. 8, on the diagonal seam. Add this leaf and stem section to the flower square to form the finished block. A twin bed-size quilt will need eight rows of ten blocks each.

This is a rather hard pattern to piece; do not try it if you have not already made several quilts.

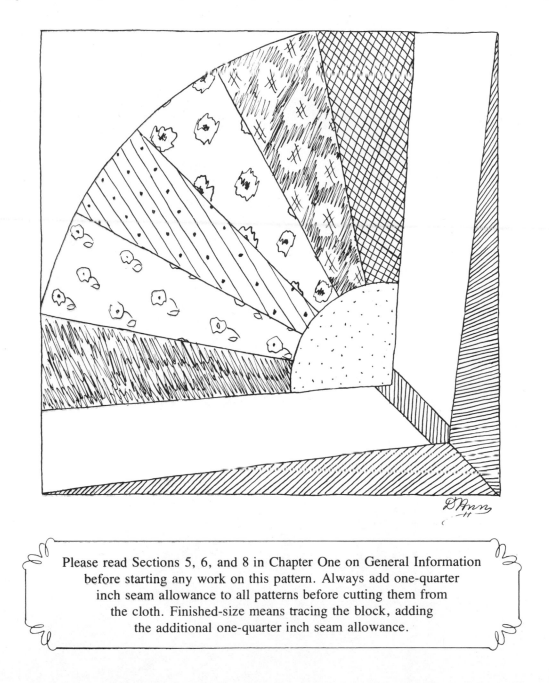

Please read Sections 5, 6, and 8 in Chapter One on General Information before starting any work on this pattern. Always add one-quarter inch seam allowance to all patterns before cutting them from the cloth. Finished-size means tracing the block, adding the additional one-quarter inch seam allowance.

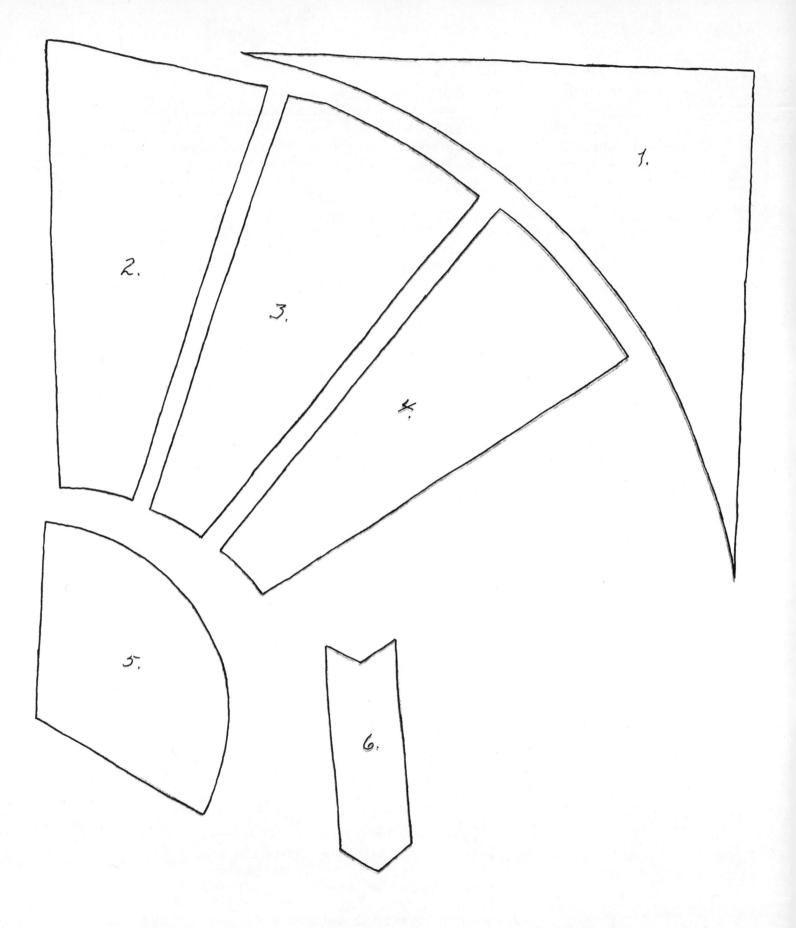

1.

2.

3.

4.

5.

6.

114

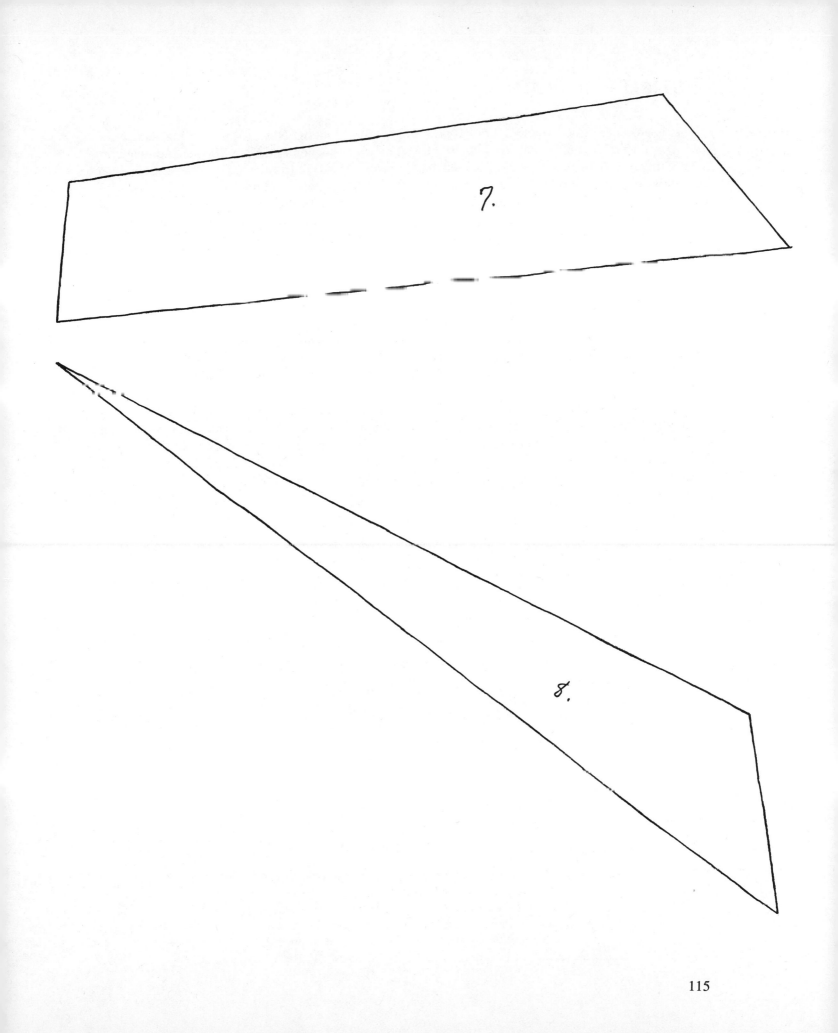

7.

8.

115

Garden Favorite

This is an Alice Brooks pattern from *Household Arts* magazine, published in the 1930s. It is an extremely hard pattern which should be tried only after you have completely mastered the art of sewing curves, but it is lovely enough to be worth the work of making it. The patterns are drawn for a 9-inch square, finished-size block. Choose your colors well. You can make this a scrap quilt if you are very careful with blending the colors. For each flower, use a light and a dark print or plain material in the same color. The leaves should be two shades of green.

As you piece this block, keep referring to the drawing to help in the placement of the various colors and patterns. Piece together two pairs of patterns Nos. 2 and 3; reverse the second pair. Sew these two sections to either side of the No. 1 diamond. Make two triangles from patterns Nos. 4, 5, and 6; reverse the second triangle. Sew these to either side of the first square. This will give you a triangle forming the lower half of the block.

Sew patterns Nos. 10 and 11 together. Now sew this section to the No. 9 petal. Add patterns Nos. 7 and 12 to each side. Make a second set of these patterns and reverse them. Sew the center petal (No. 8) between these two sections. Finish the upper triangle by sewing the diagonal seam to the top corner. Sew the two triangles together, first stitching the two curves of the seam and then sewing the straight sections. This completes the block.

Since this is an elaborate pattern, it would look best with plain blocks set between the pieced ones. This quilt should be framed with a border at least six inches wide. A fairly fancy pattern could be worked by making the top triangle, and setting a plain material triangle with it to make a strip. An inch-wide plain strip should be sewn at the top and bottom of this pieced strip, and the lower curves of the petals should be appliquéd over the bottom strip. A twin bed-size quilt will need eight rows of ten blocks each.

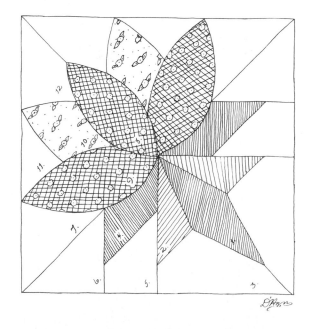

Please read Sections 5, 6, and 8 in Chapter One on General Information before starting any work on this pattern. Always add one-quarter inch seam allowance to all patterns before cutting them from the cloth. Finished-size means tracing the block, adding the additional one-quarter inch seam allowance.

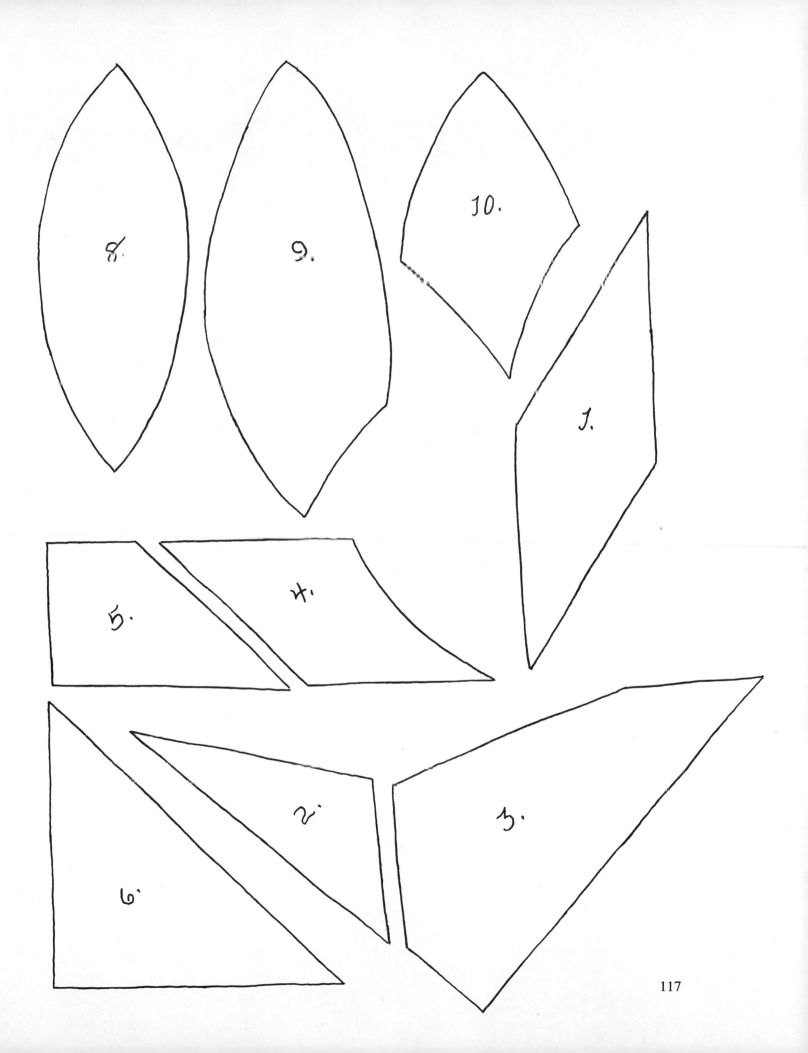

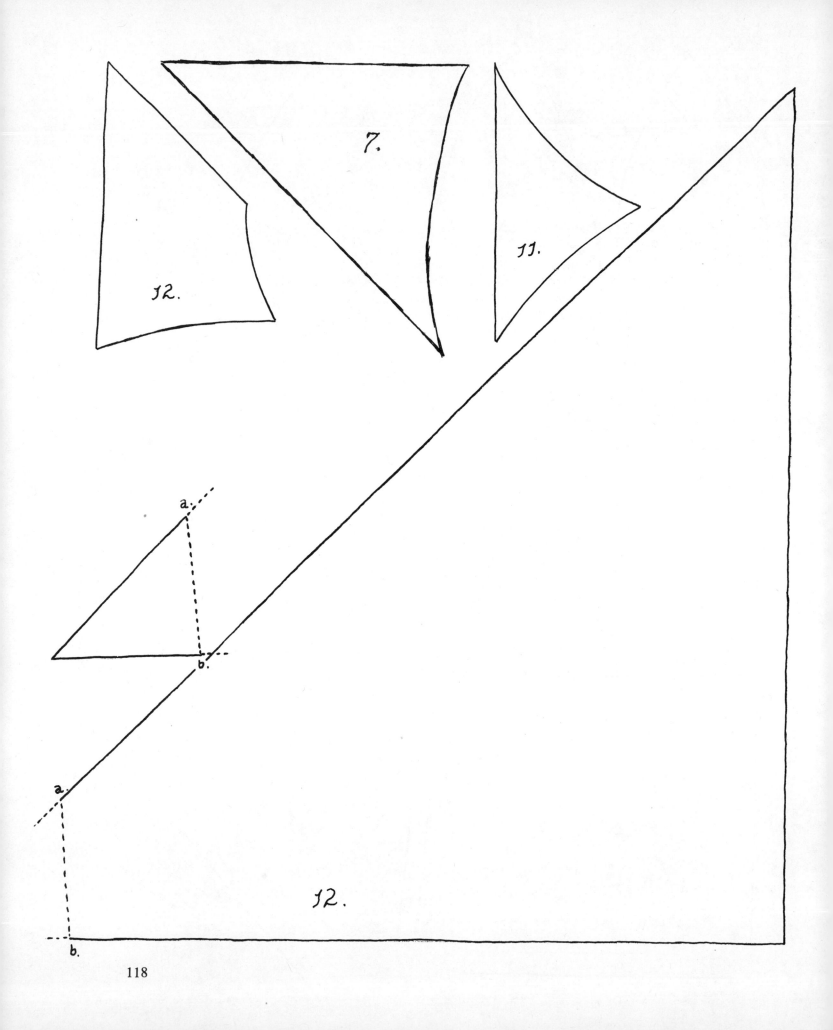

7.

11.

12.

a.

b.

a.

12.

b.

118

Milky Way

This quilt would make a lovely first quilt for a beginner. The pattern is so simple that it has only one piece that is used for the entire top. This should not be made as a scrap quilt. It uses two shades of one color in the same tone and a closely patterned matching print. We used two shades of olive green, a light and a medium tone, and the matching print has closely set roses in several shades of pink with olive green leaves and touches of rust on a cream background. The result is a quilt that has a colonial look. To complement this, we used a six-inch wide border of the print and rounded the corners. Then we quilted the pieced section by the piece and used an old braided border for the quilting on the border.

To piece the pattern, make triangles of one triangle cut from each of the three materials. Place each of the colors in the same position in each triangle you make. This will be much easier to do if you make all the triangle blocks for the quilt before you begin to put the top together. For a twin bed-size quilt you will need eight rows of 17 blocks each (143 triangular blocks).

To piece each row, place the first triangle with the point up and the print side on the left. The next triangle in the row should have the point down and the print side on top. Continue placing the blocks in exactly the same two positions with the print side exactly the same until your row contains 17 triangles. Piece the eight rows together. The two sides of the pieced center will be straight, but the top and bottom will be scalloped. Fill in the scallops with large triangles of one of the colors used in the top. Add two more rows to the sides of the quilt for a double bed-sized quilt.

Lest you think this quilt is too plain to be pretty, our quilt has been shown in three quilt shows and has won a blue ribbon each time. It looks good in a very frilly bedroom setting and is equally at home in a tailored room. Men seem to admire it as well as women, and it is one of the few quilts that looks nice in a boy's room. As I mentioned before, it has a colonial look and yet it is an optical illusion pattern that is very much in the modern mode. I think you will find that this will become one of your favorite patterns, as it has for me.

Please read Sections 5, 6, and 8 in Chapter One on General Information before starting any work on this pattern. Always add one-quarter inch seam allowance to all patterns before cutting them from the cloth. Finished-size means tracing the block, adding the additional one-quarter inch seam allowance.

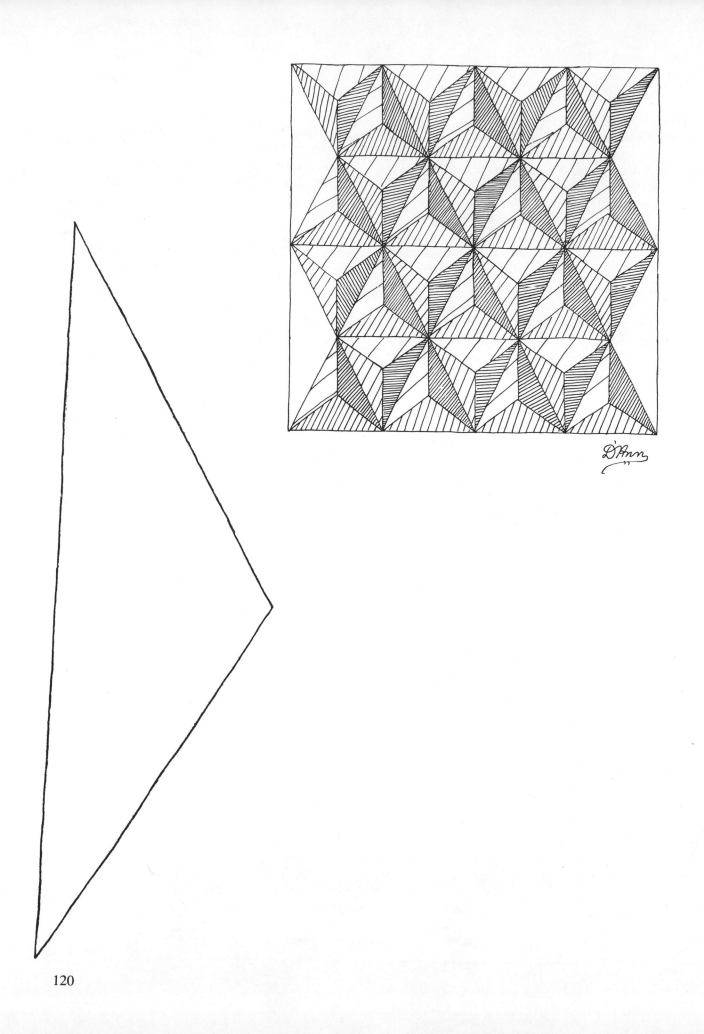

120

CHAPTER FIVE

Four Patch Patterns

General Eisenhower Star

Traditional Patterns From Diamonds

Diamonds have always been among the most versatile of the basic design shapes in quilting, and a few are included here. The oldest traditional design is the Star of LeMoine. Two variations of this are shown in drawings No. 1 and 2. The first quilts made from this eight-pointed star design are recorded by the first settlers of the Ohio and Mississippi River valleys in the late eighteenth century. It is not known if the settlers brought these designs with them, borrowed them from Amerindian designs, or created them themselves.

A later pattern, the Boxed Star (No. 3), is made in the same way as the others except that the corners are made with two triangles rather than a square. To make these patterns, choose one of the basic diamonds and note the letter in its bottom point. The diamond marked *A* gives you a square block 15¼ inches on a side. The *B* diamond makes a 9-inch square block, the *C* diamond makes a 12-inch square block, *D* yields a 6-inch square block, *E* gives another 12-inch square block (this one will be a four patch design), *F* gives a 7½-inch square block, and *G* makes a 5-inch square block. Of course, the smaller the block the daintier the quilt will be, but there will be more work in making it. A quilt made from blocks *D, F,* or *G* without lattice strips or plain blocks is called A Thousand Stars.

Now find the sets of squares and triangles marked to match the diamond shapes. Choose a square and a triangle with the same letter as the diamond. Trace all three patterns off and use these shapes for your quilt patterns. Join two of the diamonds point to point. Add a square between their upper points. Make four of these sections. Now join two of the corner sections and piece a triangle between the open points of the diamonds. Repeat for the other two sections and then join the two sections. Piece the last two triangles in place.

There are several ways to treat the color scheme of the large star. Each row of the star should be treated as a single unit from the center outward. Many lovely stars are made by starting with a light shade of one color and then making each row darker through five or six rows, then shading back to the light color at the outer point of the star. A star of two contrasting colors or a color and a matching print is also traditional, but rather rare. During patriotic times like the Centennial and Bicentennial celebrations, stars are made of repeating red, white, and blue rows. One of the nicest ways to make the star is to choose a graduated series of prints and plain colors that blend and contrast into a brilliant rainbow. The colors can be graded to the center and reversed to the outer edge, or each row from the center outward can be different. Whichever way you decide to make your star, plan your colors carefully before you begin your quilt. If you run out of a color before the row is finished, it will ruin your quilt.

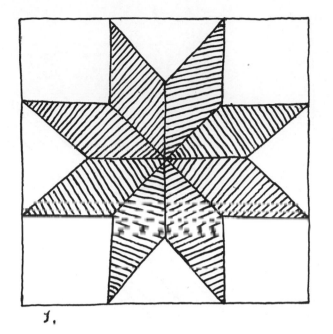

1,

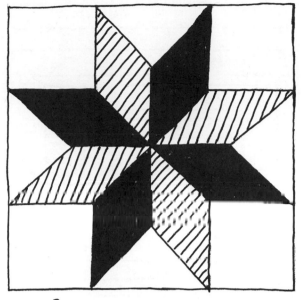

2.

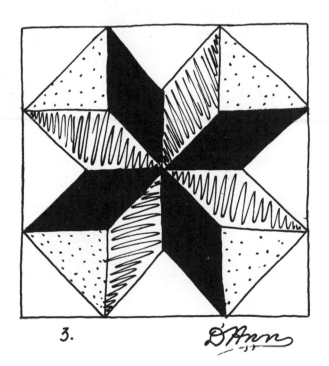

3.

D'Ann
-37

123

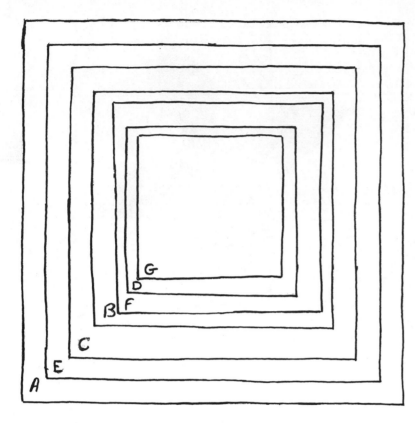

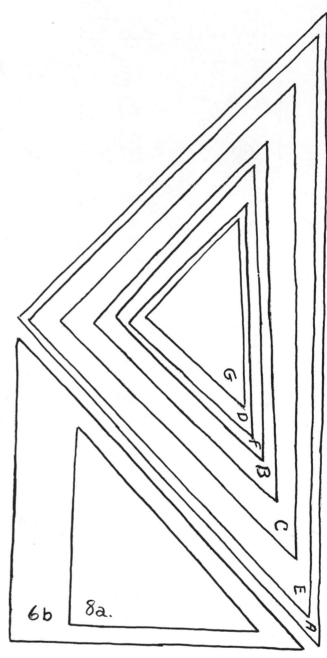

6b   8a.

124

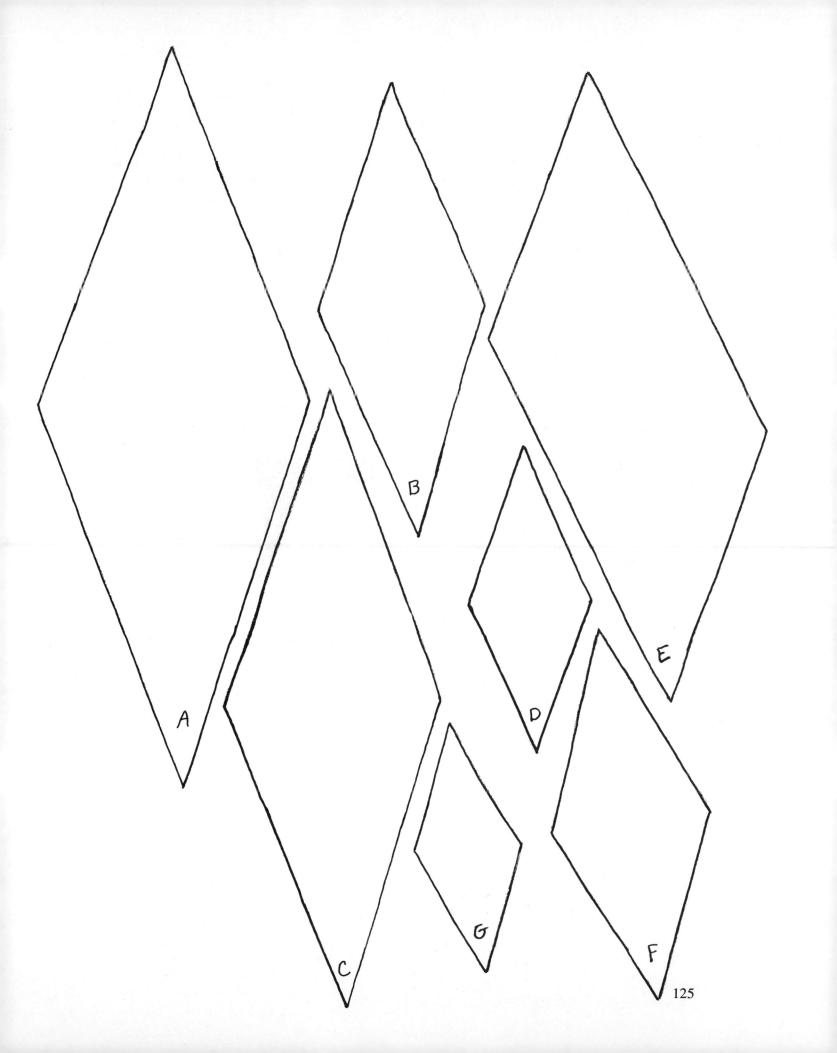

125

General Eisenhower Star

General Eisenhower, one of our first five star generals, was also President when the United States added the last two stars to our flag. A fifty state quilt is much harder to design than a forty-eight state quilt, so I was very happy when this design worked out so neatly. Count them — there *are* fifty stars in this quilt top. The multiple stars are large enough so that if you are careful and neat, they will not be too hard to sew. This is not a pattern for the beginner.

Make the center star first. Cut one gold No. 1 pentagon and five gold No. 2 triangles. Fill in between the points of the star with five blue No. 3 diamonds. This will form a center pentagon. Now make five smaller star pentagons with patterns Nos. 5, 6, and 7, with blue stars and white diamonds. Place two red No. 4 sections, one reversed, on either side of the small pentagon's point and add one large No. 8 triangle across the pentagon's top to form a triangle. Sew five of these blue star triangles to the center gold star pentagon to form the large star. Fill in between the points of the star with large white diamonds made from pattern No. 9. Only half of pattern Nos. 9 and 10 are given. This forms the large triangle that is pieced between the patterned star blocks in the outer row to form the large pentagon. Piece or appliqué this large pentagon to the center of a blue square of cloth 6½ feet on a side. Add the eight gold stars in the corners. The border is a 1½-inch wide strip of red and a 6-inch wide strip of blue.

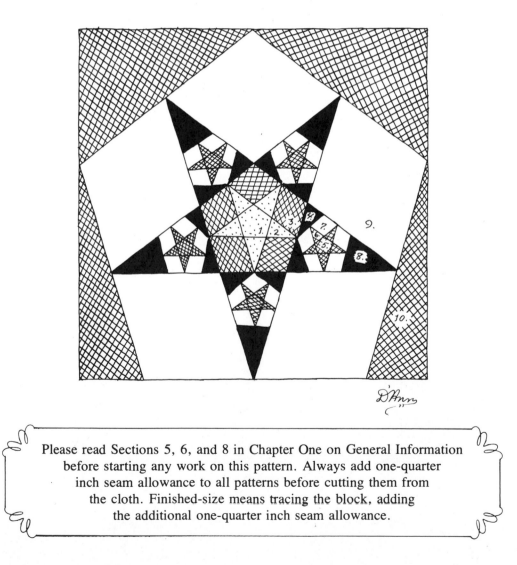

Please read Sections 5, 6, and 8 in Chapter One on General Information before starting any work on this pattern. Always add one-quarter inch seam allowance to all patterns before cutting them from the cloth. Finished-size means tracing the block, adding the additional one-quarter inch seam allowance.

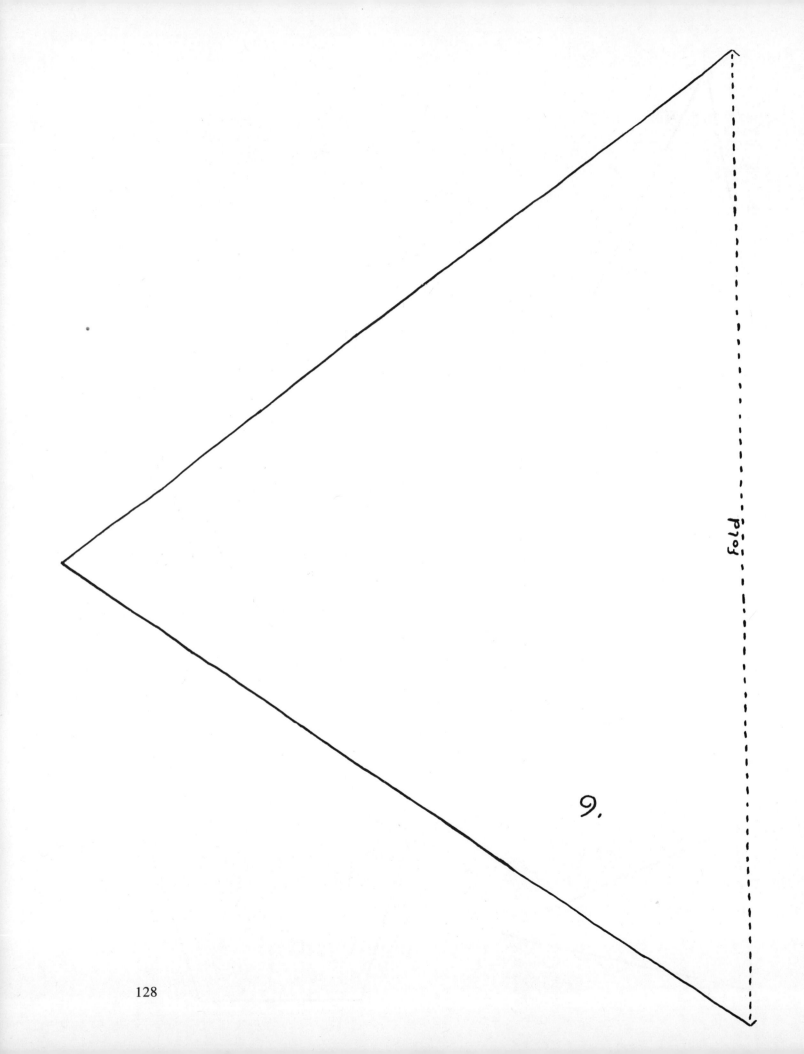

fold

9.

128

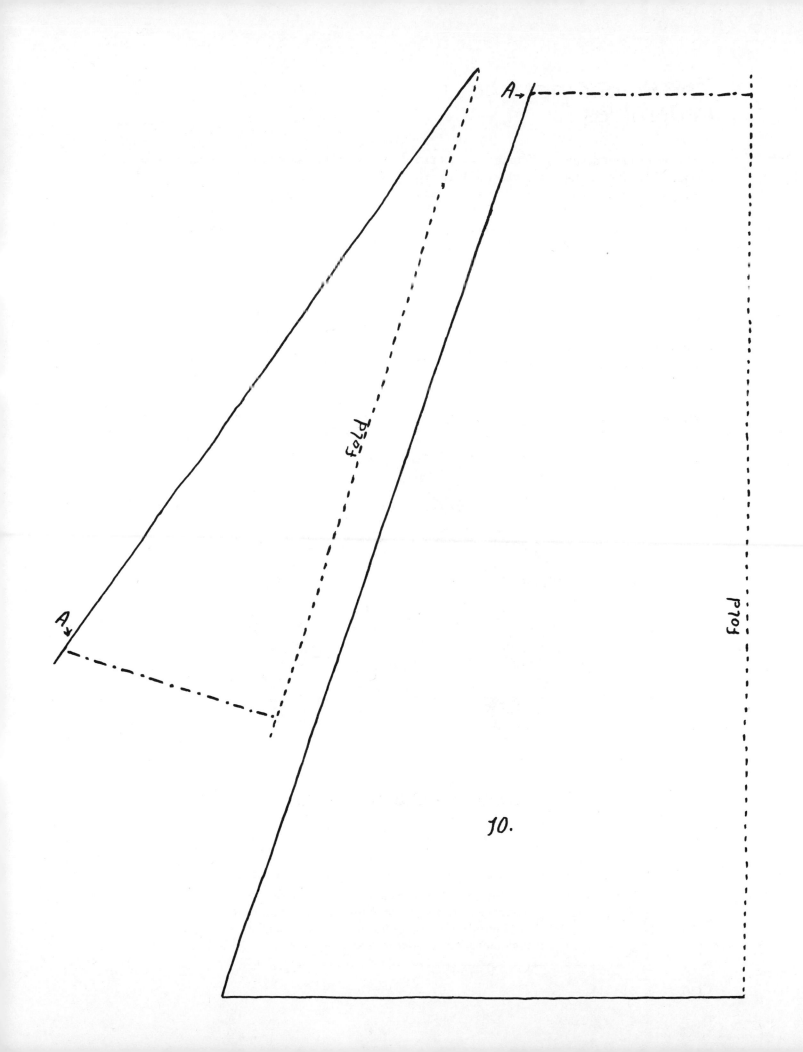

A→

Fold

A→

Fold

Fold

10.

The Star of the Pedernales

This is a pattern designed in honor of our 36th President, Lyndon B. Johnson, who was born in Texas on the Pedernales River. The large star is made of a blue No. 1 pattern and a white No. 1 pattern, reversed. Sew these two triangles together until you have made five diamonds. Then sew a gold No. 2 diamond between two red No. 3 triangles to form a large triangle (see the drawing). Sew one side of the red triangle to the long side of a blue and white diamond. Add a second blue and white diamond and sew this seam along the short side to the first diamond, from the top of the red triangle to the center of the larger star. Continue until all the diamonds and red triangles have been sewn into the large pentagon.

Several interesting quilt designs can be made from the pentagon shapes, but a beginning quilter may prefer to add the two white No. 4 triangles to the top corners and two white No. 5 triangles to the bottom corners to make this block into a square, which makes a quilt top much easier to design. Use a simple red, white, and blue border. The square is 14½ inches on a side.

A twin bed quilt will need five rows of seven blocks each, and a 1½-inch-wide border. For a larger border use four rows of six blocks and a 15- or 16-inch-wide border. A double bed quilt will need seven rows of seven blocks and a 1½-inch border, or six rows of six blocks and a 15- or 16-inch-wide border.

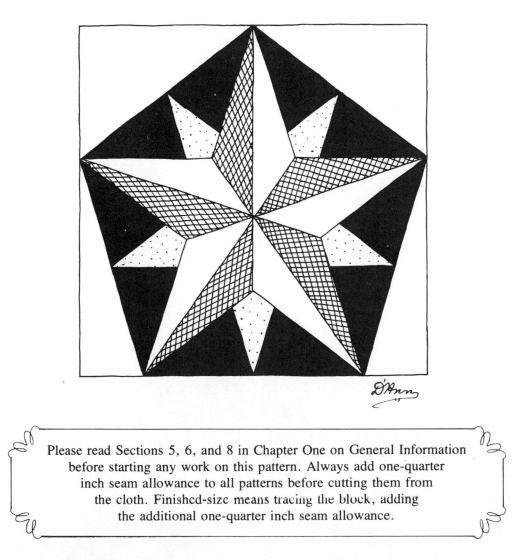

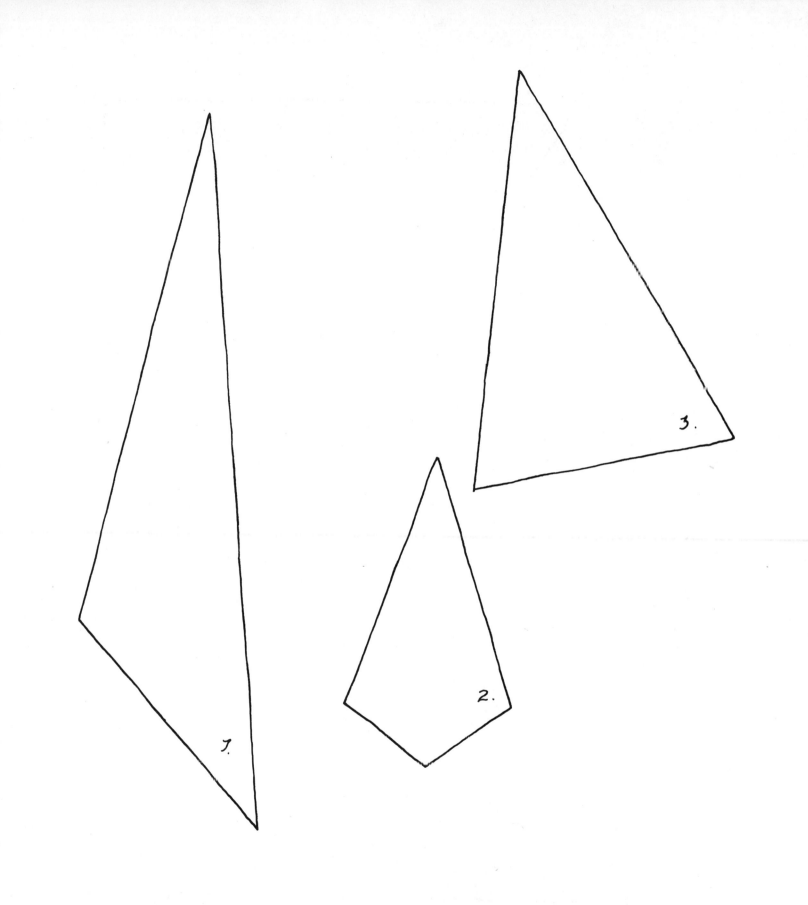

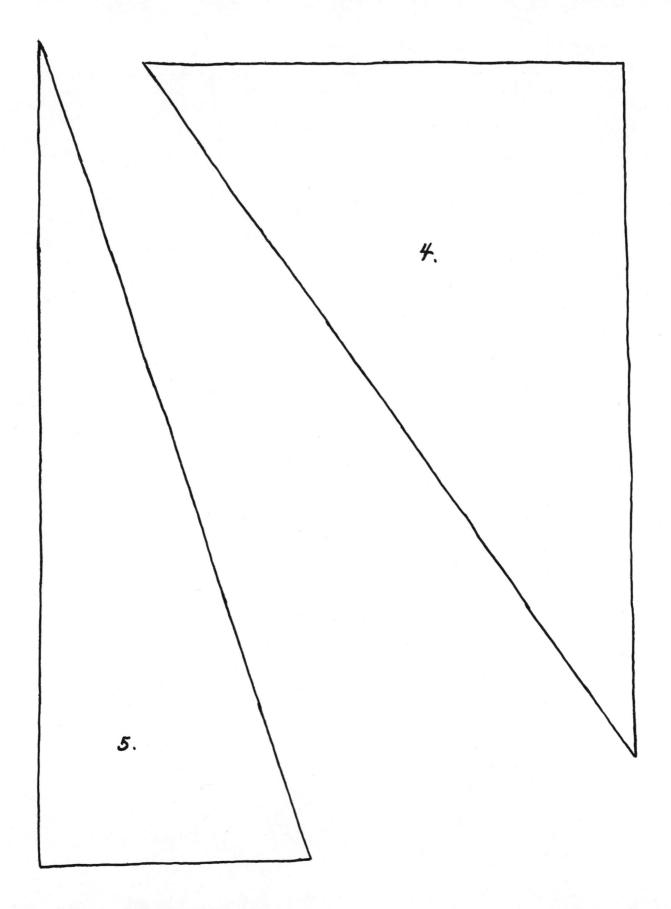

4.

5.

Rambling Road

A pattern that was very popular during the late nineteenth century is Rambling Road. It is usually done in one color, or a print, with white in each block. By piecing this pattern in a different color or print in each block, you can make a charming old-fashioned scrap quilt. The square is slightly larger than usual, since it is 12½ inches square. Your quilt (either a twin bed-size with six rows of eight blocks, or a double bed-size with eight rows of eight blocks) will also be six to eight inches larger than usual, even without a border. By removing a row of blocks each way from the quilt top, you could add a six-inch sawtooth border with a two-inch band improvised from the sawtooth border (see the section on borders).

To make the block, construct each of the four squares in it separately. First cut eight small squares of a dark and a white triangle, pattern No. 2. Take four of these squares and sew them into a row; sew the dark side of this row to a white No. 1 triangle pattern. Lay this aside. Sew together a second group of four pieced squares and add a white No. 3 square to the dark end. Sew this row to the other side of the white triangle (No. 1). Add a dark triangle No. 1 to the long side of the white triangle, and the square is finished. Make three more of these. Sew two of the finished squares together and then the other two. Sew the two units together. Study the drawing of the finished square carefully while making this block. Plain blocks between the pieced ones, lattice strips, and a top made of all pieced blocks are all possibilities with this pattern.

Please read Sections 5, 6, and 8 in Chapter One on General Information before starting any work on this pattern. Always add one-quarter inch seam allowance to all patterns before cutting them from the cloth. Finished-size means tracing the block, adding the additional one-quarter inch seam allowance.

1.

2.

3.

Fern

This is a 1930s pattern from a Nancy Page newspaper column. It would look attractive in any color and white, but a green print would match the name.

Make the center square first. Sew four green No. 2 triangles to four white No. 3 shapes. Sew these together into two units; then add the tiny, green No. 1 square. Sew the last two units together to form the center square. Make the four corner triangles by sewing a green No. 5 triangle between two No. 4 shapes. The side of the No. 4 shape which goes next to the No. 5 triangle has been marked with an *A*. Now sew a green No. 7 triangle to the No. 6 shape to form a larger triangle. Sew the two units together to form the large corner triangle; add all four of these to the center square to form the block. The finished block will be 10 inches square. A twin bed-size quilt will need seven rows of nine blocks and a simple four inch wide strip for a border.

Please read Sections 5, 6, and 8 in Chapter One on General Information before starting any work on this pattern. Always add one-quarter inch seam allowance to all patterns before cutting them from the cloth. Finished-size means tracing the block, adding the additional one-quarter inch seam allowance.

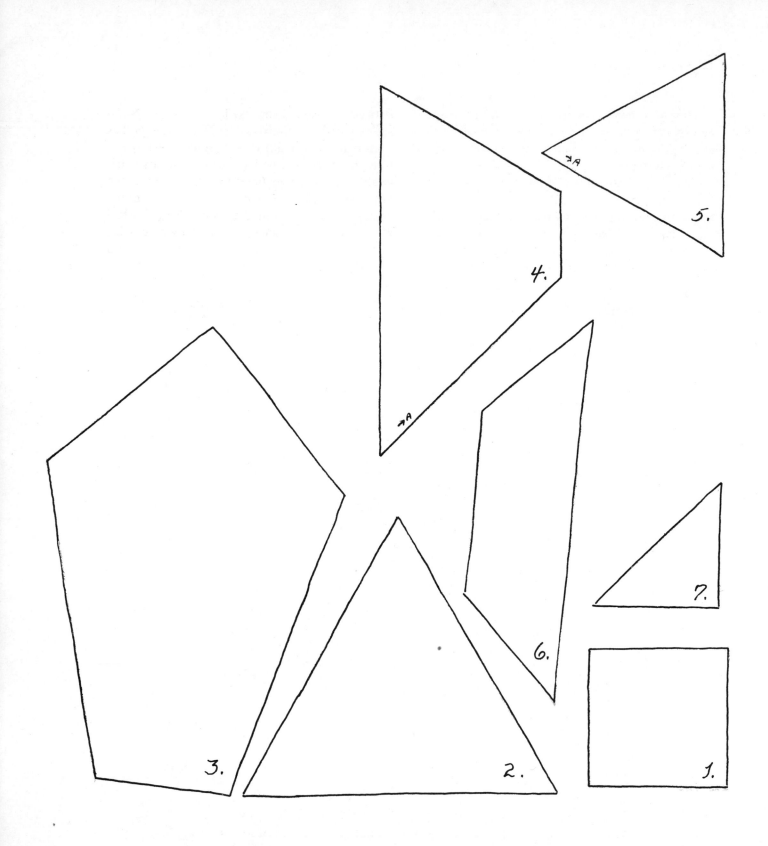

Leaded Glass

If you have ever admired stained glass windows, lamps, and other art objects, this pattern will appeal to you. It is, however, one of the hardest patterns, if not *the* very hardest pattern, in this book. Do not attempt it until you have mastered the art of sewing curves that lie flat. This is another of my original patterns; I designed it to be versatile. You may use the same colors over the entire quilt top or use the same print in all of the oval No. 1 patterns, and a different, rich, plain-colored material in each block of pattern Nos. 4 and 7 shown in white in the drawing. You could also use the same color in those patterns (Nos. 4 and 7) over the entire quilt top and use a different print in the No. 1 oval for each block. Use a four-inch-wide border of the material used for the darker sections of the pieces that represent the lead strips. For the lead strips use a dark and light gray, or a dark and medium brown, as you prefer.

To piece a block, make four curved No. 4 triangles. To give the effect of light and shadow, each strip of light and dark lead in each of the four sides of a block is in a different position. Keep these sections in the same order in each block for the entire quilt top. You might mark the top of each block with a white thread stay-stitch, so that they do not become mixed before they are sewn in place. The light lead strips in the left-hand triangles are No. 5 on the upper side, No. 3 on the lower side, and No. 8 and its reverse in the point. The light lead strips in the top block are No. 5 on the right, No. 3 on the left, and Nos. 6 and 8 on the left center section. The light lead strips on the right side are No. 2 on the right, No. 2 (reversed) on the left, and No. 6 and its reverse in the center. The light lead strips in the bottom triangle are No. 3 on the right, No. 5 on the left, and Nos. 6 and 8 on the right side of the center section. The position of the triangles is given from a point facing the drawing from the front of the page. The position of the lead strips is given facing each triangle with the straight side of the triangle at the bottom. The patterns give the right side of the triangles to the center. For the left side patterns, reverse your pattern when drawing it on cloth.

Piece each triangle in three sections. Piece sections 5, 2, and 3 around the No. 4 center. Piece the left side using the same pieces reversed. Sew the center section by sewing pattern No. 6 and its reverse and pattern No. 8 and its reverse around the diamond pattern No. 7. As you make each triangle, pay close attention to the drawing and the list of light lead strips for each triangle, given above. When all four triangles are ready, piece each one to one side of a No. 1 oval. It is easier to make these long curves lie straight if you start each seam in the center and run it out to the point on one side, then return to the center and make the seam to the other point. Now sew two of these sections together to make the two sides of the block; finally, sew the four sections together. Be very careful in this last seam to make the points of all four triangles and the four ovals come together in the exact center of the block.

These patterns are drawn for a 12-inch square block, finished-size. Six rows of eight blocks each will make a twin bed quilt with a four-inch band added to the quilt top as a border.

Please read Sections 5, 6, and 8 in Chapter One on General Information before starting any work on this pattern. Always add one-quarter inch seam allowance to all patterns before cutting them from the cloth. Finished-size means tracing the block, adding the additional one-quarter inch seam allowance.

138

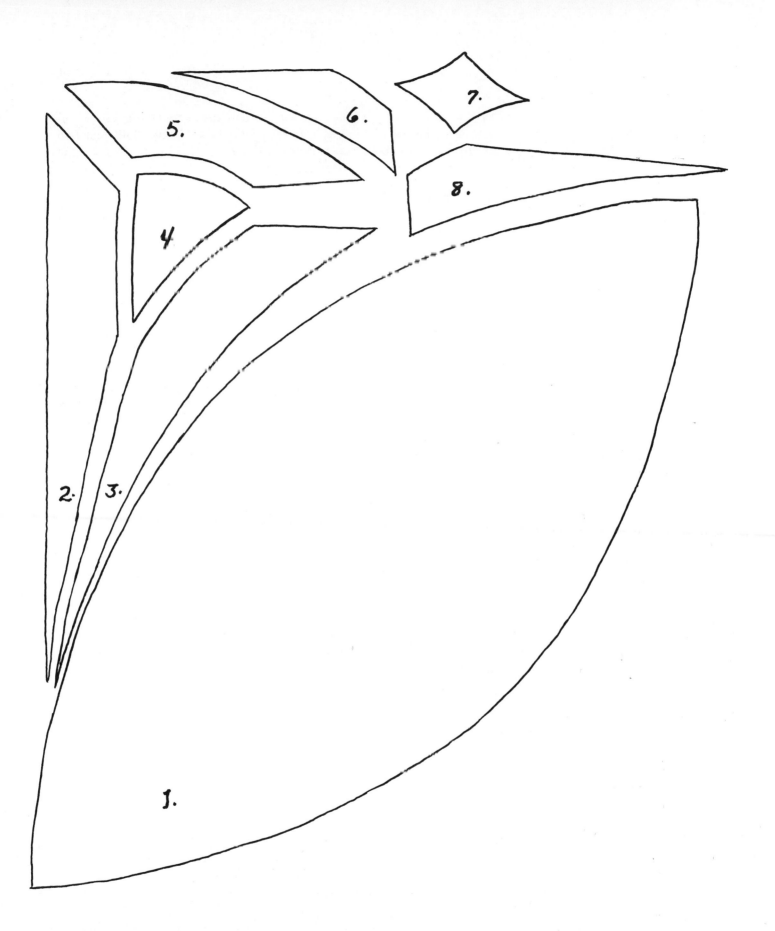

Star Flower

With a flower print in each corner and a two-tone flower in the center, this is a real garden pattern. When winters are cold and spring seems very far off, this lovely quilt will remind you of summer. A green lattice strip between the blocks would give the illusion of flower beds with garden paths between them.

This pattern is for a scrap quilt, but it will take thought to place the print materials together in a pleasing arrangement. This pattern should not be made as a first quilt. When planning your quilt, choose several flowered prints in several different colors. You will also need white, a green, either a light and dark shade in one color or in several flower colors, and a small amount of yellow. The large triangles of printed material in the four corners can all be the same, as shown, or each one can be a different flowered print. This can be an all-pieced block, or you may choose to do some appliquéing.

To make the all-pieced block, cut out pattern No. 3 (two pieces, one reversed) from white cloth. Pattern 4 is green and should be sewn between the two white No. 3 sections. Cut two green No. 2 sections and sew them on each side of the stem triangle, as shown. This is the bottom triangle for the center of the block. For the top triangle cut three dark No. 5 diamonds and two light ones. Cut out two yellow No. 6 shapes. Sew two of the dark diamonds together. Next add a yellow shape on each side, and lay this section aside. Sew a light diamond on each side of the remaining dark diamond. Now sew these

two sections of the flower together; set the finished flower aside. From white cloth, cut two sections each of pattern Nos. 7 and 8, reversing one section. Cut pattern No. 9 from white cloth also. Sew sections 7 and 8 together for each side of the pattern. Sew section 9 to the top of the flower. Sew sections 7 and 8 to either side of the flower. Appliqué the rounded ends of the No. 6 shape to the dotted lines on the No. 8 section. Do not attempt to piece these sections together as the curve of the No. 6 shape is too extreme to piece. Sew the two triangles together. Add the four No. 1 triangles in flowered materials to each side of the central pieced square.

If you wish to make this an appliquéd pattern, cut the four flower print triangles No. 1 and two more No. 1 triangles in white. Piece the flower from No. 5 diamonds and No. 6 yellow shapes, as directed in the paragraph above. Cut the stem and leaves (No. 4 and No. 2) from green. Sew the two white triangles together. Appliqué first the two leaves (one reversed) to the bottom point of the square and add the No. 4 stem in the center. Position the flower in the center of the top triangle, with its bottom point set into the No. 4 stem, as shown in the drawing. Appliqué this in place. Add the four flowered print triangles to the outside of the center square by piecing them.

These patterns have been drawn for a 12-inch square block. The quilt would be pretty with either a plain block between the pieced ones or a lattice strip.

Please read Sections 5, 6, and 8 in Chapter One on General Information before starting any work on this pattern. Always add one-quarter inch seam allowance to all patterns before cutting them from the cloth. Finished-size means tracing the block, adding the additional one-quarter inch seam allowance.

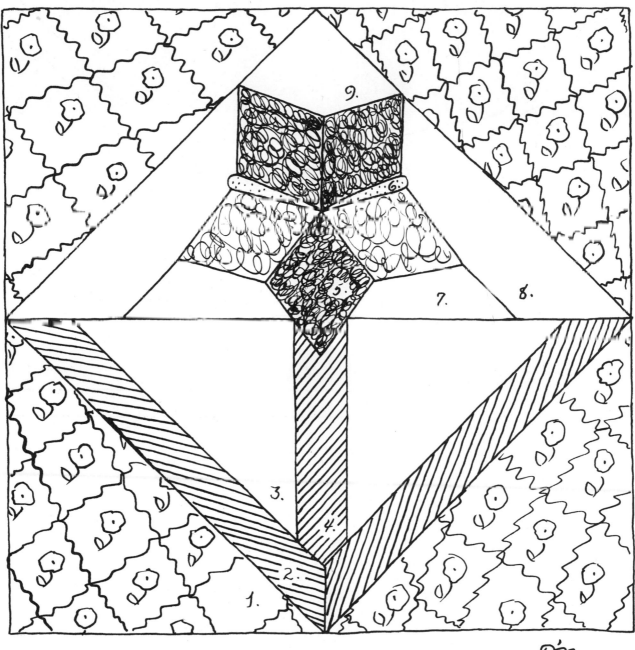

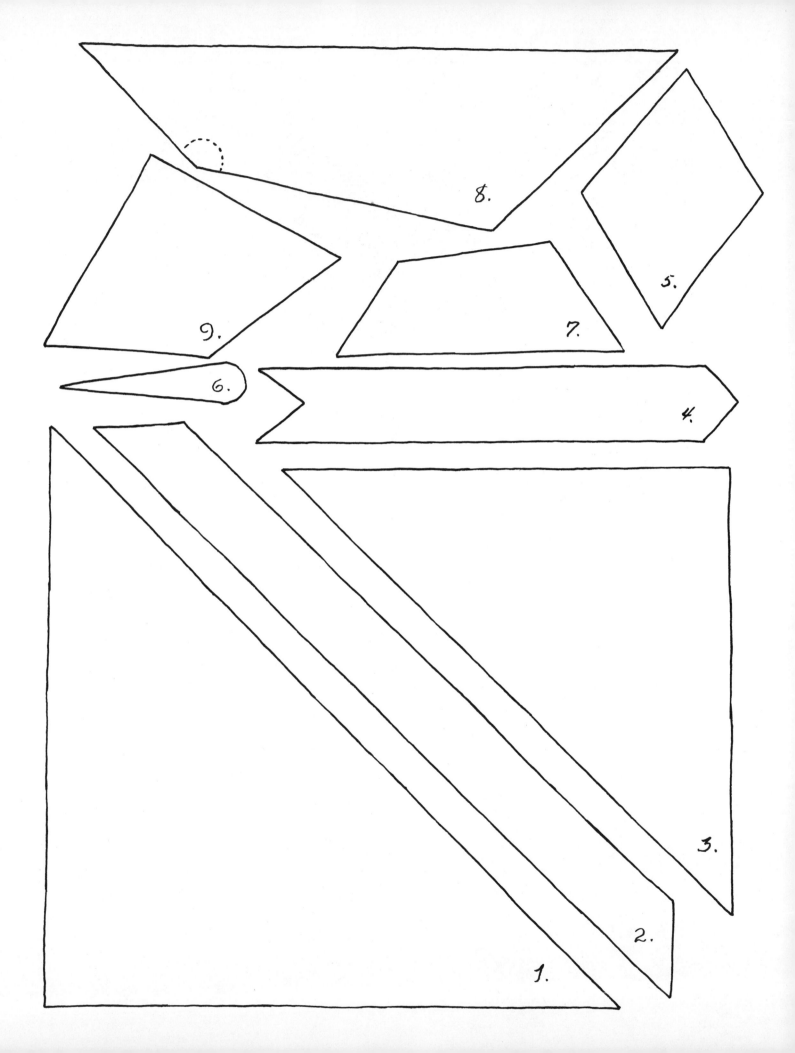

Windmill

This is an old pattern from the Alice Brooks column in *Household Arts* magazine. The design makes a lovely scrap quilt. The patterns are drawn for a 10-inch square block.

Sew a dark No. 4 shape to a white No. 5 shape. Add a white No. 3 triangle on the shorter side seam and a white No. 6 triangle on the other, longer side seam. This forms a large triangle for one side of the block. To finish this side, add a long No. 2 strip to the outside seam of the No. 6 triangle. Please look carefully at the drawing of the finished block for exact placement of the sections. Put this first section aside and make three more exactly like the first. Sew two sides together and add the very dark center square. Sew the remaining sides together; then sew them to the first two sides. This pattern would look attractive as an all-over design or with narrow lattice strips.

For a twin bed size quilt, you will need seven rows of nine blocks each and a border that is at least four inches wide. This pattern is easy enough for any beginner.

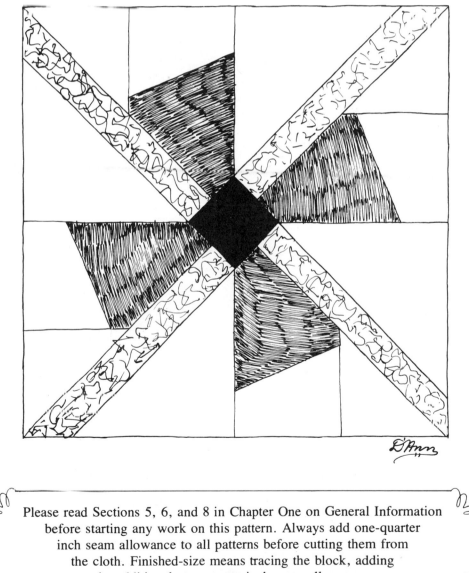

Please read Sections 5, 6, and 8 in Chapter One on General Information before starting any work on this pattern. Always add one-quarter inch seam allowance to all patterns before cutting them from the cloth. Finished-size means tracing the block, adding the additional one-quarter inch seam allowance.

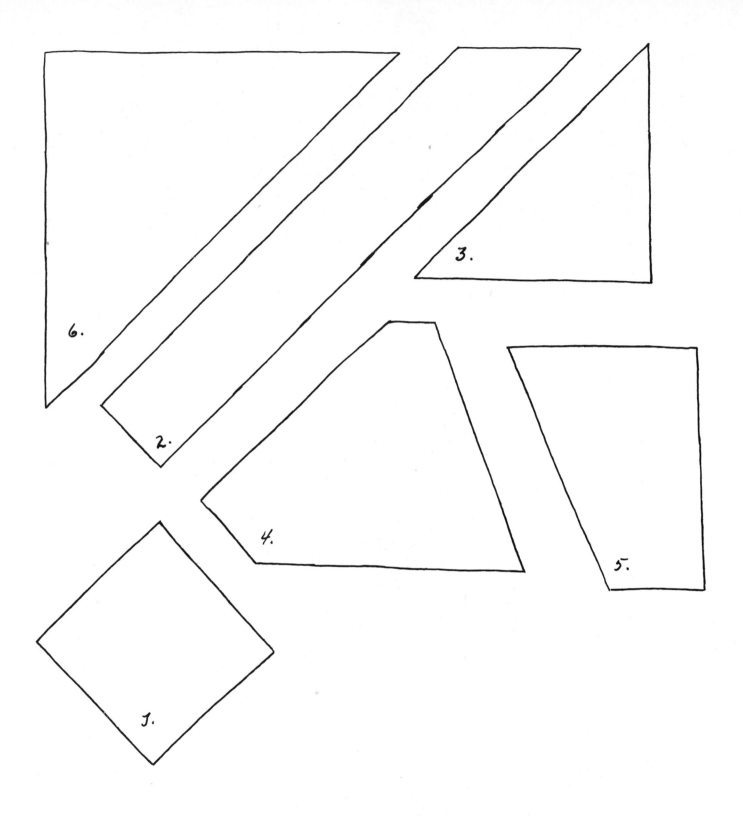

Pinwheel

This pinwheel pattern is another Alice Brooks design from *Household Arts* magazine. It is a very hard pattern, so practice sewing curved seams before starting it. This design is made to be a lovely scrap pattern, so get out all of your cotton sewing scraps and mix-and-match them in the blocks.

The finished square is large, being 14 inches square. To make this block, sew four print or colored No. 2 petal shapes to four white No. 3 shapes. Next, sew four No. 2 petal shapes to four No. 4 shapes. Look carefully at the drawing of the finished block for placement of the elements. Now sew one of the No. 2 — No. 3 sections to a No. 2 — No. 4 section along the seam that points to a corner. Sew the other three corners together in the same manner. One at a time, sew a corner section to the center circle No. 1. As each section is added, finish sewing the seams between the sections. This should be an all-over pattern. A twin bed quilt will need only five rows of seven blocks each. By adding a 12-inch-wide border to this, the quilt will be double bed-size.

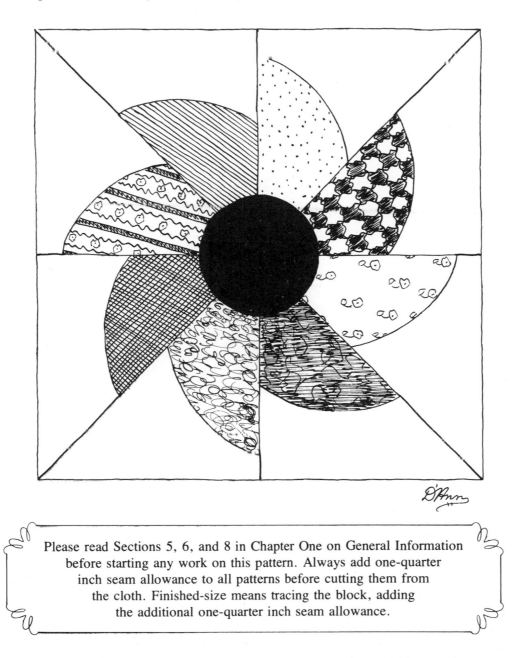

Please read Sections 5, 6, and 8 in Chapter One on General Information before starting any work on this pattern. Always add one-quarter inch seam allowance to all patterns before cutting them from the cloth. Finished-size means tracing the block, adding the additional one-quarter inch seam allowance.

2.

3.

1.

4.

146

Potomac Sun

One day, with the summer sun shining down on me in a park in Washington, D.C., I thought of how welcome a quilt would be that could remind me of the colors and heat of that day in the cold winter months. This quilt does that.

The corners meet in four blocks to form a hot, yellow, red-orange, and white sun. In the center are yellow-green paths and flower print garden beds which should be in the colors of the summer zinnias, marigolds, and nasturtiums. These flower prints may be used as scrap patterns, but all of the other colors must be those given — otherwise, your reproduction of a summer day will not shed as much warmth in your winter bedroom.

These patterns are drawn for a 10-inch square block. Sew a yellow-green No. 2 triangle to a No. 1 diamond; complete four of these for the center of the block. Sew them together two-by-two and complete the center. Lay this aside. Sew a white No. 7 triangle (one reversed) to each side of a yellow No. 6 triangle. Add a red No. 4 triangle to each of the white No. 7 triangles and a red No. 5 triangle to the top of the yellow No. 6 triangle. Make the curved section by sewing two yellow No. 3 triangles to either side of the No. 5 triangle. Make four of these corners. Start the curved seam at the point of the No. 5 triangle in the center of the seam. Sew this seam, easing the two curves together to the edge of the block. Return to the center and finish the seam in the other direction. Repeat this for the other three corners. This is the only way to make sure that a curved seam will lie flat when finished.

Choose and match your colors carefully. To be most effective, this pattern must be done in an all-over design without plain blocks or lattice strips. A twin bed quilt will need seven rows of nine blocks each. To form the border, make half suns from pattern Nos. 3, 4, 5, 6, and 7. Sew these around the edge of the quilt to match the half suns produced by the edges of the blocks. This design is not for a beginning quilter because of the curved seams.

Please read Sections 5, 6, and 8 in Chapter One on General Information before starting any work on this pattern. Always add one-quarter inch seam allowance to all patterns before cutting them from the cloth. Finished-size means tracing the block, adding the additional one-quarter inch seam allowance.

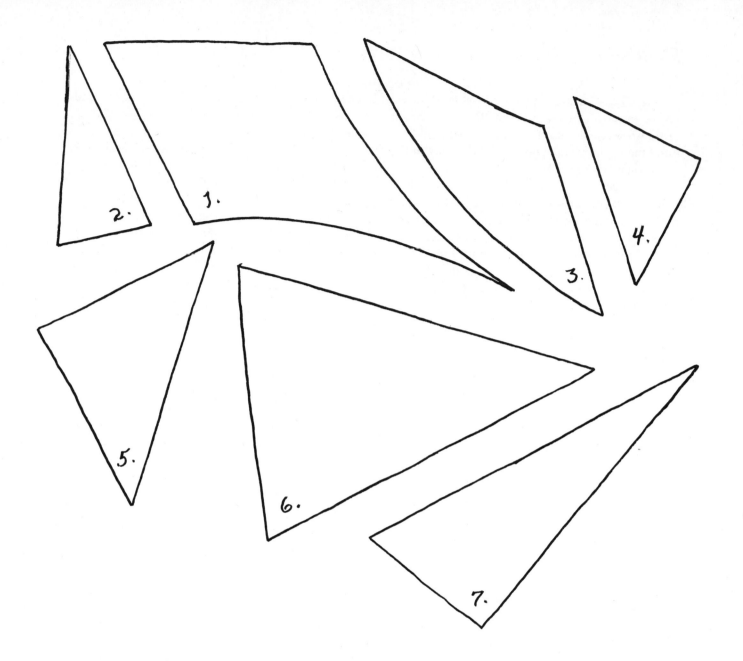

The Spinner

This original pattern is not quite as simple to make as it looks and is very definitely not for a beginner. I have given the colors as brown, yellow, and white. This should make a very nice scrap quilt if you leave the blank areas either white or a very light shade of a plain color. You may use an all-over pattern, plain blocks, or lattice strips. This quilt can be made with or without a border. A twin bed quilt will need six rows of eight blocks each. The patterns are drawn for a 12-inch square block.

When cutting the patterns for this block, cut four each of patterns 1, 3, 4, and 5, then reverse the patterns and cut four more of each. Look very closely at the drawing of the finished block and notice the placement of the elements. Sew together a No. 1 shape and its reverse to make the corner seam at the top of the cone-shaped No. 2 pattern. Finish the other three of these sections. The top of pattern No. 2 and the section just finished is a very tight curve. Fold the cloth No. 2 cone in half lengthwise to find the exact center of this curve. Place this point at the end of the corner seam. Sew this seam starting in the center and working to the outer edge. Then return to the center and sew to the other edge. You must make short stitches and carefully ease the two curves together. Do not hurry. Complete all four of these corner sections before going on. Stitch together pattern Nos. 3, 4, and 5 and their reverse. Sew the center seam and add the tiny No. 6 triangle. Make all four of these sections. Sew the tiny No. 7 square to the end of the fourth section. Now sew one of these sections to the corner sections. This forms one-quarter of the finished block. Sew two of these quarter square sections together, including the seam of the center square No. 7. Repeat with the other two sections and then finish the center seam.

Please read Sections 5, 6, and 8 in Chapter One on General Information before starting any work on this pattern. Always add one-quarter inch seam allowance to all patterns before cutting them from the cloth. Finished-size means tracing the block, adding the additional one-quarter inch seam allowance.

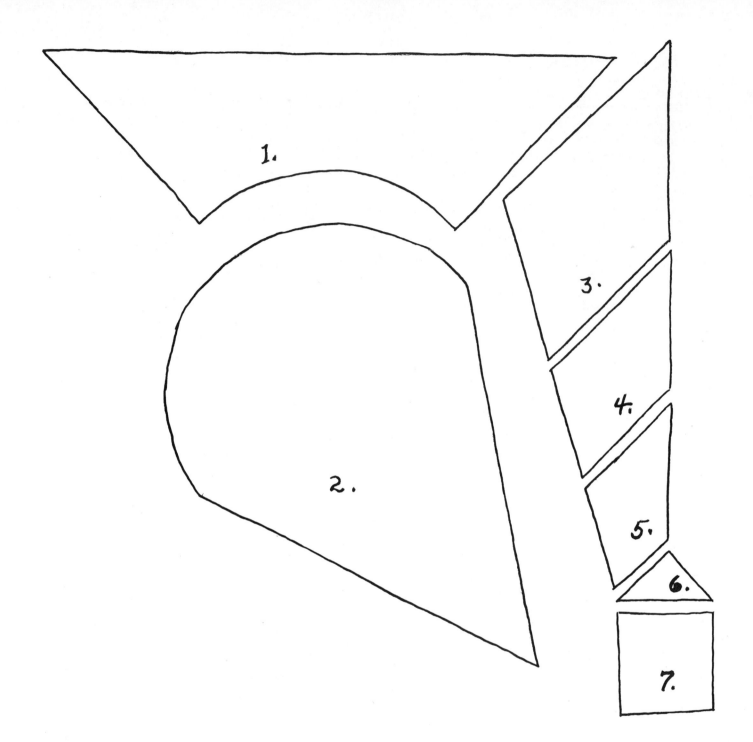

Snow in the Summer

I wish you could see this block made into a finished quilt. It stops traffic whenever I show it because the dark background, accented with a bright yellow, not-quite-gold color, sets off the white flowers so they seem to sparkle. My quilt made with this pattern has won four blue ribbons. I used one of the reproduction calicos with a black background and tiny flowers that gave a hint of green and warmer tones to the block when seen from a distance. This is not a quilt for beginners because of the slight curve in the flower petals. This is, however, one of the easier curved patterns and would be a good one to make for your first pattern with curved seams.

The patterns are drawn for a 12-inch square block. Do not use plain blocks or lattice strips with this pattern. A twin bed-size quilt will need six rows of eight blocks each and a two-inch border of a plain strip in one of the materials used in the top.

First, make the flower center from one dark No. 5 square and four light No. 6 triangles. Put this to one side. Make four units from two light No. 2 shapes (one reversed) and one dark No. 1 diamond. Sew one white petal shape to each side of this unit, and then finish the seam between the two petals. Sew one of the No. 3 corner shapes to one of the petals. When all four of these side units are finished, sew one of the units to the flower center along one side of the square. Repeat with the next unit; then sew the seam between the two units. Continue until the block is finished. Be very careful to match the corners of the pieces exactly, and watch the curves so they will lie flat when the block is finished.

Please read Sections 5, 6, and 8 in Chapter One on General Information before starting any work on this pattern. Always add one-quarter inch seam allowance to all patterns before cutting them from the cloth. Finished-size means tracing the block, adding the additional one-quarter inch seam allowance.

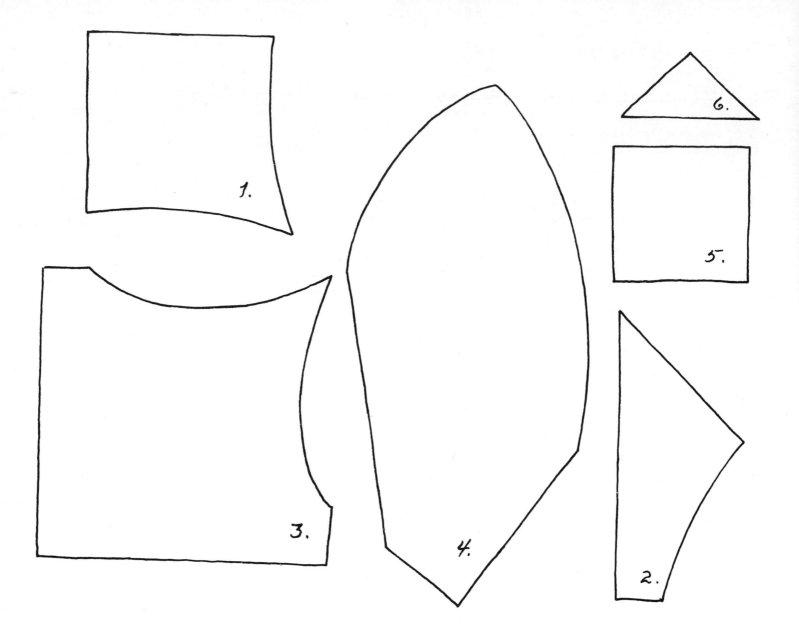

1.

2.

3.

4.

5.

6.

Columbia Star

At a showing of nineteenth-century quilts in Tennessee, I found this pattern in a quilt that was between 125 and 150 years old. It is a variation on the Star of LeMoine and was originally done in dark rose, green, and white. It has two-inch lattice strips in white between the blocks, which are 12 inches square.

Sew a rose and a green No. 2 diamond together. Starting at the bottom point between the two diamonds, sew each side seam of the No. 3 square to the two diamonds. Repeat this until you have four of these units. Sew two units together and add a No. 4 triangle between them, starting at the bottom point between the two diamonds for each stem. Sew the other two diamond units together and add triangle No. 4 in the same manner. Sew these two halves together and add the other two No. 4 triangles to each side in the same way. Put this center square aside. To make each of the four corner pieced triangles, make a square of a rose and a white No. 1 triangle. Make three of these squares for each corner triangle. Sew the three squares together with the dark sides all pointing the same way (see the drawing of the finished block). Add a dark No. 1 triangle to fit between the two bottom squares. On this same side, add a dark No. 1 triangle to each of the squares to make this section a triangle. Sew each of these triangles to the sides of the center square. You can make this quilt with or without a border.

A double bed quilt will need six rows of seven blocks and two-inch lattice strips.

Please read Sections 5, 6, and 8 in Chapter One on General Information before starting any work on this pattern. Always add one-quarter inch seam allowance to all patterns before cutting them from the cloth. Finished-size means tracing the block, adding the additional one-quarter inch seam allowance.

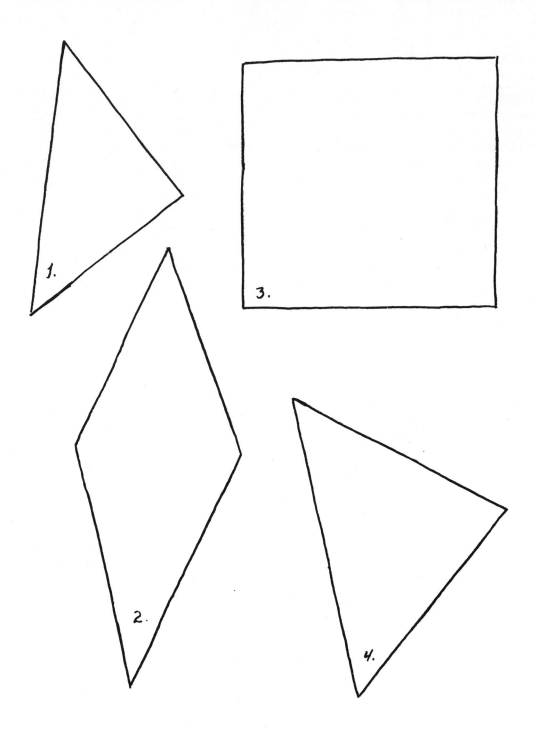

Twisting Star

Despite appearances, this original pattern is one of the harder patterns in this book. Be very careful in fitting the corners because neatness is of prime value in making these blocks. I made my quilt in an off-red salmon and gold with white; it was most effective.

Sew a No. 2 triangle to the point of shape No. 3, forming a larger triangle. Repeat this three times with white and dark. Add a large, yellow No. 1 triangle to form a triangle of double the size. Make four of these units and lay them aside.

Sew a No. 2 triangle to one of the slanted sides of the No. 3 shape, forming an oblong shape. The small triangle should be yellow and the shape dark. Now add a No. 1 triangle to the oblong to make a large triangle the same size as the ones you made first. Make four of these units. Sew one of the first and one of the second units together to form a square. Make three more squares from the other units. Now sew the squares together two-by-two and then down the center seam to form the finished 12-inch square block.

Please read Sections 5, 6, and 8 in Chapter One on General Information before starting any work on this pattern. Always add one-quarter inch seam allowance to all patterns before cutting them from the cloth. Finished-size means tracing the block, adding the additional one-quarter inch seam allowance.

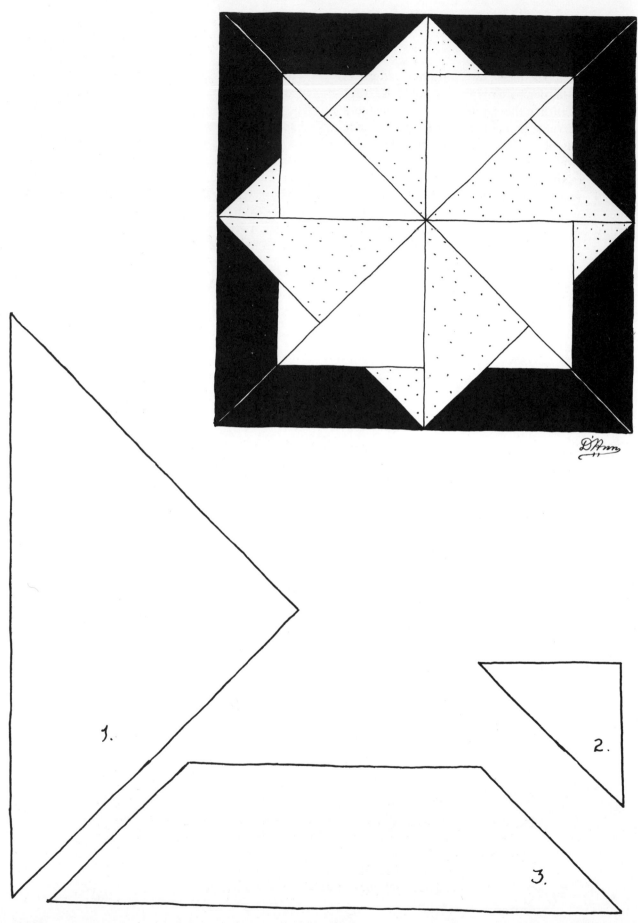

1.

2.

3.

156

Stars and Squares

This is one of the Nancy Page patterns from the 1930s. I have given the colors as red, yellow, and green on white, but any color combination would look attractive. It should be easy enough for a beginning quilter to master.

The center and outside blocks are made with the same directions. Sew together two No. 5 triangles on either side of a No. 6 triangle; make four of these. Sew two of these units to either side of a No. 1 square. Lay this aside. Sew two No. 4 squares to either side of one of the remaining units and repeat for the other unit. Sew the resulting strips together on each side of the first strip. This square will form the center square of the larger outside square. Use triangle Nos. 2 and 3 for making the first units and square No. 1 for the corners. The finished block will be 12 inches square.

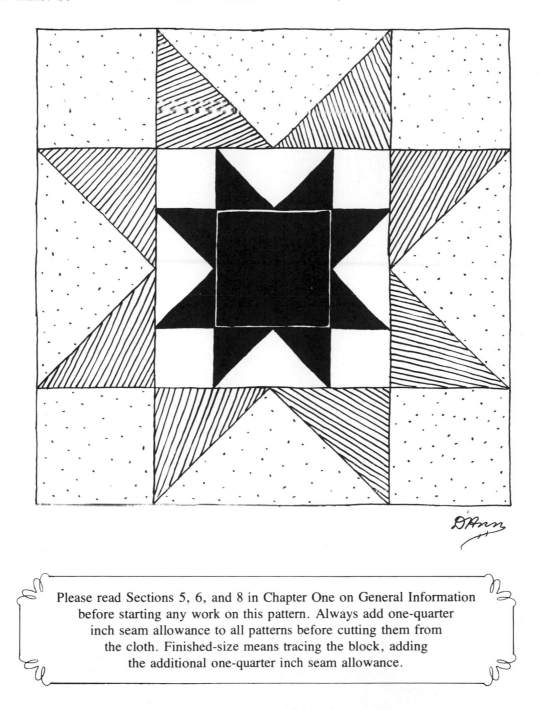

Please read Sections 5, 6, and 8 in Chapter One on General Information before starting any work on this pattern. Always add one-quarter inch seam allowance to all patterns before cutting them from the cloth. Finished-size means tracing the block, adding the additional one-quarter inch seam allowance.

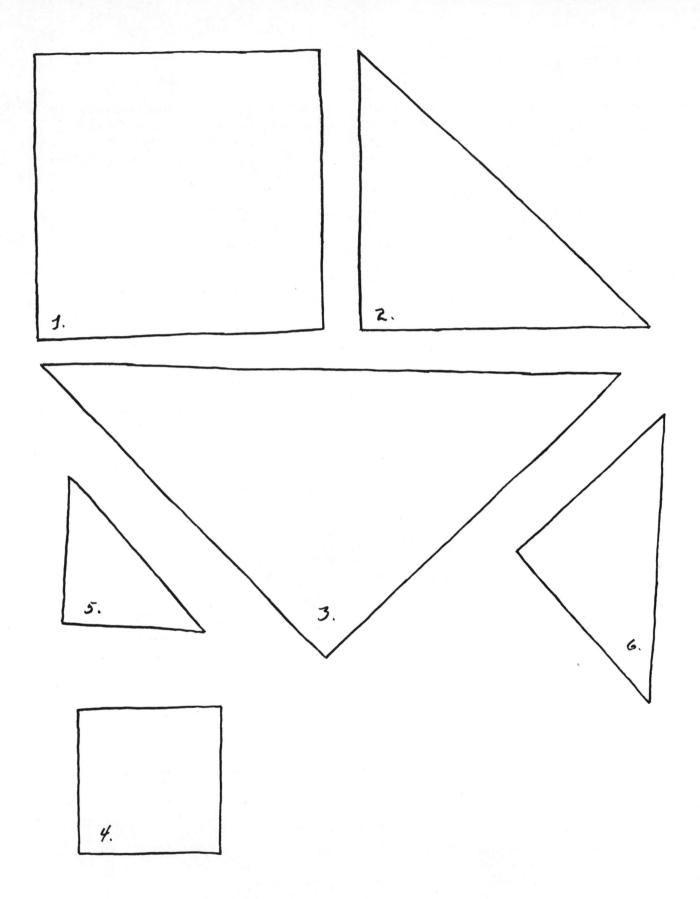

Square and Star

This pattern is a 1930s block from the Nancy Page quilt column. The colors given are red, green, and yellow on white, but it would look attractive in almost any combination.

Piece four No. 4 triangles around the large No. 5 square. Now piece two yellow No. 2 triangles on a red No. 3 square to form a large triangle. Next, piece together two white and two green No. 2 triangles to form two triangles. Place these on either side of the large pieced triangle to form an oblong. Add a yellow No. 1 square to one side of the oblong. Make three more strips just like this, and sew all four to the center square to form the finished 10-inch square block. This pattern is not quite as hard as it looks, but it should not be a first quilt.

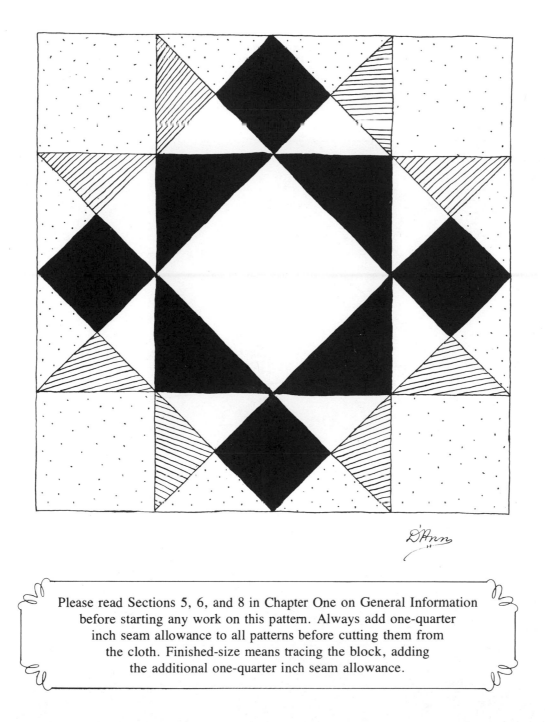

D'Ann

Please read Sections 5, 6, and 8 in Chapter One on General Information before starting any work on this pattern. Always add one-quarter inch seam allowance to all patterns before cutting them from the cloth. Finished-size means tracing the block, adding the additional one-quarter inch seam allowance.

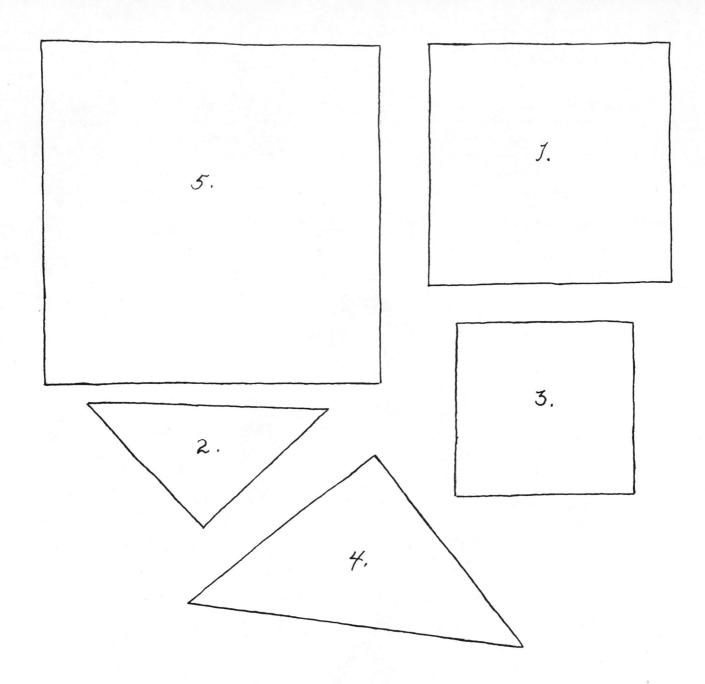

Constellation

This is an original pattern that looks very complicated, but is really easy enough for any beginner to construct. Do not use lattice strips between the blocks as there are already lattice strips in the blocks. You may use plain blocks between the pieced ones, but this pattern looks best in an all-over design. Use a good, strong, dark color and white. The dark color may be one of the fine ginghams, but a plain material will give a stronger pattern to the top. This pattern will make a tailored quilt that is very suitable for a man's or boy's room. It would also look bright and neat in a cabin or boat bunk. Trimmed with white eyelet frills, this quilt would enhance any room.

Constellation is the pattern that is used to illustrate section 8 of General Information; full instructions and illustrations are given there for this pattern. Do not use a border with this quilt unless you wish to use a one- or two-inch wide band of the dark color.

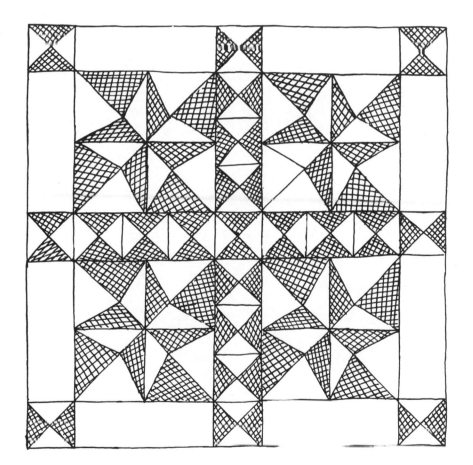

Please read Sections 5, 6, and 8 in Chapter One on General Information before starting any work on this pattern. Always add one-quarter inch seam allowance to all patterns before cutting them from the cloth. Finished-size means tracing the block, adding the additional one-quarter inch seam allowance.

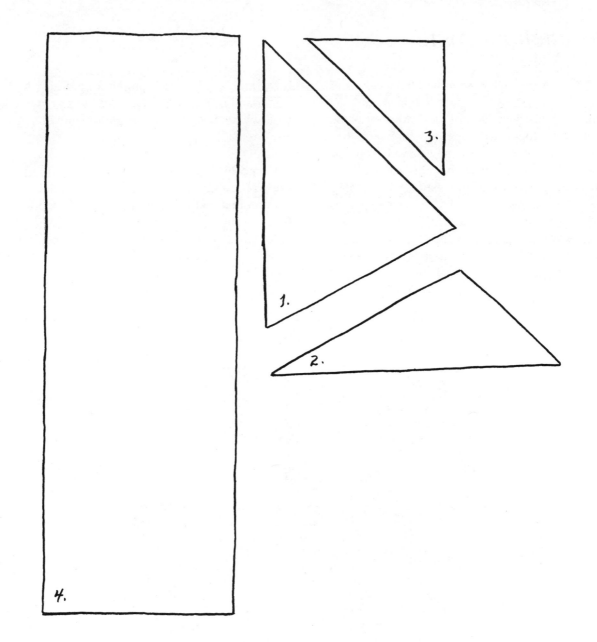

1.

2.

3.

4.

Maryland Puzzle

If you enjoy the play of light and shadow, you will like this pattern. When I designed it, the alternate ways of using two shades of one color and white seemed endless, and I covered a sheet of paper with them. The four drawings shown are the ones that made the most interesting designs when used in an all-over pattern for quilt tops. Do not use more than one design in a quilt top. This is not a scrap quilt. If you decide to use a border on your quilt, make it a simple dark band two or three inches wide at most. When done in blue and white, these patterns give the impression of water in motion. Read the description of the ways to use quilts made from the Constellation pattern. These patterns may be used in exactly the same types of rooms.

Decide which variation you wish to use for your quilt. In putting together each block, look carefully at the drawing of your variation and follow the placement of light and dark colors and the white pieces. The No. 1 square is always the same color in a variation. The shapes No. 2 and 3 are sometimes faced with a reversed section in another color, in which case you must use the patterns as they are shown. At other times the reversed pieces are the same color. When this is the case, cut the pattern so the line marked *A* is used as a fold. In other words, the No. 3 triangle will then be cut as a diamond. This will eliminate a sewn seam. You may sew the blocks as shown, or you may start at one corner and add the pieces in turn as if you were making a one-patch quilt. This last method will enable you to use two pieces of either pattern Nos. 2 or 3 as one piece to eliminate those seams.

This is not an easy pattern to piece because the individual shapes do not build to easily pieced sections. Sew a No. 2 piece to each side of a No. 1 square and sew the seams between the two No. 2 pieces on each side. Add a triangle or diamond, pattern No. 3, on each side. When sewing a V-shaped seam, sew from the center to each end in two seams so these pieces will lie flat. Continue in this manner until the block or the quilt top is finished. Be very careful of color placement. In this, as in all pieced quilts, you must be very careful to get corners to join exactly.

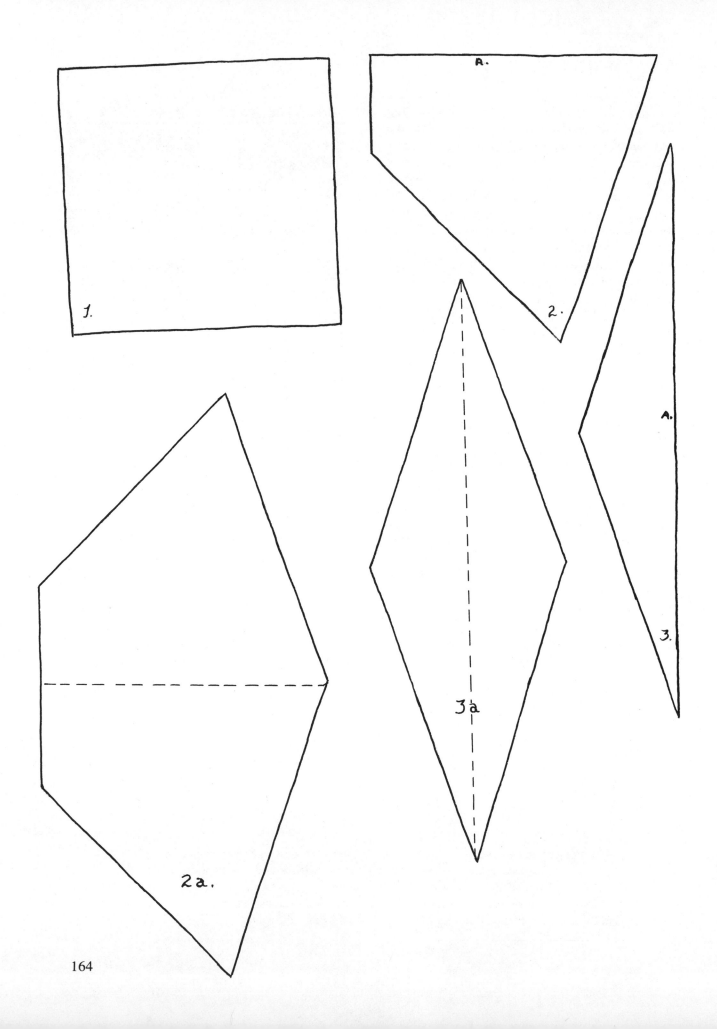

1.

A.

2.

A.

3.

2a.

3a

164

The Boondocks

The boondocks are underdeveloped land, and this is a quilt which will use up lots of scraps you'd otherwise waste. I have drawn the block using green, yellow, and brown, with a white square in the center. You may choose any color combination but keep the dark, medium, and light portions in each block as they are shown in the drawing. Your quilt will look coordinated if you use one color for the piece Nos. 1 and 5 in all the blocks for one quilt. You may or may not use a border with this pattern as you choose. It is an easy quilt, but not quite easy enough to make as a first quilt.

The patterns are drawn for a 12-inch square block. Sew a light No. 6 strip to each side of a white No. 7 square; then sew the four diagonal corner seams. Set this unit aside. Sew a dark No. 4 piece to a light No. 2 piece. Match the shapes carefully to the drawing. Now add a light No. 3 piece in two seams from the point of the No. 4 piece to one edge and then from that point to the other edge. Make eight of these pieces with four sections reversed. Sew two pieces together on the seam between the two No. 3 pieces. Add a medium No. 5 triangle by sewing two seams from the center point to the outer edge. Make four of these double units. Add a medium No. 1 square to the right side of each unit. Sew each of the four units to one side of the center that was pieced first. Finish the block by sewing the four side seams. Be very

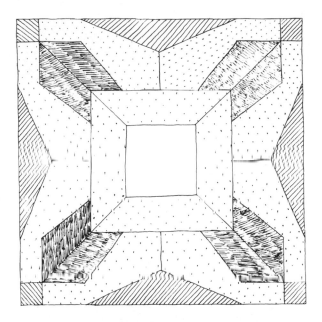

careful that the corners of all your pieces meet exactly.

A twin bed-size quilt will need six rows of eight blocks each. You may use plain blocks, an all-over design, or lattice strips, as you prefer. Lattice strips in the same color used for pattern Nos. 1 and 5 would look very nice. If you use three-inch lattice strips in the medium color, the corner blocks could be a white square cut from pattern No. 7. A twin bed-size quilt with these lattice strips would need five rows of six blocks, with a three-inch lattice strip between each row and on the outside.

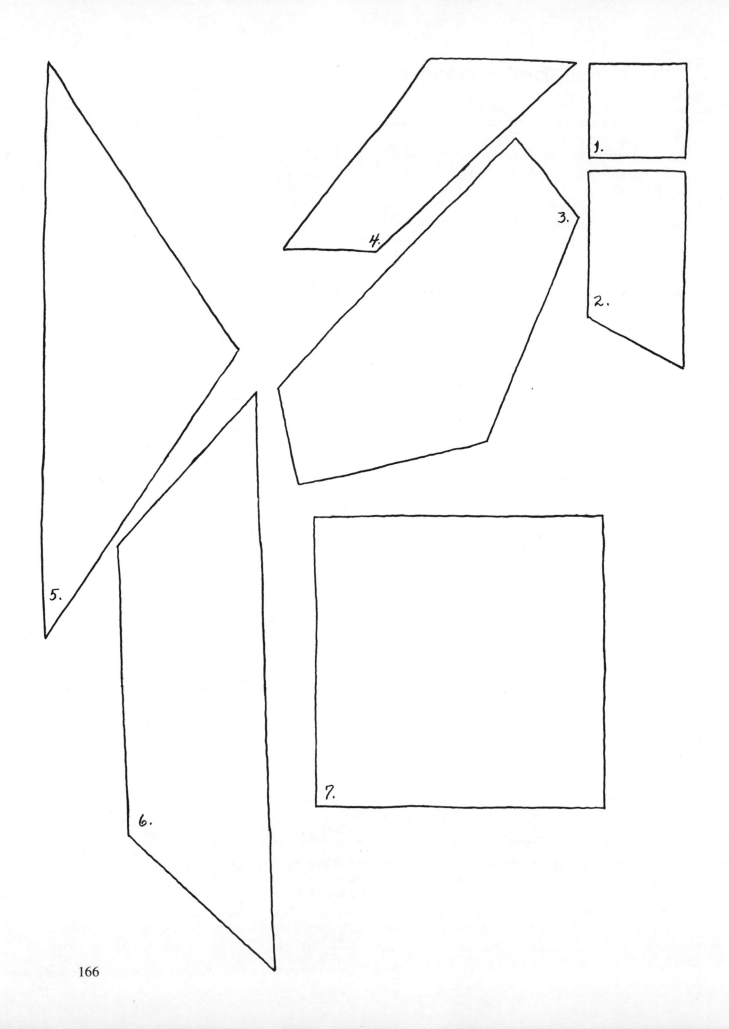

CHAPTER SIX

Nine Patch Patterns

Spring Flower

Spring Flower

This original pattern became my mother's favorite quilt. It was entered in two quilt shows and won blue ribbons in each. Everyone thinks that it is a nineteenth-century Double Tulip pattern, but I collected all of the Double Tulip patterns I could find and then designed something different.

This pattern is much easier to piece than most of the older patterns. The stem and leaves form a geometric unit in one corner with geometric tulips in each of the other corners. The blocks may be made in any suitable color combination. We chose four different red calico prints for different blocks in the top. This made an antique-looking quilt. One hundred and fifty years ago when these quilts were at the height of their popularity, a quilter seldom had enough of one kind of cloth to finish an entire quilt. The mixture of color and cloth has now become a classic part of this pattern.

We used yellow calico for the centers of the flowers, a blue-green for the leaves and stem, and unbleached muslin (brown domestic) for the backing and background of the quilt. Another traditional color is a yellow-green. A white block was placed between each of the pieced ones and the blocks were arranged on the diagonal, facing the two sides in a traditional manner. A simple quilting design was used in each of the plain blocks and the pieced blocks were quilted by the piece. This quilt is stunning in a colonial or traditional style bedroom.

This is one of the easier quilt patterns in this book. To make it even easier for beginners, I have given the patterns in two sizes. Do not confuse them — the different sizes necessitate some pattern changes. This means that there is one more pattern piece in the smaller pattern. The small pattern will make a block 12½ inches square. The larger pattern will make a 15-inch square block. A beginner will find the smaller block a little harder to sew.

Make the three tulip squares first, by sewing together two squares made from one red and one white No. 1 triangle each. They should be sewn together along their long side. Sew one of the pieced square's red sides to a white No. 2 square and the other to a yellow No. 2 square. The pieced squares should be at the right of the white and the left of the yellow square. Check carefully with the drawing of the finished block to make sure your squares are in the correct position. Now sew these two elements into a square, with the white square at upper left and the yellow at lower right. Next make two oblongs.

If you are using the large patterns, make the oblongs from a red No. 3 diamond and a white No. 1 triangle. If you are using the small patterns, make the oblongs from a red No. 3 diamond and a white No. 3a triangle. Sew the long side of the white triangle to the left side of one diamond and to the right side of the other. Sew the first diamond to the right side of your finished pieced square. Sew the other diamond to the lower edge of the square and finish by sewing the diagonal seam between the two diamonds. When three tulips are finished, lay them aside.

The fourth corner of the block is the leaves and stem. Sew two No. 5 triangles to the right and lower sides of a green No. 6 square to form a large triangle. Repeat by sewing two white triangles to the upper side and left side of the other green square. Sew these large triangles to either side of the green No. 4 stem.

Sew one tulip square to each side of a white No. 8 oblong. Then sew the stem square to the left and the last tulip to the right of a second No. 8 oblong. Check the drawing for placement. Now make a long strip by sewing one white oblong No. 8 on either side of a green No. 7 square. Sew the tulip strip to the top and the stem strip at the bottom of the long center strip.

The drawing of the finished quilt top is a scale drawing of a twin bed-size quilt made from the smaller patterns. The 15-inch pattern will make a large double bed-size quilt.

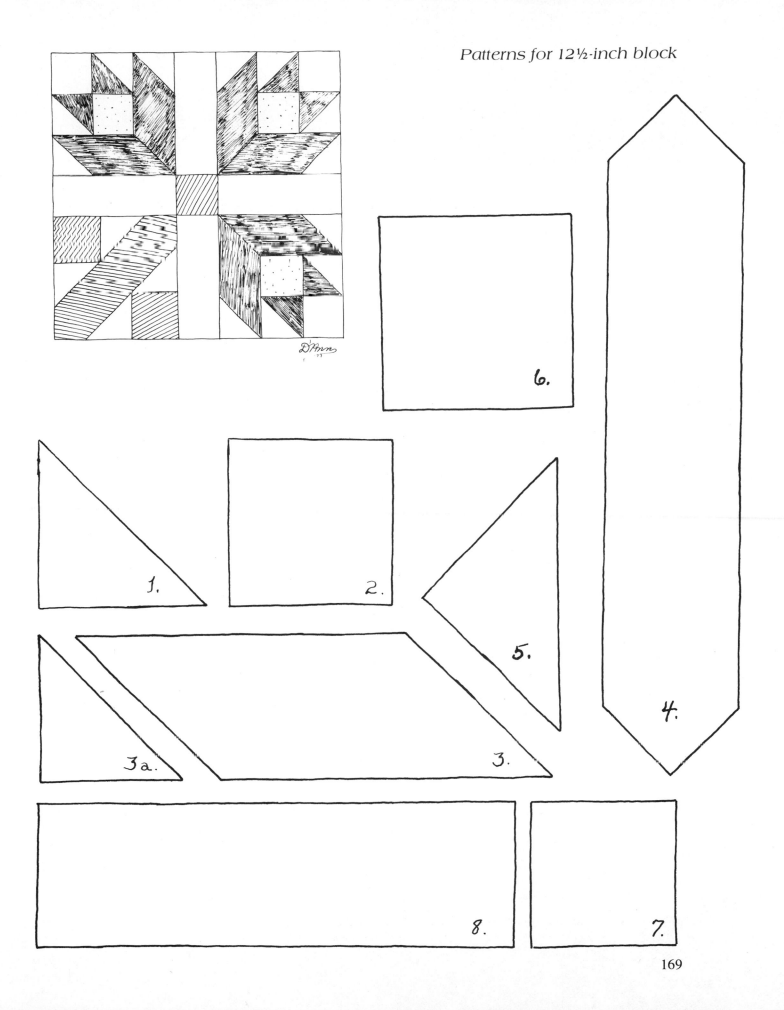

Patterns for 12½-inch block

6.

1.

2.

5.

4.

3a.

3.

8.

7.

169

Patterns for 15-inch block

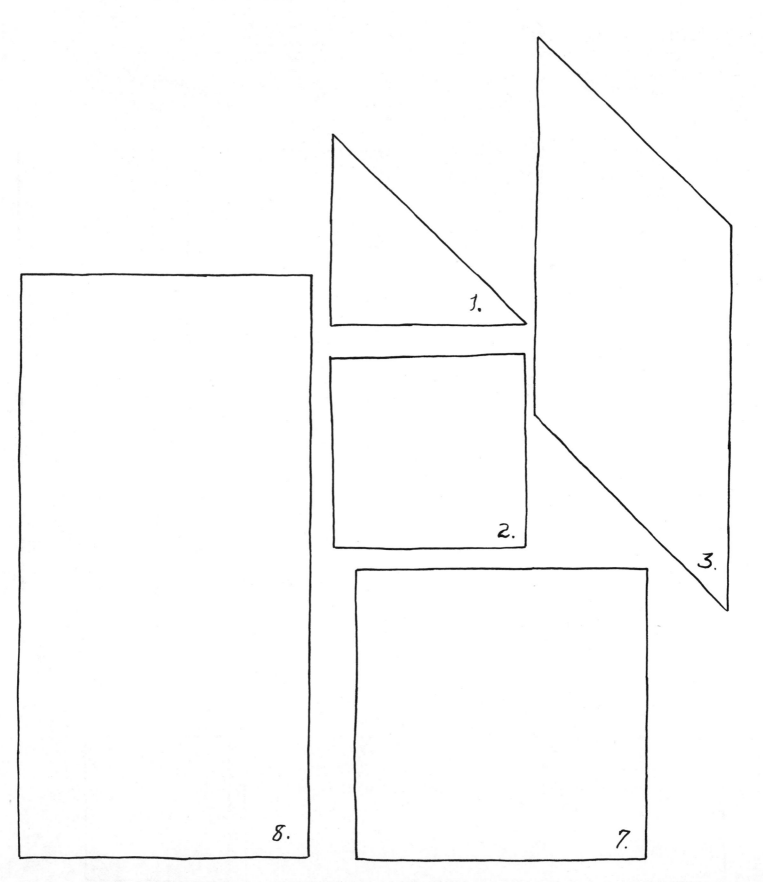

1.

2.

3.

8.

7.

170

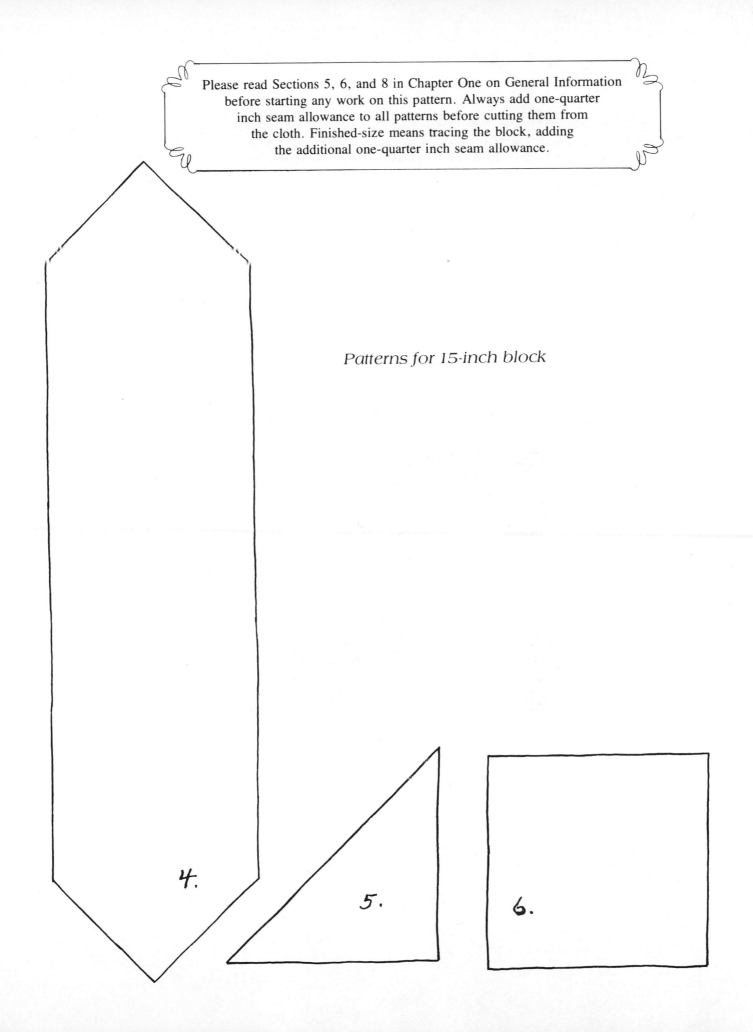

Please read Sections 5, 6, and 8 in Chapter One on General Information before starting any work on this pattern. Always add one-quarter inch seam allowance to all patterns before cutting them from the cloth. Finished-size means tracing the block, adding the additional one-quarter inch seam allowance.

Patterns for 15-inch block

4.

5.

6.

Clever Patch

This is another original pattern based on a traditional one. It is very easy to piece. I have listed the colors as red and white, but this may be made in any color or print and white. The top should be put together either with plain blocks between the pieced ones or lattice strips. There should be a narrow band as a border.

The pattern looks complicated, but it is quite easy when it is divided into the four corner squares, four side blocks, and the center nine patch. Make the center nine patch from four white and five dark No. 5 squares. Sew these together in three rows; then sew the rows together. Lay this aside. The four side blocks are next. Sew a dark No. 3 triangle on each side of the white No. 4 triangle (reverse one No. 3 triangle when drawing it from the pattern). Make

four of these and lay them aside, also. The corner squares are made as follows: take a white No. 1 square and sew it to a white No. 2 shape. Add a second No. 2 shape in white and fit into the corner where the two No. 2 shapes join. Add a dark No. 2 shape and finally a second dark No. 2 shape to fill in the square. Make four of these corner squares.

To make the finished square, sew two strips with a corner square on each side of one of the side blocks. The third strip has two side blocks on either side of the center nine patch. Sew the two strips with corner squares on each side of the center strip.

A double bed quilt will need eight rows of eight blocks each, as the finished-size block is 12 inches square.

Please read Sections 5, 6, and 8 in Chapter One on General Information before starting any work on this pattern. Always add one-quarter inch seam allowance to all patterns before cutting them from the cloth. Finished-size means tracing the block, adding the additional one-quarter inch seam allowance.

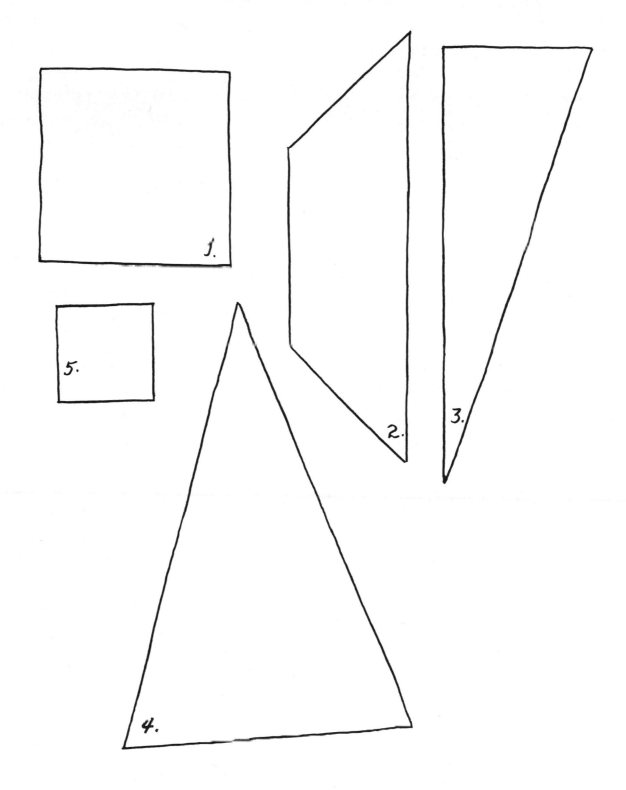

Cross and Recross

Red, white, and blue will make a striking combination in this design. The patterns are cut for a 12-inch square block. When you piece this design, be sure to keep the corners as even as you can. If you do this, the pattern will turn out well, even for a beginner. The pattern does not need a border; the binding will be enough to finish it. This is one of my original designs.

A quilt in this pattern with an all-over design will look attractive, and so will one with plain squares between the pieced ones. Try the plain blocks in the darkest color — this will add an interesting design to your top. The way I have visualized a quilt from this pattern is to use a 2-inch-wide lattice strip and corner square with the blocks. The lattice strip should be in the darkest color and the corner squares in white. For the lattice strip and square patterns use No. 8 extended to a 12-inch length and a No. 1 square. You will be quite surprised at the pattern this combination produces.

To make the block, first make the following sections. Cut a dark No. 3 square and four medium No. 4 oblongs. Sew the square to the right side of one side of an oblong. Sew a second oblong on the seam at the end of the square and the oblong. The next oblong is sewn to the third side of the square. The ends of the second and the fourth oblongs fill in the remaining side, forming a larger square. Make four of these and lay them aside. Now cut two No. 5 shapes in medium color and one pointed No. 2 shape in white. Starting at the point, sew a No. 5 shape to one side of the point of the No. 2 shape. Again start at the point and sew the other No. 5 shape (reversed) to the other side of the point of the No. 2 shape. Finish the seam between the two No. 5 shapes. Make four of these and lay them aside. Make a strip by sewing a medium-colored No. 6 triangle to either side of a dark No. 8 oblong.

Look closely at the drawing to see how to place the triangles. Sew one side of a white No. 7 diamond to the long side of each triangle. Make four of these strips and lay them aside.

You now have all the elements to make a square. Sew them together in the following order. Sew a section made of one No. 2 shape and two No. 5 shapes between two squares that have a No. 3 square at the center. Repeat this for a second strip. Next sew a white No. 1 square between two sections made of a No. 2 shape and two No. 5 shapes. Make sure that the edges of the white No. 2 shapes touch the white No. 1 square. Now sew these three strips together, placing the white square in the center. Consult the drawing for the exact placement of these pieces. Sew the four strips that have a dark No. 8 oblong center to the four sides of the block's center. Finish the block by sewing the diagonal seams between the white No. 7 diamonds at the corners. A twin bed-size quilt will need six rows of eight blocks each.

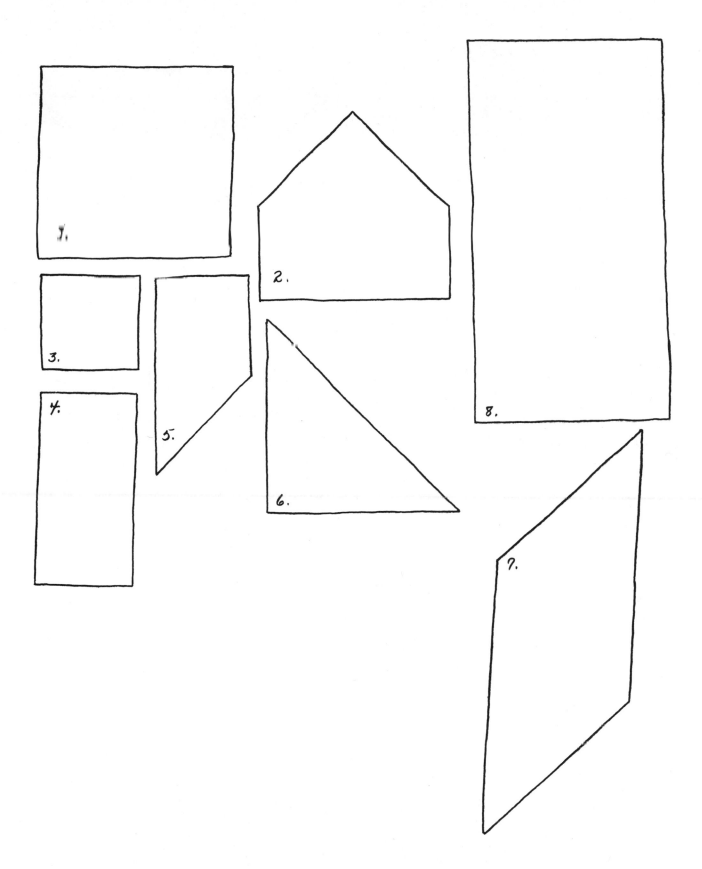

1.

2.

3.

4.

5.

6.

7.

8.

Formal Gardens

In the eighteenth century, gardens were laid out in geometrical beds of flowers and herbs. Each bed was separated from the next by a strip of grass or walkway, and each bed was surrounded by a hedge which was usually yew or boxwood. I have used this idea in an unusual quilt pattern that combines the rigidity of the arrangement with the beauty in color which were the hallmarks of the colonial gardens. The color of the outer and inner walkways should be a soft brown or rose to imitate either dirt or brick. The pieces representing the hedges should be a blue-green and a contrasting yellow-green that do not clash. Each bed or pair of beds in the original gardens was filled with a different plant. To achieve this effect, use prints with different background colors and try to frame at least one flower of the print. I have shown two boxes of light green, two of lavender, two of yellow, and two of blue in the flower beds. In the center is a single red print. These beds usually had a sundial or a bird bath in the center. This center square could have a bird, rather than a flower, to represent the bird bath.

To make the basic block, sew four green No. 7 triangles to the four sides of the No. 8 square, which should be a bird or flower print. Sew four No. 6 shapes to each side of this center. Lay the center aside. Next, sew two dark green and two light green No. 3 shapes to each side of a No. 5 square in a flower print. Make four of these. Sew three light and dark green No. 2 and 3 sections to three sides of a No. 4 oblong flower print. When making these sections, consult the drawing carefully for the placement of light and dark

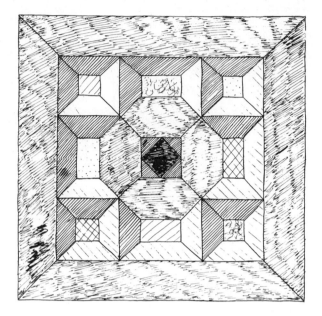

greens, as these give the effect of sunlight and shade that will give the finished block a three-dimensional appearance. Sew one corner square with a No. 5 center to each side of a unit with a No. 4 oblong center. Make two of these strips. Sew the remaining two units with No. 4 oblong centers to each side of the center of the block. Add one of the strips to the top and the bottom of the center. Add a No. 1 strip to each of the four sides of this pieced center to finish the block.

Be very careful when fitting the corners and joining the corners of the pieces. These patterns are drawn for a 14-inch square block. Five rows of seven blocks each will make a twin bed-size quilt. Add a two-inch-wide green band for a border.

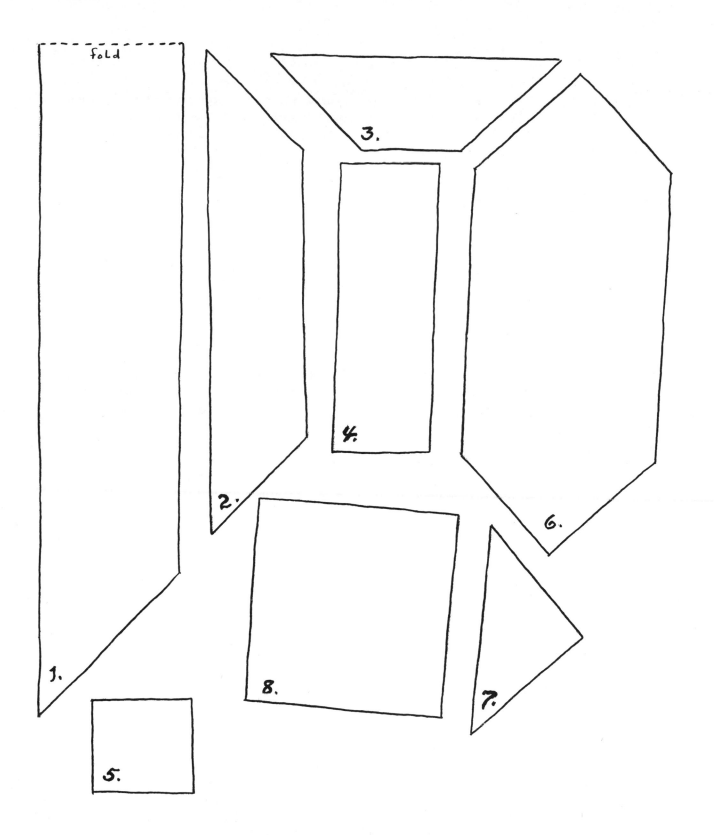

fold

3.

2.

4.

6.

1.

8.

7.

5.

Michigan Star

This original pattern is a little too hard for a beginner, but it has only straight seams. With a little care, it could be tried as a second quilt. Be very careful to have the corners of all the pieces meet exactly. I have given the design's colors as green and white. It might also be effective in two colors or two shades of one color and white. Lattice strips or plain blocks should be used between the pieced blocks, and a simple border or plain band should be used on the top. An interesting variation would be to make the outer sections of all the blocks match and have each star a different color. The patterns are drawn for a 12-inch square, finished block.

Sew the star in the center first. Sew a white No. 6 triangle to the slanted side of a No. 7 green piece. Sew a second green piece (reversed) by starting the seam at the point of the triangle and sewing to the edge of the triangle. Return to the point of the triangle and sew a second seam between the No. 7 pieces. This method ensures that the piece will lie flat when finished. Make three more of these pieced squares. Sew two white No. 5 squares on either side of one of the pieced squares. Repeat with two more white squares and another pieced square. Sew two pieced squares to the last white No. 5 square. Sew the first two strips on each side of the last strip to finish the center star. Lay this aside. Make each of the four corner squares in the following manner. Make a strip of one white No. 2 triangle, one dark No. 3 square, and one white No. 3 square. Make a second strip of one white No. 2 triangle and one dark No. 3 square. Sew these two strips together and add a white No. 2 triangle to finish the corner of the pieced triangle thus formed. To each of the pieced triangles add a dark No. 1 triangle (see the drawing of the finished block). Sew two dark No. 4 strips on each side of a white No. 4 strip. Make four of these units. Sew one corner square on each side of a unit of No. 4 strips. Repeat this for the bottom of the block. Now sew a unit of No. 4 strips on each side of the center star square. Sew the strips with the corner squares to the top and bottom of the strip with the center star. Look carefully at the drawing to make sure the placement of the pieces is correct.

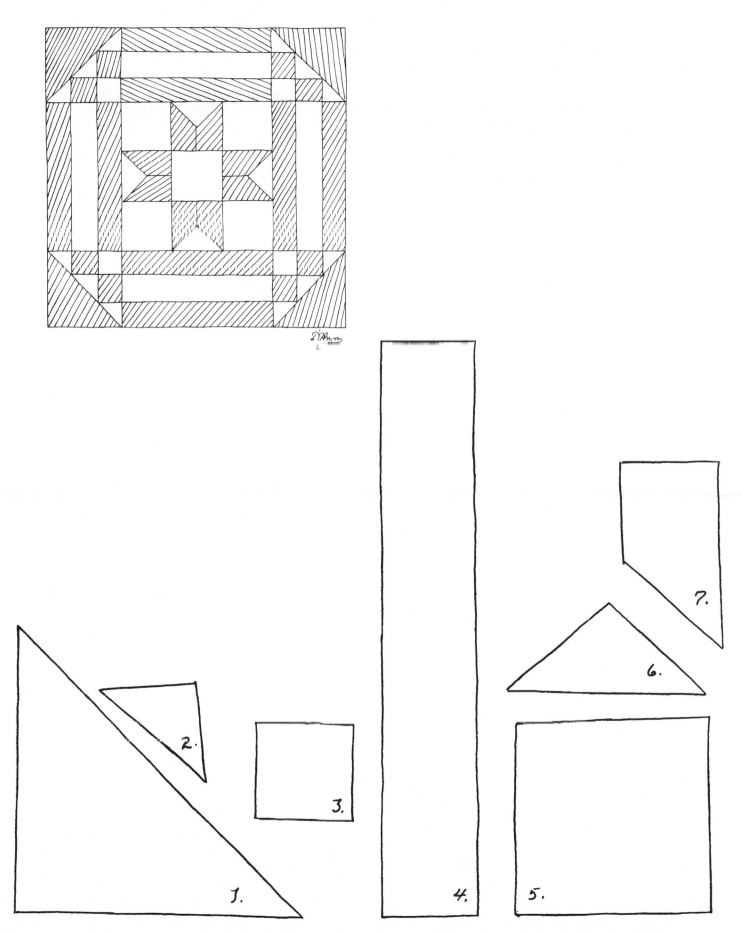

1.

2.

3.

4.

5.

6.

7.

Tile Puzzle

This is an old pattern, but I don't know its exact age. It should be done in two shades of the same color and white. This is a little too hard for a beginning quilter.

The whole block is made with one pattern. Cut six white, 24 light, and 18 dark diamonds for one block. Make two different units from four diamonds each and make six of each of the units. The first unit should be made from two light and two dark diamonds with the dark units at top and bottom and the light diamonds at the sides. After making six of these, lay them aside.

The second unit is made from two light, one dark, and one white diamond. In this unit the light diamonds are at the top and bottom, and the white and dark diamonds are at the sides.

Sew the first units together three at a time with the dark diamonds to the center. Sew the two triple units across the center. This will form a star. Now fill in the points of the star with the second unit, placing the white diamonds on the outside. Neatness is a must with this pattern. All of the corners must match exactly for the finished quilt to look good.

Please read Sections 5, 6, and 8 in Chapter One on General Information before starting any work on this pattern. Always add one-quarter inch seam allowance to all patterns before cutting them from the cloth. Finished-size means tracing the block, adding the additional one-quarter inch seam allowance.

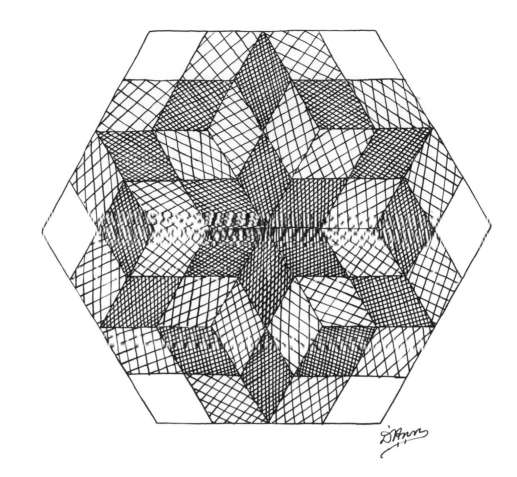

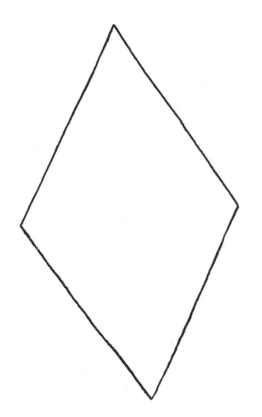

Wake Robin

One of the most beautiful American wild flowers is the trillium of the deep woodlands. There are white trilliums with pink throats, small yellow trilliums, and then my favorites, the medium-sized red trilliums that have several names. The name I chose for this pattern is Wake Robin.

This is the easiest of all the pieced hexagon patterns in this section; with care, even a beginner could make this charming quilt. The colors are those of the flower, red and green with a white background. This pattern should be done in an all-over design. There will be 53 pieced blocks needed for a twin bed-size quilt. These should be arranged in four rows of eight blocks, alternating with three rows of seven blocks. These rows with seven blocks will need a plain white half-hexagon cut from the pattern given for The Dove at the top and bottom of the rows. Pattern No. 3 should be used for the zig-zag

sides of the quilt, and a straight band two inches wide can be used on the top and bottom of the quilt. If you make this band red, use a green binding to finish the quilt edges. If you decide on green for the border, use red for the binding.

To make the block, sew together a green and a white No. 1 triangle to form a diamond. Make three of these. Sew together the green and white diamond with a red and a white No. 2 diamond. When adding the white diamond to this unit, start at the lowest point between the first two diamonds and sew to the edge. Then return to the lowest point and sew to the other edge. This will insure that the unit lies flat when finished. Make two more of these hexagon units. Sew the three units together. Look at the drawing of the finished block to make sure the colors are placed correctly. Add the last three white No. 2 diamonds to finish the block. Be sure to sew them in two seams from the middle point outward.

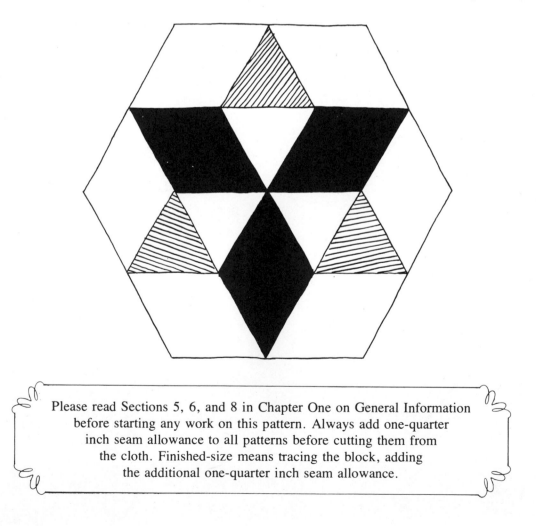

Please read Sections 5, 6, and 8 in Chapter One on General Information before starting any work on this pattern. Always add one-quarter inch seam allowance to all patterns before cutting them from the cloth. Finished-size means tracing the block, adding the additional one-quarter inch seam allowance.

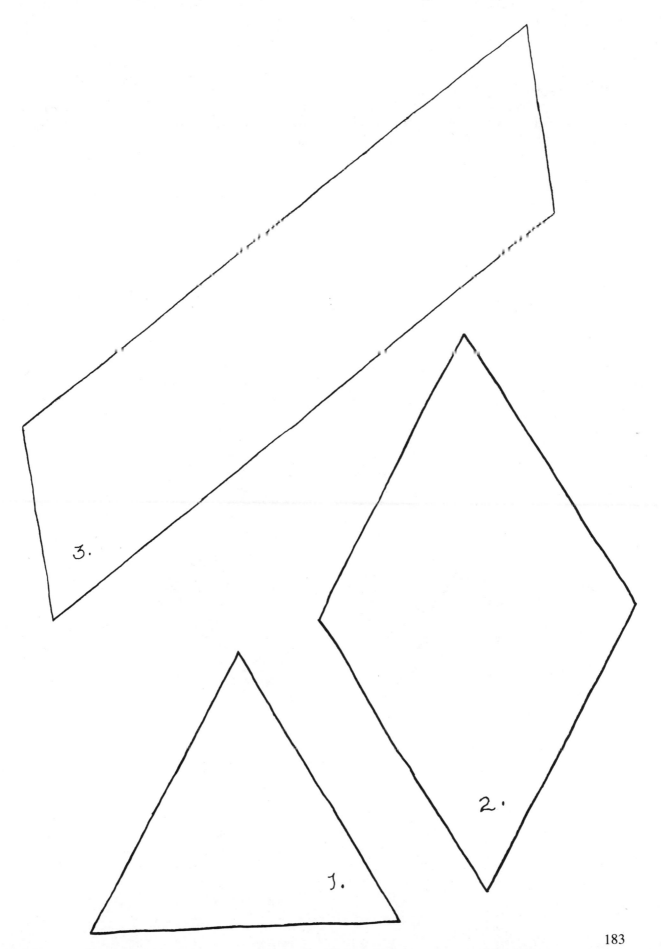

3.

2.

1.

Star Design

This is one of the most versatile of the hexagon designs I originated and included in this book. I have listed the colors as green and red on white, but as long as you keep the dark and light sections the same in each block of your quilt this could be used as a scrap quilt pattern. You may use it as a hexagon block, in which case a twin bed-size quilt will need 53 blocks arranged in the same manner as The Dove. This block is slightly larger than The Dove and the half hexagons will need ½ inch more added to each size if you decide to use it for plain and half blocks for this quilt. Another variation is to use pattern No. 3 in each of the corners (two reversed) of the hexagon. This makes it a square. In this case you will need only five rows of seven blocks and a two-inch wide border to make a twin bed-size quilt. The third variation is a combination of both of the first two. Piece the hexagons together into a top and then add pattern No. 3 to the sides of the quilt to make them straight. This will allow you to use any kind of border you prefer.

Make three diamonds from a red and a white No. 1 triangle and three diamonds from a red and a green No. 1 triangle. Take one of each of these two combination diamonds and sew them together. Add a white No. 2 triangle by starting at the center point and sewing to the edge. Return to the center point and sew to the other edge. By sewing an inverted seam in two sections, you make sure it lies flat when finished. Make three of these units and then sew them together. Finish the block by sewing the other three white No. 2 triangles in place with two seams each.

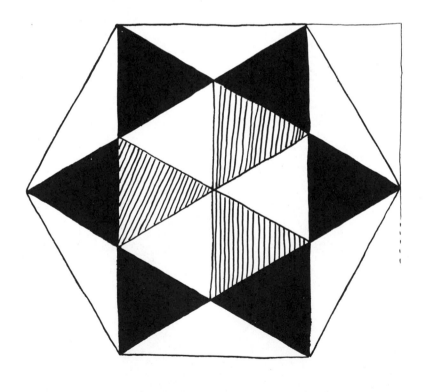

Please read Sections 5, 6, and 8 in Chapter One on General Information before starting any work on this pattern. Always add one-quarter inch seam allowance to all patterns before cutting them from the cloth. Finished-size means tracing the block, adding the additional one-quarter inch seam allowance.

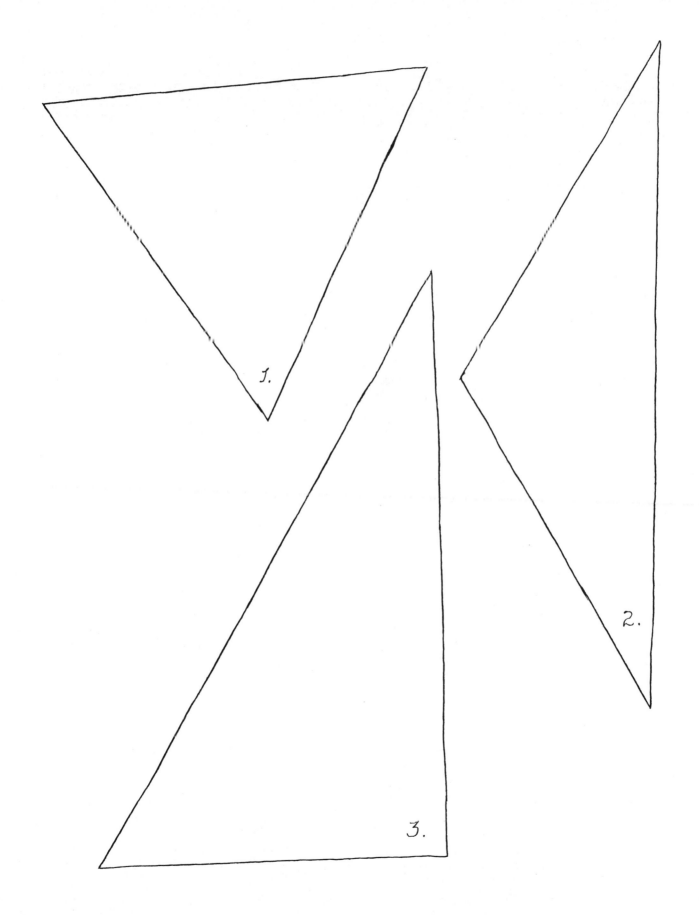

The Airport

This is one of the hardest original designs in this book. I drew the block in brown, yellow, and white. When I finished it, the design looked like the terminal at one of the larger airports with landing strips fanning out in all directions. This pattern is quite interesting if the blocks are arranged in an all-over design. The patterns are drawn for a 12-inch square block. You may use a border if you like. Six rows of eight blocks each will make a twin bed-size quilt.

Sew five light and four dark No. 1 squares into the center nine patch. Add four white No. 2 triangles to each side of this nine patch, and set the unit aside. Make four corner units by sewing together two light No. 5 shapes (one reversed) along the line marked *a*. Sew these to the point of a white No. 3 shape by starting at the point and sewing to the edge, and then returning to the point and sewing the other seam. On each side of the No. 3 shape, sew a No. 4 strip with its point up, as shown in the drawing. This strip should also be light-colored, and one should be cut with the pattern reversed. When you have four of these units, set them aside.

For the last set of four units, sew a white No. 8 strip to the long side of a light No. 7 shape. Cut another No. 7 and No. 8 strip with the patterns reversed, and sew them together in the same manner. Sew these two sections together and fill in the V-shaped opening between them with the dark No. 6 triangle. Sew this in two seams also,

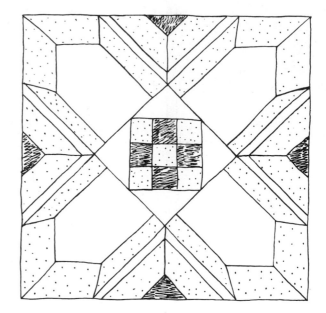

from the point to each edge. To put the block together, sew one of the units with a No. 3 shape to two sides of the center nine patch square, making a long strip. Set this aside. Now make a large pieced triangle for each side of the block by sewing one of the pieced sections containing a No. 6 triangle to each side of one of the units with a No. 3 shape. Sew these large pieced triangles to each side of the center strip. Look carefully at the drawing of the finished block as you piece each unit and section to help you arrange the pieces correctly.

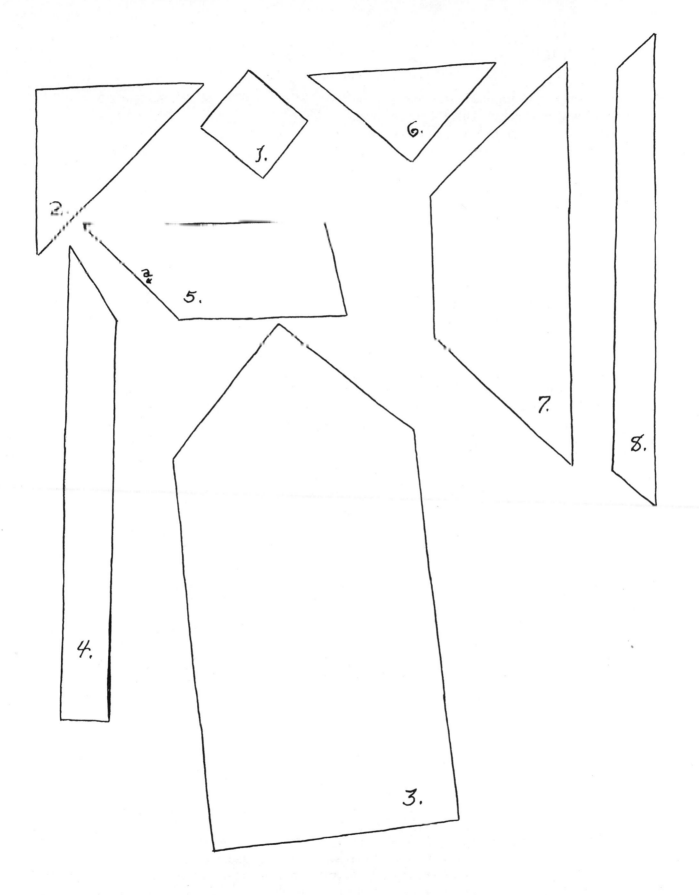

The Dove

The doves in this original design are white on light blue with gold beaks. There should be plain blocks alternating with the pieced blocks. Since this is a hard top to visualize, I have drawn a diagram of part of the top for a twin bed-size quilt. In the diagram the shaded blocks are the plain blocks and the white blocks represent the pieced blocks. There will be three plain half blocks at the top and three more at the bottom. This quilt does not need a border. This is one of the harder patterns in this book.

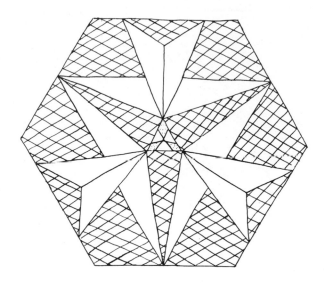

Pattern No. 8 is used for the plain block. Trace off section 8A and then place the traced pattern so the dot-dash line marked *a — b* on each piece matches. Trace the top of pattern No. 8, section 8B, on the tissue paper. When making a cutting pattern, place the dotted line marked "fold" on a fold and cut it. The twin bed-size quilt design will need 35 pieced blocks, 18 plain full blocks, and six plain half blocks.

To piece the block for this pattern, first make the small triangle in the center. Piece three gold No. 1 diamonds and three white No. 2 triangles into the triangle shown by sewing two diamonds on each side of one triangle, and then sewing two triangles on each side of the remaining diamond. Now sew these two pieces together. Sew two white No. 5 triangles together (one reversed). Starting at the lowest point of the triangle formed between these pieces, sew a blue

No. 6 triangle first to one side, then return to the center and sew the other side. Make three of these units and lay them aside. Next sew a blue No. 3 triangle to a white No. 4 triangle and add a blue No. 7 shape to the other side of the No. 4 triangle. Make three of these units. Sew the three units made with a No. 5 triangle to each one of the second three units. Sew the triangle center to the first of these double units; then sew the other two units to the first one. Match the block carefully to the drawing as you sew. Neat work is a must in making this pattern.

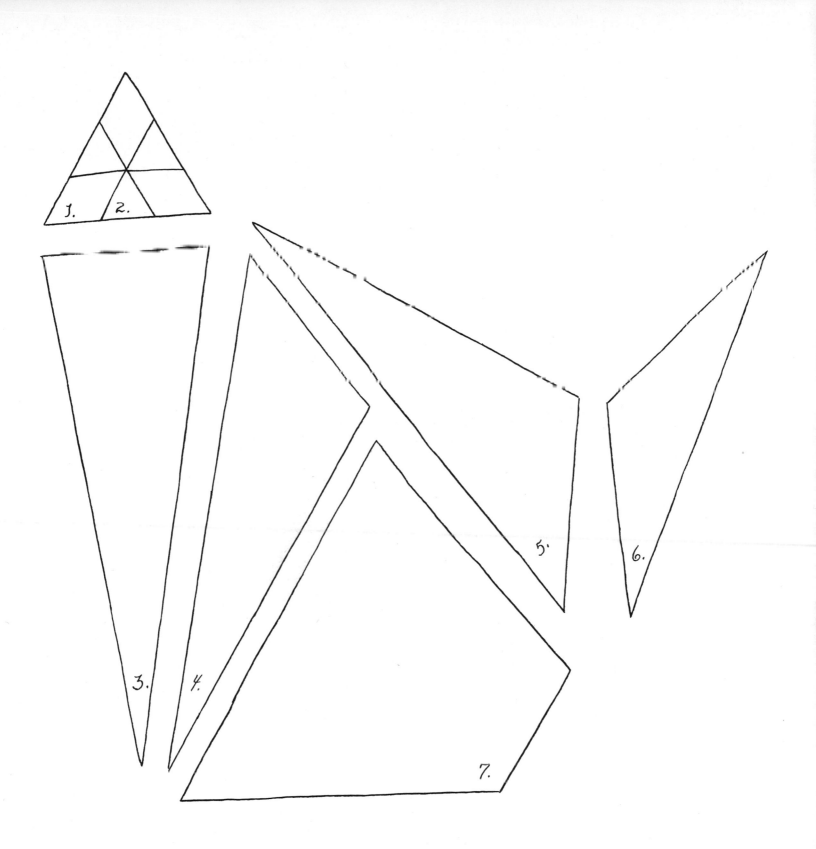

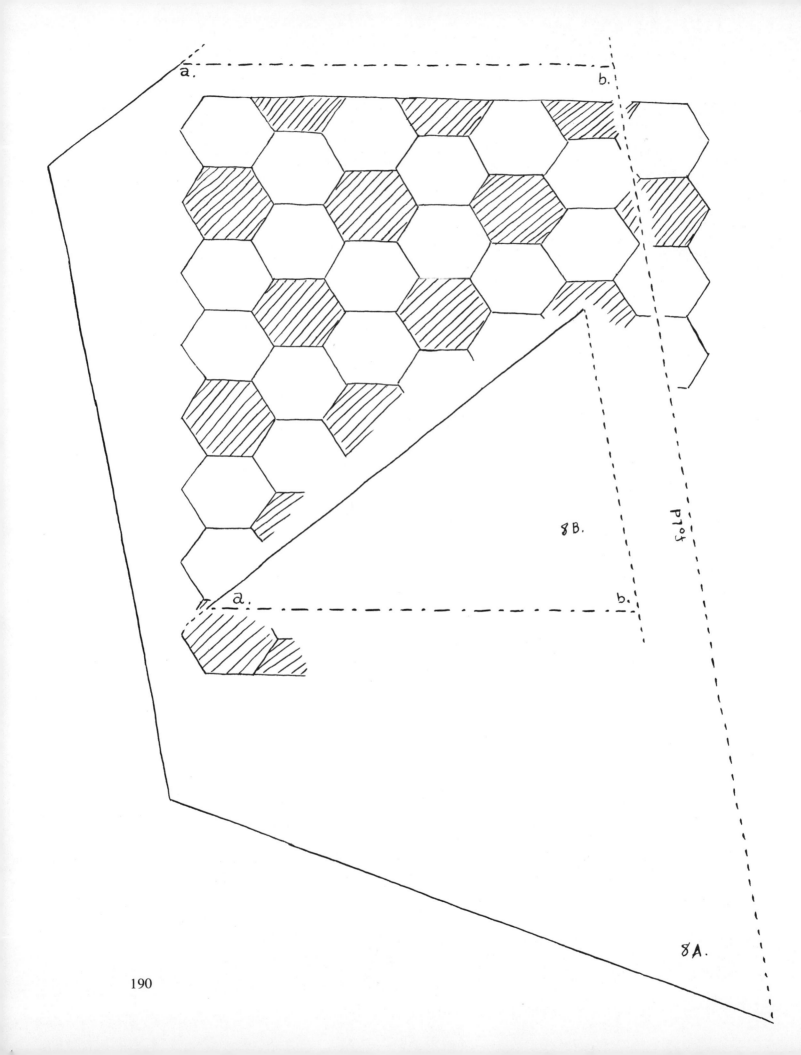

a.

b.

a.

b.

8B.

sold

8A.

190

CHAPTER SEVEN

Borders

Not all quilt designs need borders, as when the binding at the edges of the top finishes them admirably. Other quilt patterns, however, seem to need the formal design of a border to hold the pattern in place and surround it, much the same way that a hedge or picket fence surrounds and finishes a flower garden. The size of some blocks makes it difficult to piece a quilt of the proper size. This happens when a certain number of blocks makes the top too small and adding another row of blocks makes the top too large. The answer to this problem is to fill in the needed inches with a border that will make the quilt top just the correct size. In sections 3 and 4 of General Information, the sizes and variations in top design are given. Each block size is given with the patterns. Multiply the size of the blocks to give the length and width nearest the size top you wish to make. If the blocks are ten inches and the width needs to be eight feet, the border will need to be three inches wide on each side. If you prefer a much wider border, a block can be eliminated from the row and the border can then be eight inches wide on each side. You might wish to have an even wider border and a quilt larger than eight feet. The finished size of the quilt is entirely up to the quilter. Just remember that a very large quilt can be unwieldy to use and will wear badly at the edges if it drags on the floor around the bed.

This section describes two patterns that can be used for lattice strips as well as for borders, eight pieced borders, one half-pieced, half-appliquéd pattern, and three appliqué patterns. Strips in various widths can be added to the inside or outside edge of a border to make it larger. The meander vines are the most versatile border patterns a quilter can own. These can be utilized for any appliqué quilt by using the flower and leaf patterns given for the blocks and arranging them in a pleasing design along the meander. Remember that if your quilt seems to need a pieced border to finish an appliqué quilt, or an appliqué border for a pieced quilt, and the results please you, it is then a perfectly correct procedure. Quilting is a *folk art*. In folk art there are no hard and fast rules that must always be followed. If the folk artist tries something and the results are pleasing, then the artist was right even if what was done was never tried before.

You might be interested in making an old type of quilt that was popular during the seventeenth century. This type is a Medallion quilt. A center of pieced or appliquéd work two or three feet in width and length is surrounded by several borders. These may all be pieced borders in different widths with plain strips between them, they may all be appliqué, or they may be mixed. All Medallion quilts are *one-of-a-kind quilts*, and there are never any patterns for them. There are Medallion quilts illustrated in many fine quilt picture books.

Meander Lattice and Corner

This meander is drawn for use with 12-inch blocks. The background strip should be four inches wide by 12 inches long, finished-size. The background square for the corner square should be four inches on a side, finished-size.

When using this meander on a border, it can be cut to the same length as the border without using seams. To do this, draw lines with a pencil and ruler on the cloth to be used for the meander itself. These lines should be 2⅛ inches apart. Leave room for seam allowance between each set of two lines. Draw the pattern for the meander by tracing the No. 1 pattern on tissue paper.

Turn the tissue paper over and place one end of the traced pattern in the unfinished section given. Trace the meander again. This will give two sections of the meander, which is now 12 inches long. By turning your tracing paper over each time and fitting the just-finished tracing in the unfinished portion of the pattern given, you may trace as many six-inch-long sections to make the pattern as long as the finished pattern material will accommodate. By placing the finished pattern between the lines 2⅛ inches apart, the meander can be made up to eight to ten feet long, and the direction will remain a straight line.

Please read Sections 5, 6, and 7 in Chapter One on General Information before starting any work on this border.

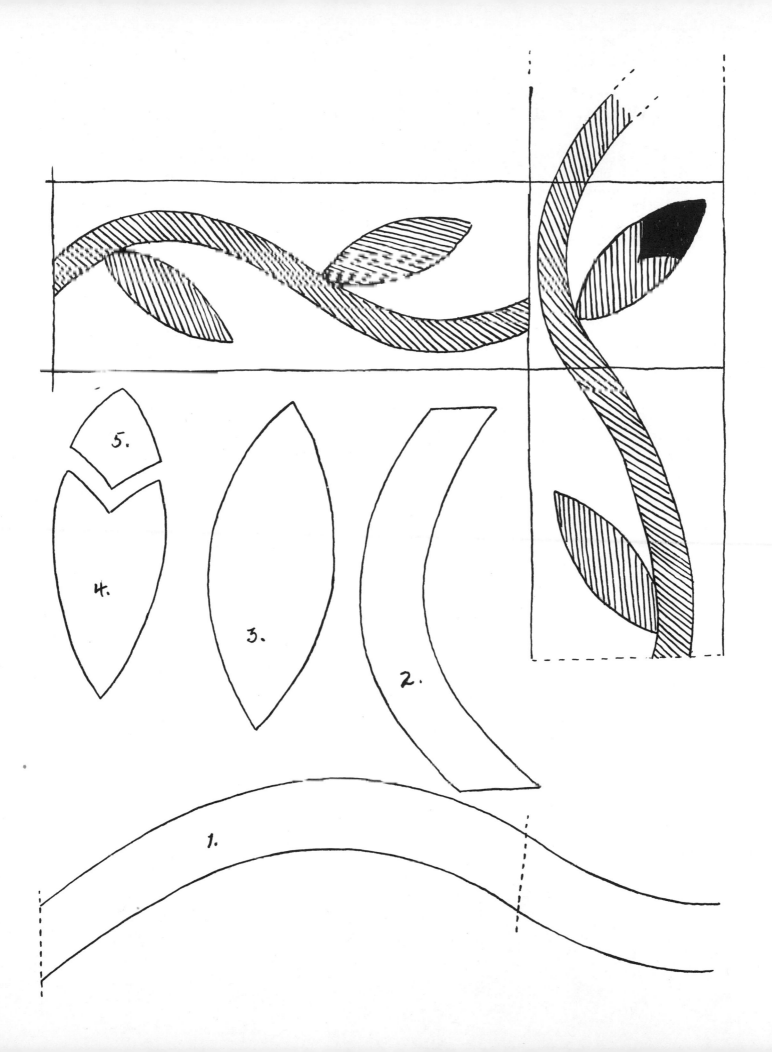

Plain Lattice with Windmill Corner

This is a second four-inch-wide lattice, but because it is plain it may be cut long enough or short enough to fit any size block. The section given is six inches long.

The windmill corner pattern is given. It is merely four light and four dark triangles. The colors used in lattice strips or borders should always match those used in the quilt. This four-inch square can be used to make doll quilts, as shown in Plate No. 1 of General Information. Four of these squares in the same colors make an eight-inch block of the traditional windmill.

Please read Sections 5, 6, and 7 in Chapter One on General Information
before starting any work on this border.

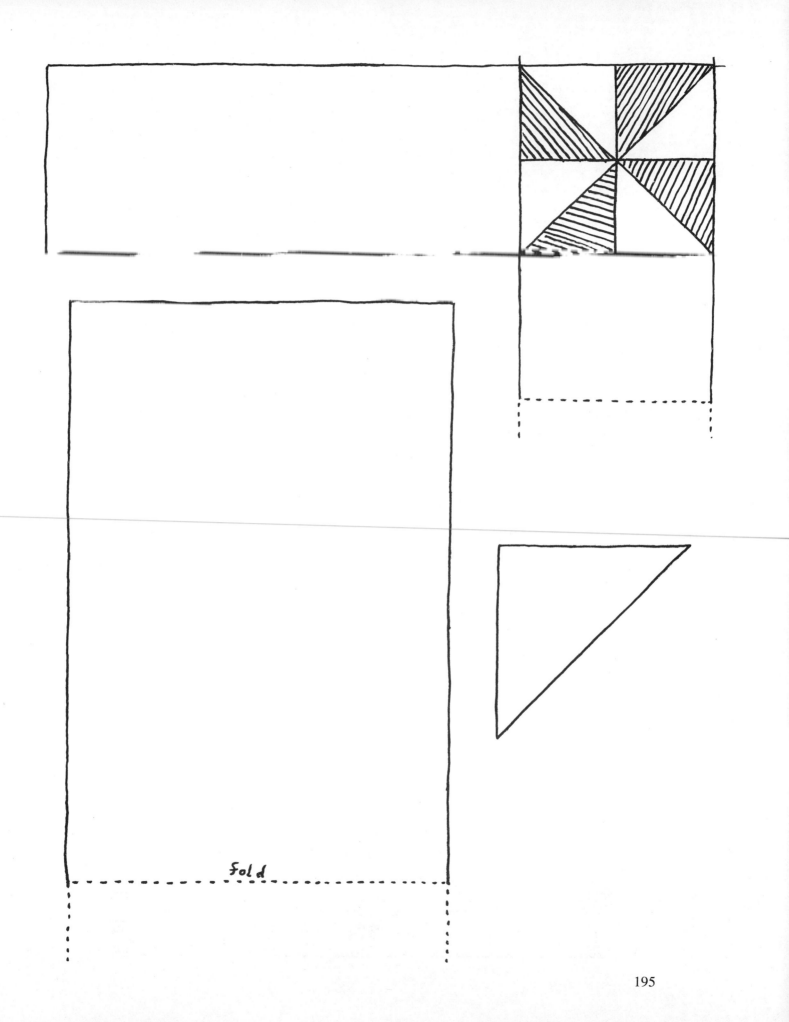

Fold

Straight Vine and Flower Border

This is a charming, primitive form of the meander. Its very simplicity makes it a perfect appliqué flower border for some patterns. This would look very attractive on a simple pieced quilt. For an appliqué quilt, use the straight vine pattern in the length needed. Then use the flower and leaf patterns from the quilt top patterns to compose a pleasing border design.

I have given one-fourth of the flower pattern. To trace this into the full pattern, place a dark dot at the point of the two dotted lines. Next trace the solid outline on your tissue paper. Move the paper to align the end of the solid line with the one drawn on your paper, and see that the dot on your paper covers the one in the book. Trace this line and repeat until the entire flower is traced. The length of the straight vine pattern will depend on the length of the four sides of the border for the quilt. Lay out the cloth for one side of the border. Cut paper circles with 9-inch diameters and lay them along the border at measured intervals. One flower must go in the corner on each side, as shown in the drawing. If the flower centers are 18 inches apart, the vine will need to be 12 inches long. If you do not want many flowers along the border, more leaves can be used along the vine. The leaves may be opposite each other as shown, or they may alternate.

This vine may be used on a 12-inch-wide border, but it might be rather crowded. An 18-inch-wide border would look better.

 Please read Section 5 in Chapter One on General Information before starting any work on this border.

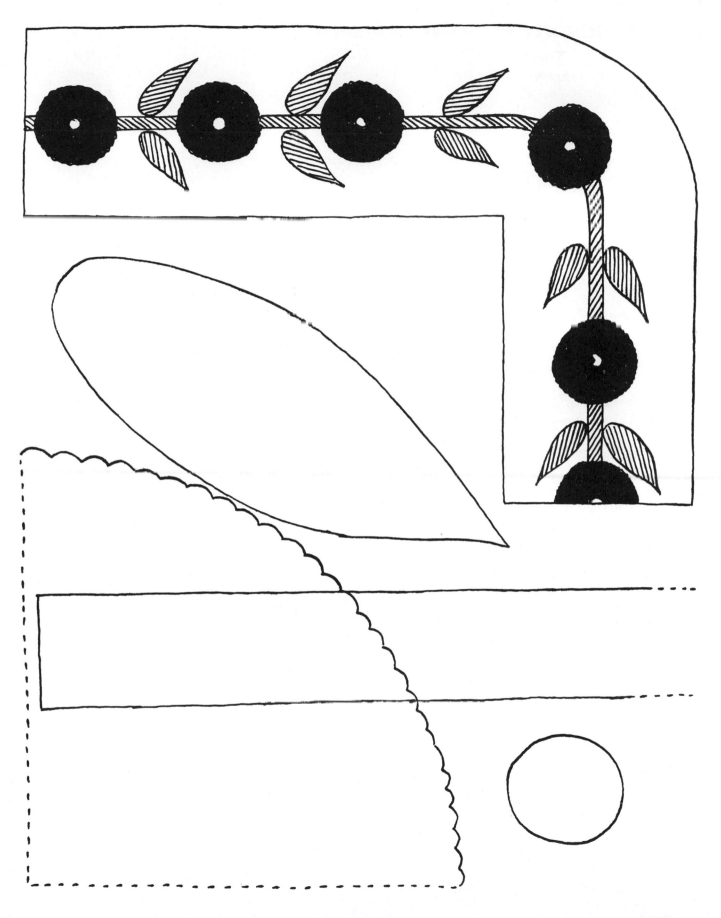

Elaborate 1840 Border

During the early decades of the nineteenth century, it was fashionable to use large, elaborately appliquéd borders on quilts with large appliquéd blocks. These quilts had either four or nine blocks that were sometimes 30 inches square or more. The borders for these quilts were 18 to 24 inches wide. The pattern was usually based on a vine meander with fruit, flowers, leaves, insects, birds, and butterflies. Sometimes even animals and people were worked into the pattern. This particular border is actually rather restrained for the type, having only a peony and bud, several leaf shapes, a grape cluster and tendril.

The chief difficulty in making meander borders is that the meander is not always at the same place in its arc when the corner is reached. Solving this problem by starting the meander at exactly the same place at each of the four corners then poses another difficulty: the meanders from each side will not meet correctly in the center. Most quilters making the borders in the early nineteenth century matched the meander down each side and improvised as best they could at the corners. This quilter solved the problem in a much simpler manner. The meander was taken from corner to corner, and then the corner was filled with a flowered square. The original border was made in the very popular color combination of green and red on white. The patterns were drawn for an 18-inch-wide border.

Make four corner squares, 18 inches square. The patterns are marked a, b, and c. Cut out the stem in dot-dash outline marked a. Flower a goes with this stem. The leaves in dot-dash outline should be cut out separately. The stem, leaves, and bud marked b should be cut out next and laid aside, and finally the c stem, bud, and leaves should be cut. Look carefully at the drawing of the corner square. Place the b stem on the background square as shown. The stem marked a should be placed over this at the lower dot-dash place indicated on stem b. Stem c should then be added, crossing stems b and a at the indicated places. Place the leaves, flower, and buds on the background where the drawing and patterns indicate.

The long sides of the border and the top and bottom should be done in the sections a, b, and c. Lay out the cloth of the border background. At one end of the a section of vine there is a straight line. This line should be placed on the seam of the background cloth. Start at the right side of the cloth, keeping at the upper end the side that will be sewn to the edge of the quilt center. This section has the grape cluster (dotted lines on a from g to h). The large leaf j should be placed at the indicated spot. Add the small leaves and grapes.

The next section is b. This has another large leaf placed across it. You can also draw the first section of vine with the leaf attached and add the short section of vine under the end of the leaf. There is another cluster of small grapes. Last are two more small leaves.

The last section is c, and it contains the peony, two buds, a tendril (e), an unusual leaf shape and a small leaf. Continue the vine with section a turned upside down, and add b and c, also upside down. If more sections are needed, always start them at a, adding b and c in turn. Turn the sections upside down each time section a repeats. Stop the vine wherever the end seam interferes, even if it occurs in the center of one of the sections. A small part of a bud or leaf may extend over the seam as shown.

Please read Sections 5, 6, and 7 in Chapter One on General Information before starting any work on this border.

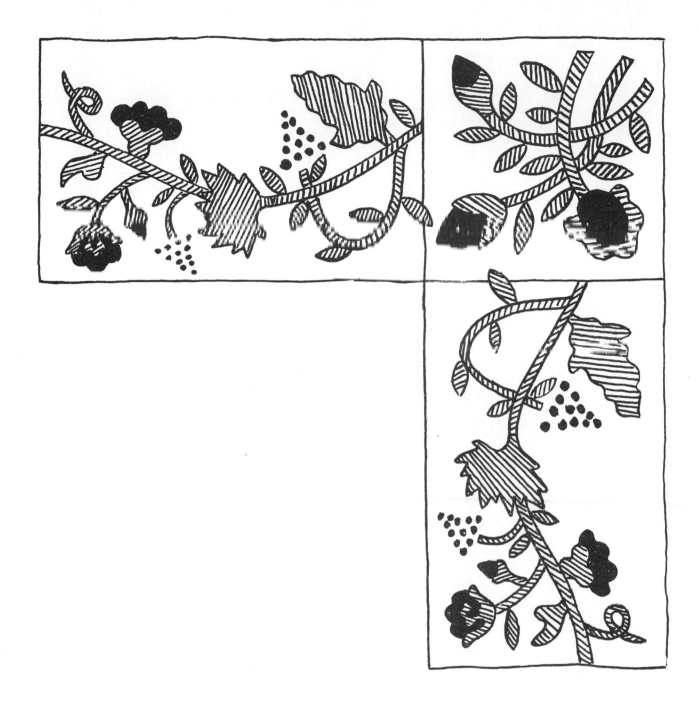

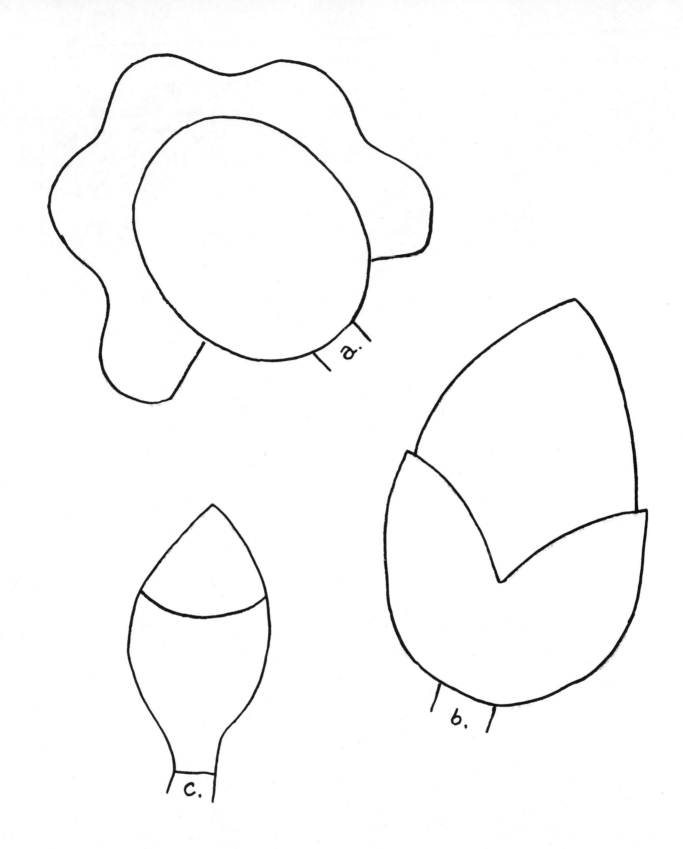

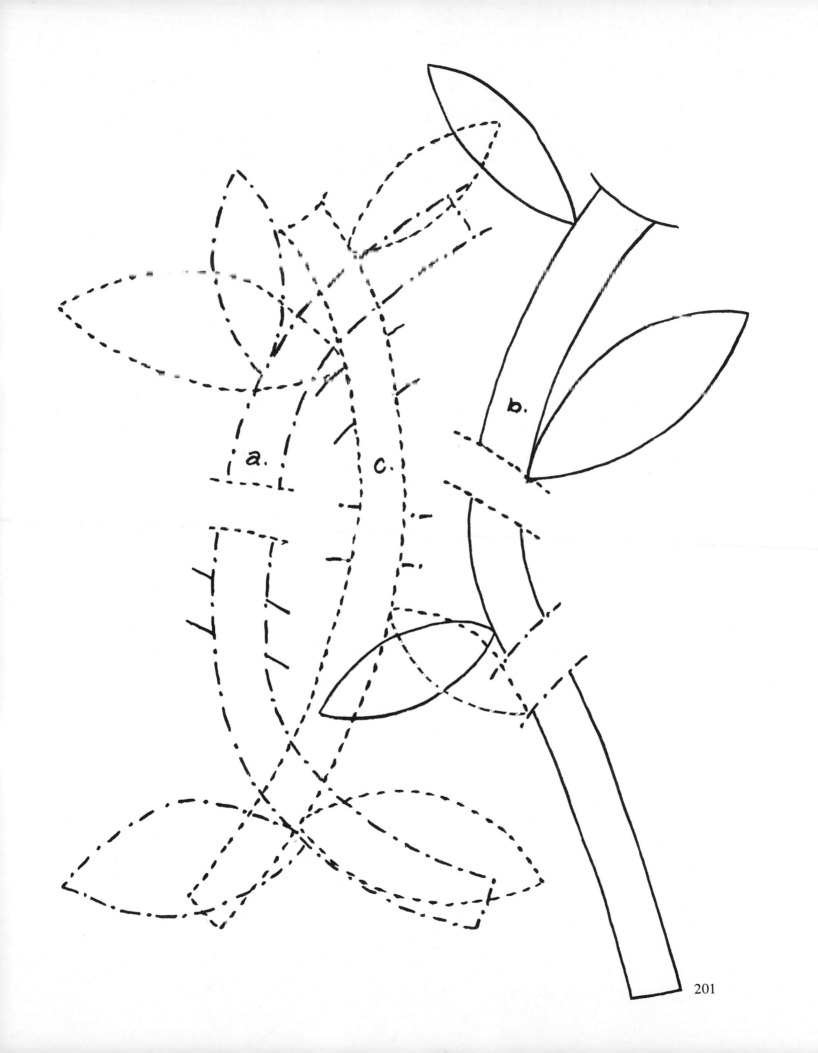

a.

c.

b.

201

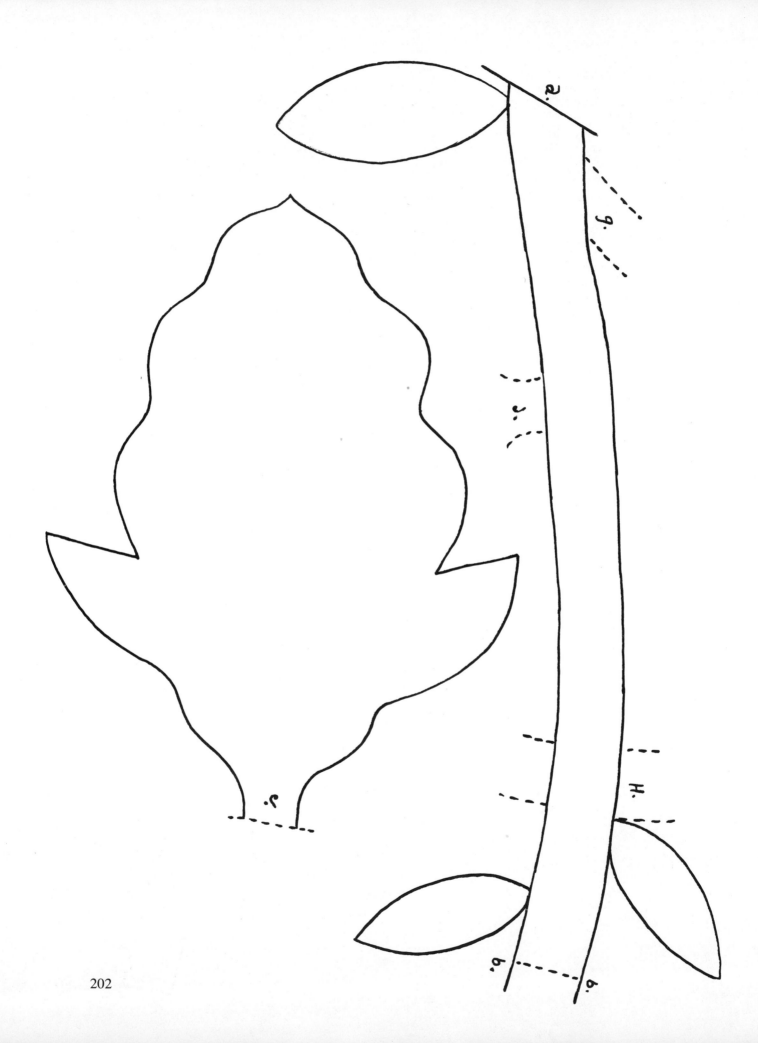

203

Spring Leaf Border

I found this delicate border on an old quilt. I am including it because it is a little different from the usual type of border. Borders similar to this were made in the nineteenth century.

Remove every other top leaf and replace it with one of the flowers or buds from your quilt pattern. Choose a flower or bud that does not overpower the stem and leaves. Another similar nineteenth-century border replaced some of the top leaves, or even all of them, with a small, brightly colored bird shape.

There are two ways to make this border. If you are an expert seamstress and do not mind difficult work, you may cut the white strip 9 inches wide and the green or dark strip 4½ inches wide.

Using the curve, mark the lower edge of the white strip and the upper edge of the dark strip to fit together, remembering to add seam allowances. Using great care, piece the curves as you would a small sleeve in a garment.

Since this method is much too hard for most sewers, I would advise that the green strip be appliquéd to the bottom of a 9½-inch-wide white strip to make the border 12 inches wide in all. Add a stem and the leaves to the top of each dark curve. This border may be reversed to put the dark strip on the outer edge of the quilt, but then the corner should be turned at the bottom of the dark curve rather than at the top as shown.

Please read Sections 5, 6, 7, and 8 in Chapter One on General Information before starting any work on this border.

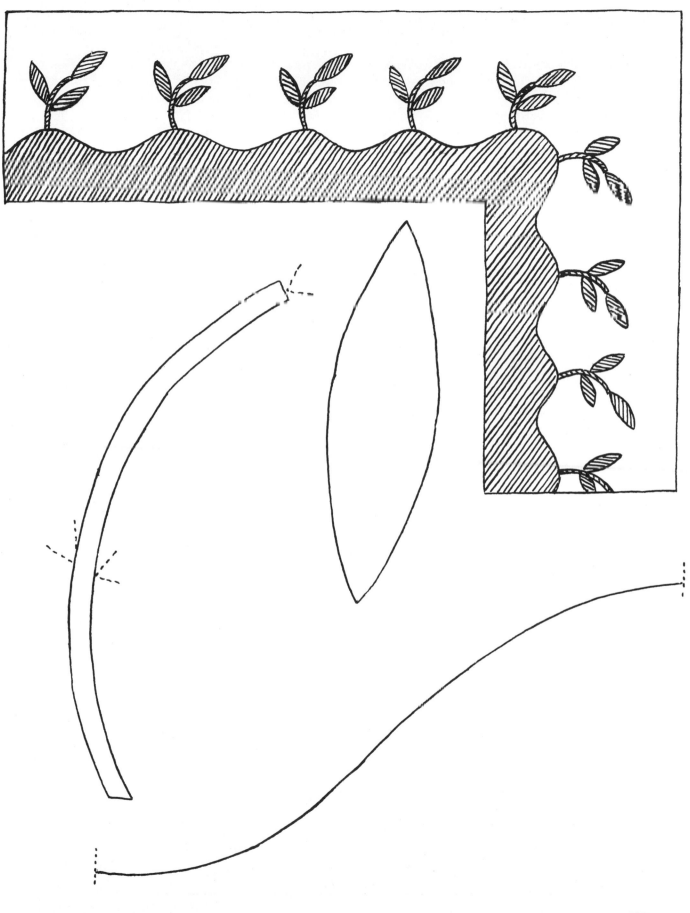

Arrowheads Border

This is a simple pieced border that would look attractive by itself or with bands of color added to the top and bottom. It may be made in any length because corner-turning poses no problem at all. It is so easy and so versatile that I have given the basic pattern in two sizes, one for a four-inch and the other for a six-inch border. You might also use half of the border width as a border between two dark strips to form still another simple border.

To make this border, choose one of the diamond patterns. Make a strip of alternating light and dark diamonds the length of one side of the quilt border. Piece a second strip the same length. If you began the first strip with a light diamond, start the second with a dark diamond. Piece the two strips together, making sure the seams between the diamonds on both strips meet exactly. To turn the corners, cut triangles from the diamond patterns along the dotted lines. Look carefully at the drawing for the placement of the triangles.

Please read Sections 5, 6, and 8 in Chapter One on General Information before starting any work on this border.

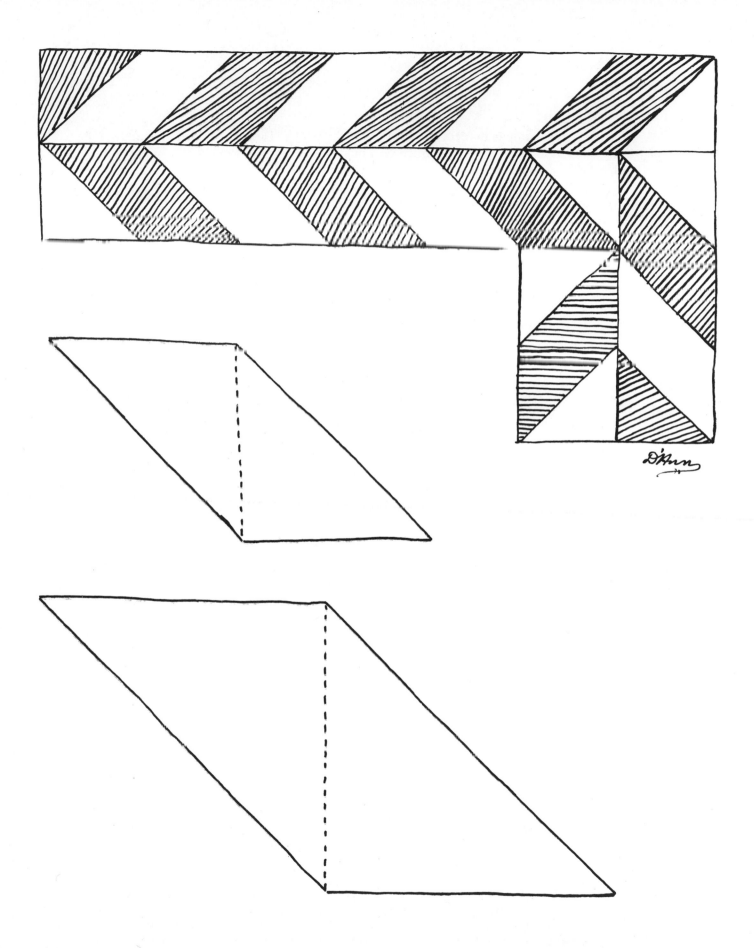

209

Sunlight and Shade Border

This is another very simple border without complicated corners. I have given the two triangles in different sizes. The larger will make a strip four inches wide that you can expand to any width you like by varying the width of the two strips. The other triangle will give a three-inch-wide strip. If the triangle is three inches wide, the strips are one inch wide. If the four-inch triangle is used, the strips are each 1½ inches wide.

I have pictured the most difficult corner you might have. Measure the length that is needed for the border. Do not overlook the width of the inner border strip. If the length is not a multiple of either three or four, divide the excess between the two ends and add this onto the end of a triangle as shown by the dotted lines.

To make the pieced strip, just make squares of one light and one dark triangle each and piece them into a strip as long as is needed for the border.

Please read Sections 5, 6, and 8 in Chapter One on General Information
before starting any work on this border.

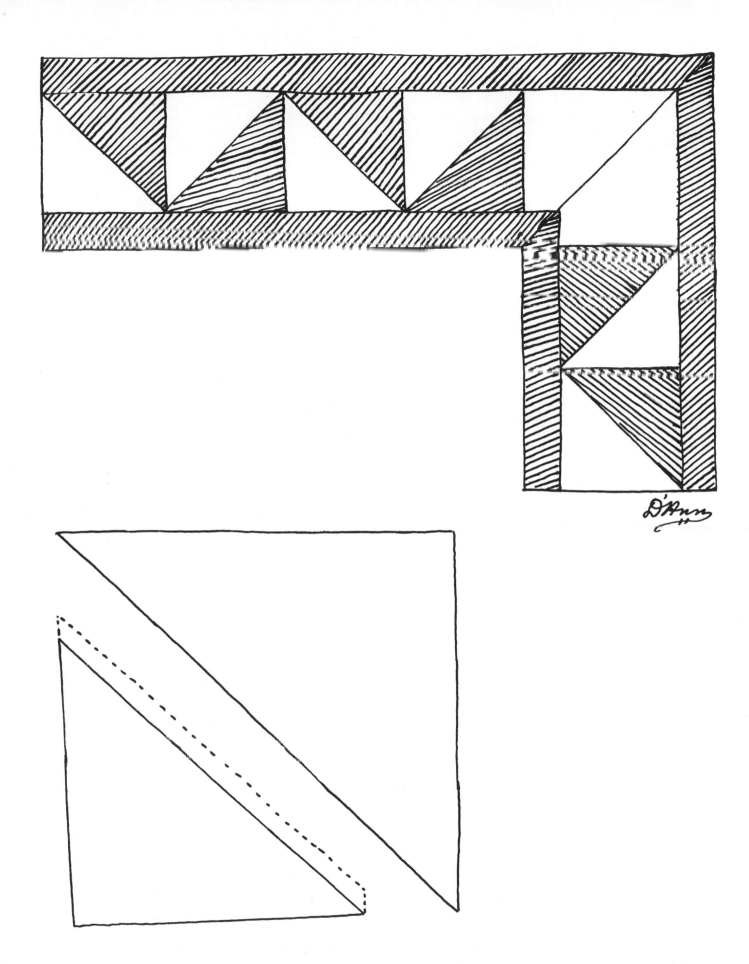

Castellated Border

The dark squares in this design make this border look like the skyline of an old castle. You can place these squares either toward or away from the center of the quilt. Here they are shown pointed toward the quilt's center. The dark sections may be made in any color to harmonize with the body of the quilt; a small print may also be used effectively. The large squares are six inches on a side. To make this border come out correctly, the quilt's dimensions must measure to the half-foot — for example, 7½ feet or 8½ feet. Measure the center of the top carefully and add a strip of white if the border is to look as I have drawn it. If you plan to reverse the castella-tion, add a matching dark strip. This strip should add as many inches as necessary to make the length one foot shorter than the finished quilt size. If the finished quilt is to be 8½ feet long, the strip should make the top 7½ feet long.

For an 8½-foot side, cut eight full squares (solid line No. 1). There will be seven half-dark and half-white rectangles. The pattern for these is the top half of the square to the dotted line (No. 2). Each corner has a square made from half of the rectangle (dotted line and dot-dash line No. 3). The dark sections of the corner meet in a mitered seam at the corner. Cut No. 3 plus No. 4 for this pattern.

Please read Sections 5, 6, and 8 in Chapter One on General Information before starting any work on this border.

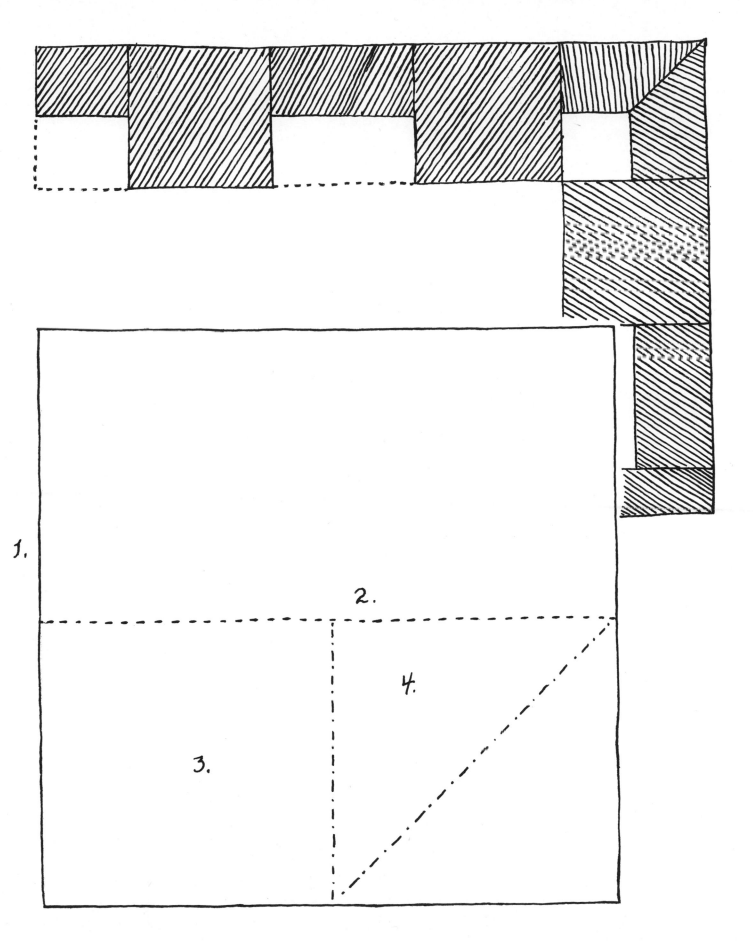

Checkered Border with Star Corner

This is a 17-inch border that will need a dark plain strip at least on the outer edge. The length of the border may be multiples of 17 inches. If the result is within six inches over the length needed, overlap the two end squares by the same amount at each end of the border. If you have more than six inches left over, eliminate a pieced square of four and place a white strip the same width at each end of the border. The corner is also a square, 17 inches on a side. The eight-point star is pieced (see the directions for Star of LeMoine), and then it is appliquéd to the center of the corner square. Measure the square

and place a dot in the center. Place a pin-point down in the exact center of the star, and then put the point of the pin through the dot on the cloth to center the star.

To make the pieced strip, sew together squares made of two light and two dark No. 2 squares. Sew these into a strip by adding a large No. 3 triangle to the top and bottom of one side of the square; then add another set of the pieced squares. At each end of the strip place two of the half-triangles cut from the large triangle pattern along the dot-dash line (No. 4). Study the drawing carefully.

Please read Sections 5, 6, 7, and 8 in Chapter One on General Information before starting any work on this border.

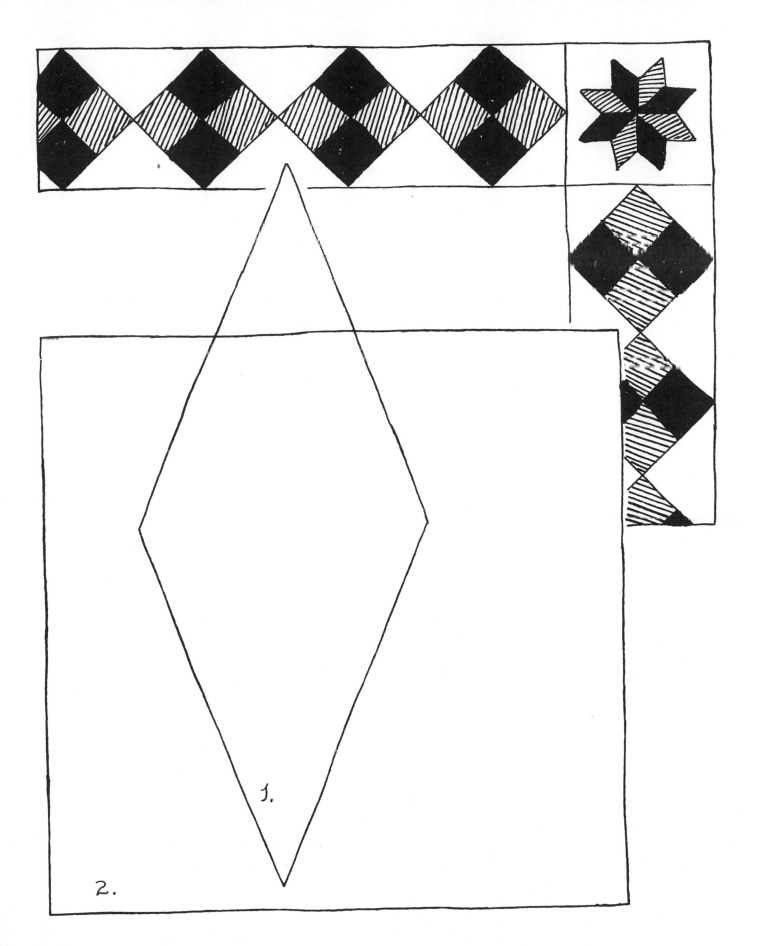

1.

2.

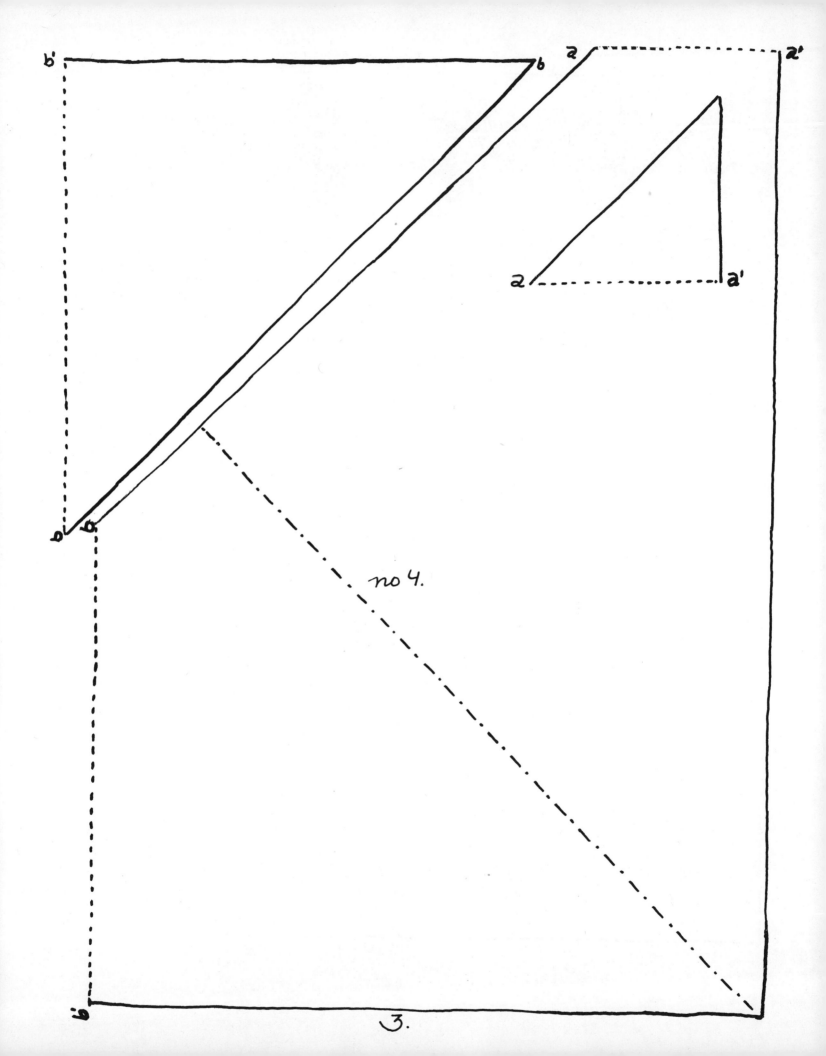

b'

b

a

a'

a

a'

b

b

no 4.

3.

Picket Fence Border

One of the most charming quilt innovations devised in the 1920s was piecing a picket fence border around appliquéd flower quilts. The pattern for the open gate can be placed either in the center of one side or the center of all four sides.

Consider the drawing carefully. Pattern No. 1 is the pickets. Their length should be one inch less than the width of the border. If the border is 12 inches wide, the picket should be 11 inches long. The 10-inch-long picket shown would be correct for an 11-inch-wide border. Pattern No. 2 is for the strips between the pickets that correspond to the laths the pickets are nailed on. Pattern No. 3 is the pattern for the two partial pickets at each side of the corner post. Pattern No. 4 is the corner post. The corner posts should be the same length as the pickets. Their top corners should touch the two whole side pickets just one inch below their top corner, as shown. Cut the partial pickets to fit.

The gates may be placed anywhere, but they look best at the center of a border side. The gate consists of two No. 5 posts with No. 6 balls on top. These posts should be 1½ inches shorter than the pickets. The top of the ball will touch the top seam of the border. The gate consists of three pickets: one picket in the usual length, the second made 1½ inches shorter, and a third 1½ inches shorter than the second. Place two No. 2 squares between the post and the longest picket. Four No. 7 shapes take the place of the squares between the three gate pickets. The gate latch is pattern No. 8, given in dot-dash outline. Two inches from the smallest gate picket, place the other post with its ball top and continue the picket fence to the next corner.

This border usually had a light blue background (to simulate the sky) and white pickets. Suit the color scheme to your quilt.

Please read Sections 5, 6, and 7 in Chapter One on General Information before starting any work on this border.

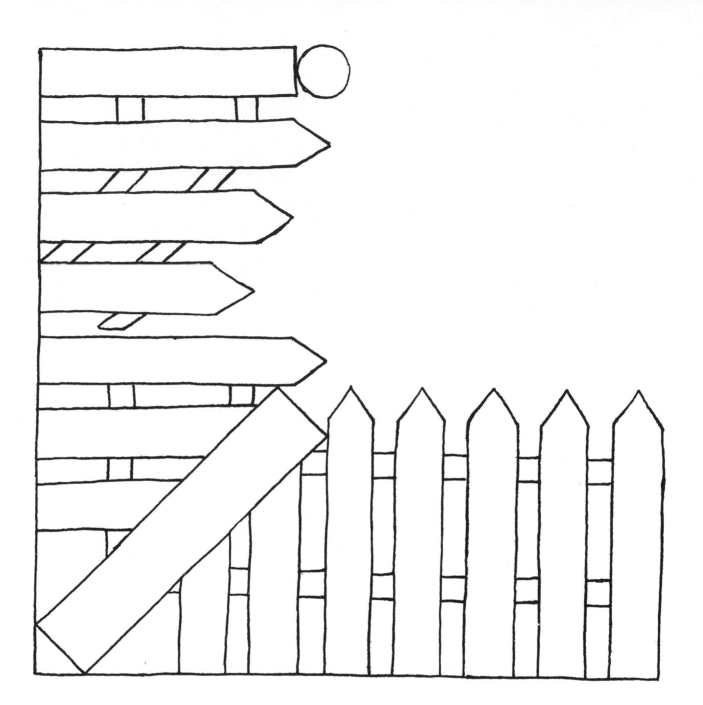

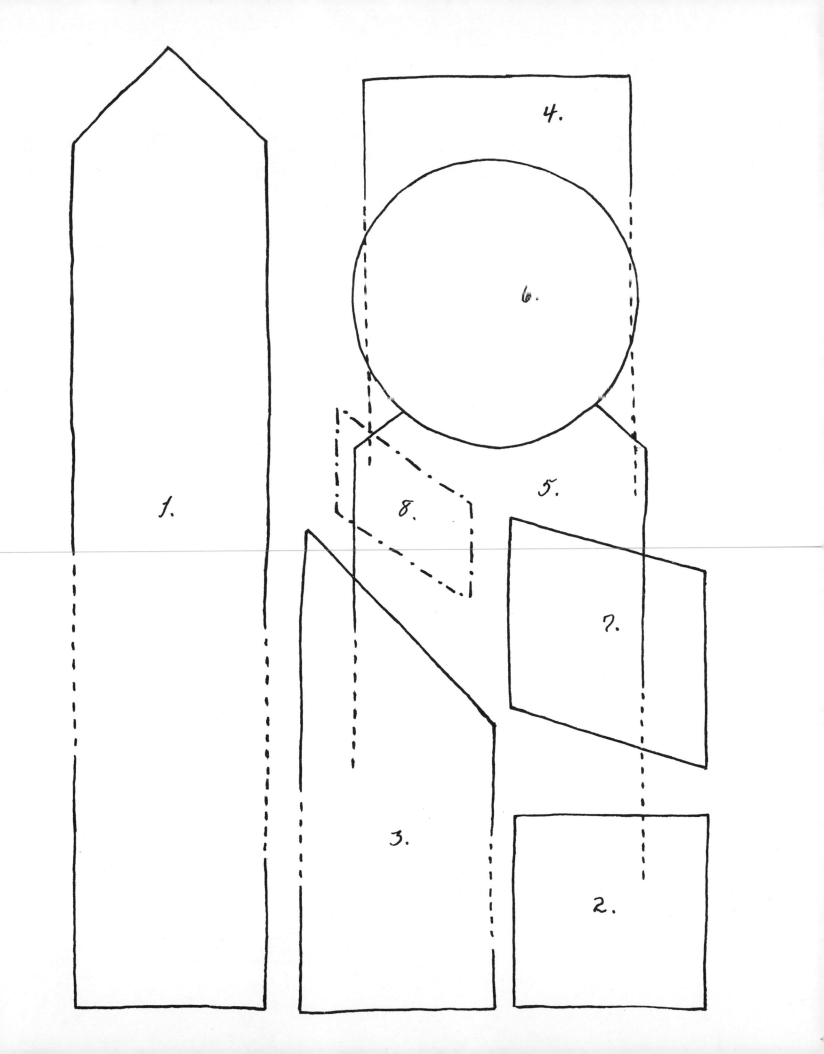

Ribbon Border

This border is an old one, and I could not find a description of the corner treatment anywhere. I improvised a corner that I think will be satisfactory. This is such a pleasing design that I have given the patterns in two sizes. Those marked 1 are for a 6-inch-wide border. Those patterns marked 2 are for a 12-inch-wide border. These directions use the No. 2 border pattern.

The corners are pieced in a 12-inch square made from a large triangle in the principal color and three white background triangles. The large dark triangle is marked 2c. Piece this to a white 2a triangle with the bases of the two triangles together. Cut two triangles in white from pattern 2e, reversing one. Sew these to each side of the large dark 2c triangle to form a square.

The sides of this border are pieced in two strips each. Look carefully at the drawing. Cut three white and one very dark triangle from pattern 2b. Sew these together into a large triangle with the dark triangle in the center. A side for an 8-foot quilt will be 6 feet long. This will take 12 whole, large, light-colored triangles, pattern 2a. The second strip will start with a half-triangle (dotted line), then there will be 11 whole, light-colored triangles. The strip ends with another half-triangle.

Alternate the pieced and light-colored triangles to make the strips, then sew the strips together. Finish each end of the outer strip with one white small triangle, one very dark triangle, and one small, white half-triangle. Sew them together, then sew the half-triangle to the corner square and overlap this with half of the very dark triangle. Appliqué this half to the corner square. Be sure to study the drawing carefully.

This border could be widened with dark bands on either side to make your quilt top as wide as needed.

Please read Sections 5, 6, and 8 in Chapter One on General Information before starting any work on this border.

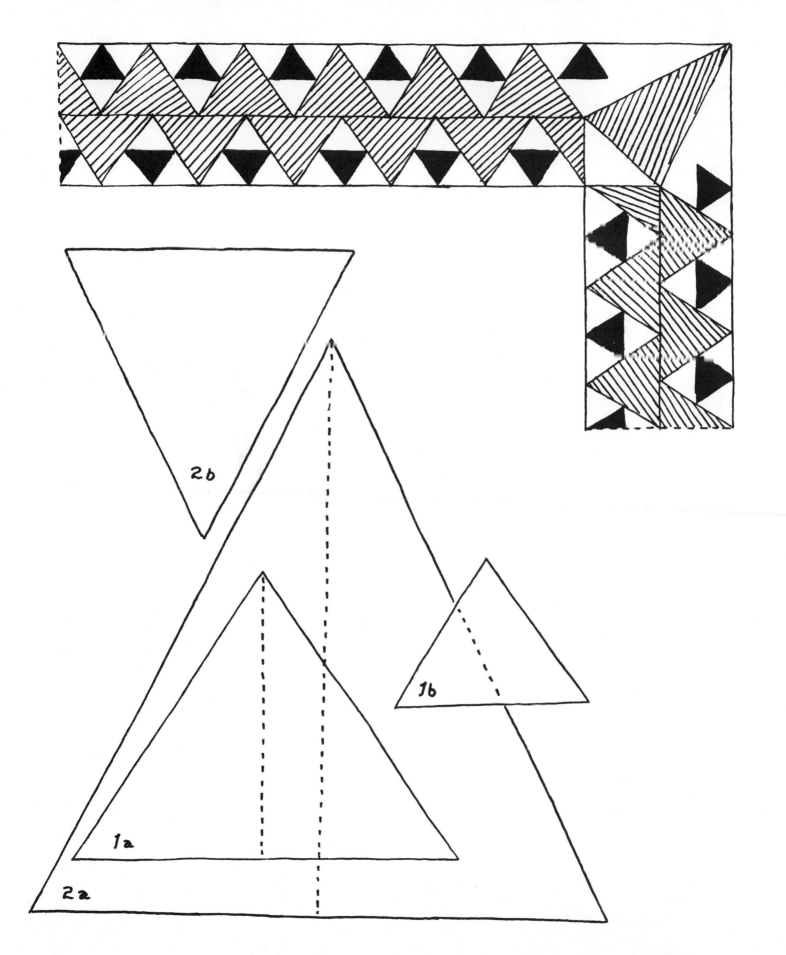

221

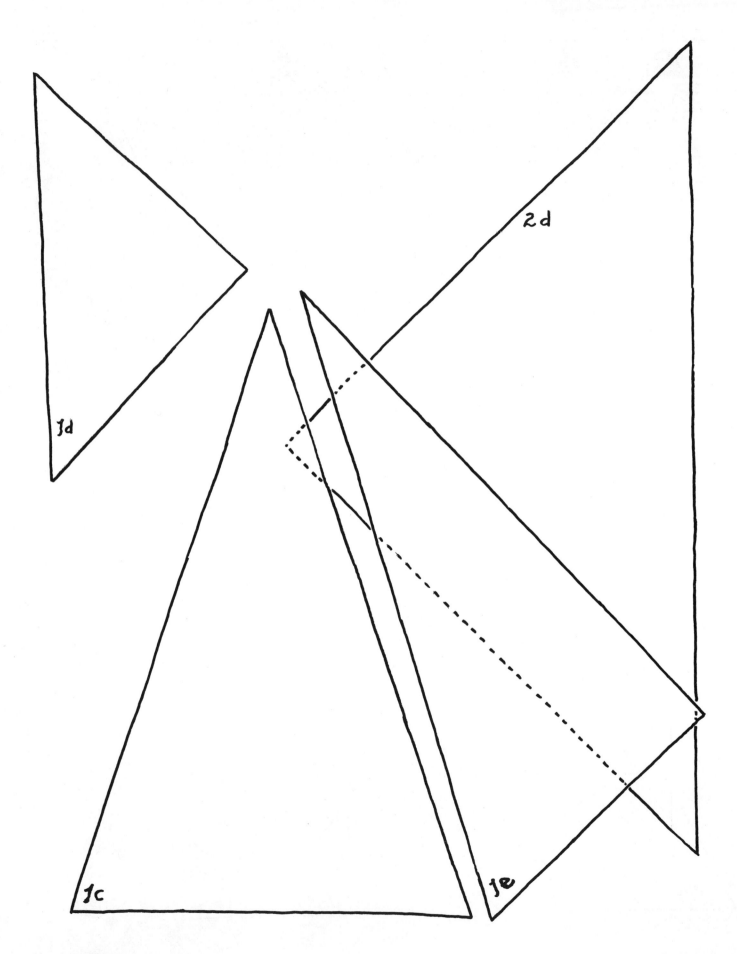

1d

2d

1c

1e

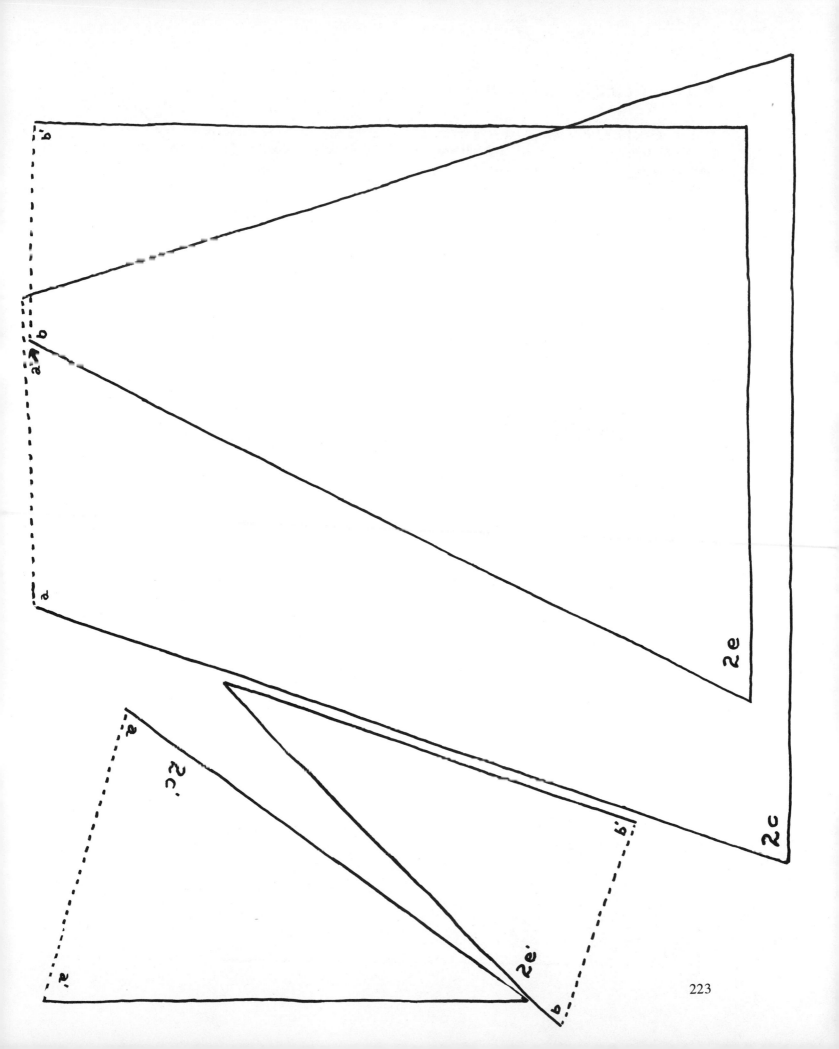

b

b

a

a

2e

2c'

2e'

2c

a

b'

b

223

Double-Chained Border

This is one of the more formal types of colonial pieced borders. It goes well with almost any kind of pieced or appliquéd pattern. The border is made up of two rows of chained squares and three rows of plain cloth, two white and one the same color as the squares. If your quilt has two main colors, the dark strip might match the second color to make the border match the quilt.

The patterns are drawn for three different border sizes. The smallest is 9 inches, the second is 12 inches, and the largest is 15 inches. The size of the chained square strips remains the same in all three, but the width of the three plain strips changes for each size. The drawing shows the 15-inch-wide border.

Measure the size of your top. The first strip of chained squares should be six inches longer than the length of the quilt. Sew a white triangle, half of square *A* (dotted line), to each side of square *A*. Continue this until the strip is the length needed. The squares on each end of the chain should not have a triangle on the lower end. Repeat for the top strip of chained squares, but make this strip the finished length of that side of the quilt (8 feet long for an 8-foot quilt).

Choose the pattern for the width of the border needed. The smallest, 9 inches wide, should be cut from the pattern for the plain strip that is marked one inch. Sew a white strip to the top of the inner chain. It should overlap by a little more than one inch at each end. The next strip should be dark and it also should overlap the previous strip by an additional inch at each end. Add the second white strip and overlap this strip again by an additional inch on each end. Finally, add the outer chained square strip. It should overlap the last white strip by three inches on each end. Join the two strips for two sides so that the corner is mitered. Cut off the triangles of cloth for the plain strips on the back of the top. This border forms a corner much easier to make than most.

To make the 12-inch border, use the 2-inch pattern. These strips should each overlap two inches further on each end. The 15-inch border shown in the drawing will take the three-inch pattern. The overlap at the ends will be three inches for each row.

Please read Sections 5, 6, and 8 in Chapter One on General Information before starting any work on this border.

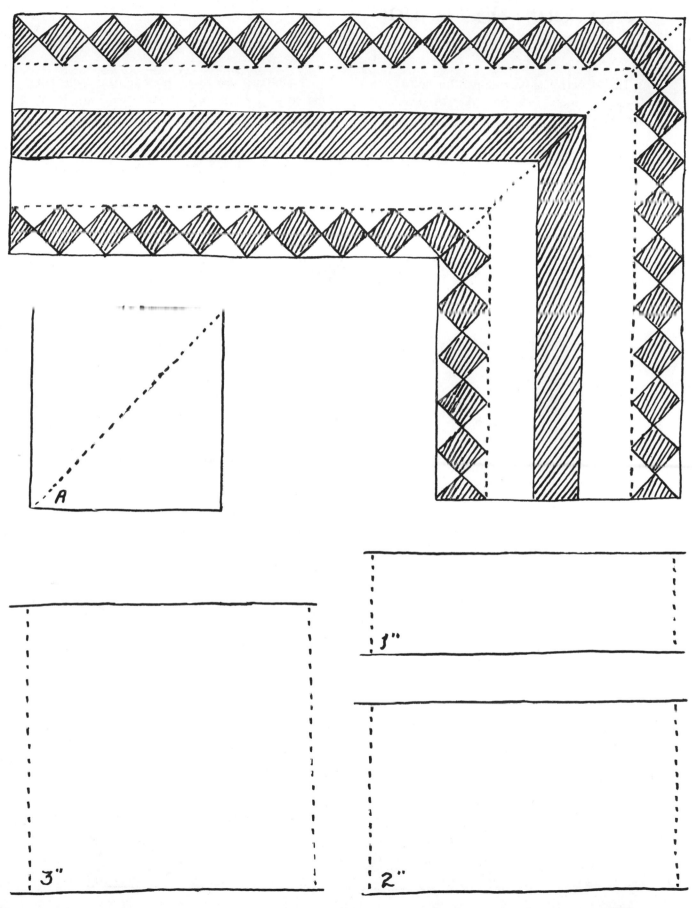

A

1"

3"

2"

225

Saw-Tooth and Bands Border

This pattern has been drawn for both 12- and 16-inch borders. The only patterns needed are the triangles and a pattern the same width for the bands. The patterns for the 16-inch border are marked 1, and those for the 12-inch border are marked 2.

The saw-tooth strip is made up of squares of a light and a dark triangle each (see the drawing). This strip should overlap the side of the quilt center by four inches on each end. Study the corner treatment.

Cut the two strips four inches longer each than the strip inside it on the quilt. This will leave enough cloth for a mitered corner. You may prefer the corner with the four-inch square inset if you are a beginning quilter. This treatment, shown in the white band, eliminates the miters in the corners.

If the 16-inch border is used, change the above directions by substituting six inches everywhere four inches has been used.

Please read Sections 5, 6, and 8 in Chapter One on General Information before starting any work on this border.

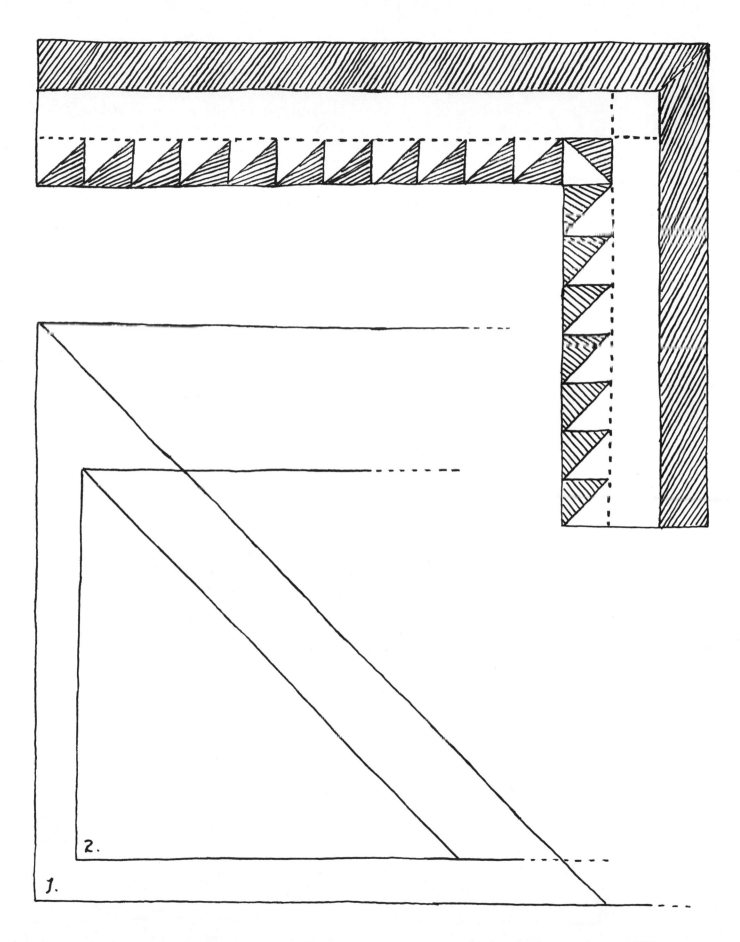

1.

2.

Scalloped Border

This is an interesting variation on the border usually used for a Dresden Plate quilt, which uses one of the petal patterns from the design to form its border. However, this border could be used on almost any dainty quilt. I can see it used in gingham and white on a little girl's quilt. It is only six inches wide and could be used effectively on a crib quilt.

This pattern is easily sewn together by just alternating the two patterns, No. 1 and No. 2. I am quite sure a beginner could use this design on her very first quilt. Simply turn the corners as shown by using three of the No. 1 cones.

Please read Sections 5, 6, and 8 in Chapter One on General Information before starting any work on this border.

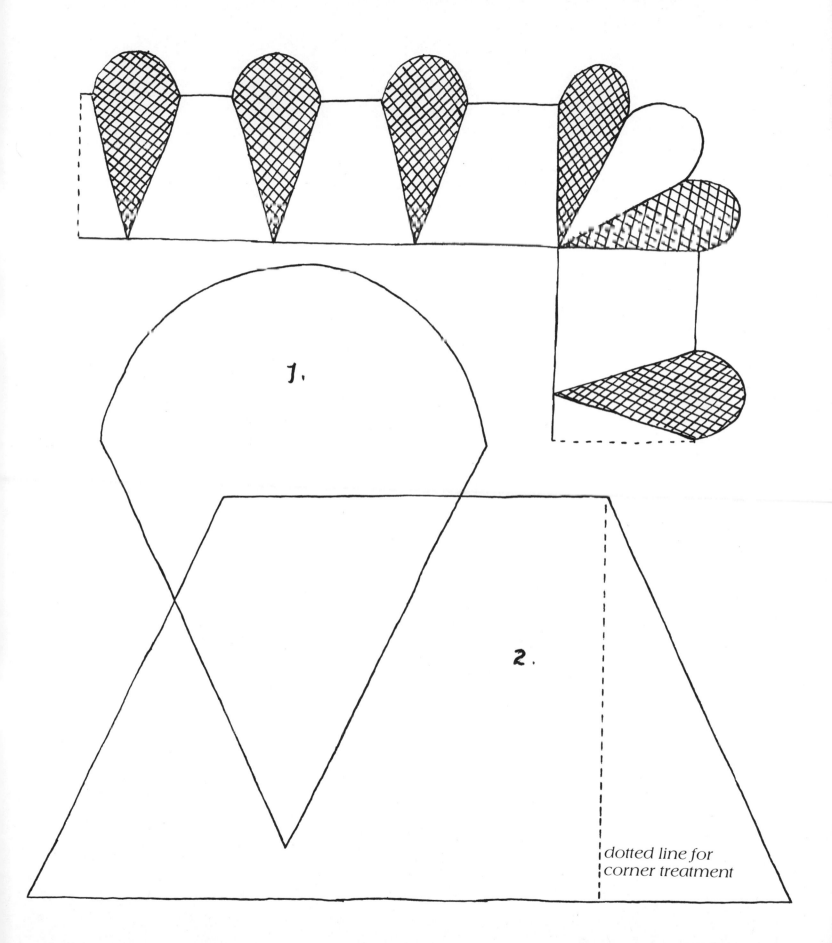

1.

2.

dotted line for
corner treatment

CHAPTER EIGHT

Quilting Patterns

One of the unofficial rules traditionally observed by most quilters is: "A fancy quilting pattern should be used with a plain quilt top pattern, and a simple outline or all-over quilting pattern is used with a fancy-patterned top."

The quilting pattern is very important to the overall charm of a quilt. Of course, the main purpose of the quilting is to hold the three layers — top, filler, and backing — together. A pattern also makes shadows that give the surface of the quilt the look of fine bas-relief carving. The spaces of closer quilting contrast with the open spaces to accentuate the beauty of the pieced or appliquéd patterns in the top.

I have given 23 patterns for quilting. Most of these patterns are full-sized. The graphed patterns should be redrawn on graph paper with one-inch squares. The patterns with dotted lines show one-half or one-fourth of the pattern. (See section 5 of General Information for instructions on how to complete these patterns.)

Outline and all-over patterns should be drawn on the top. Those patterns that fit into white or plain spaces may also be drawn on the top. The fancy patterns that overlap the pieced patterns or ignore the top design entirely are best drawn and worked on the plain backing. To do this the quilt should be placed in the frame upside down.

There are many ways to reproduce the design on the cloth for quilting. The best way for each quilter may be found by experimentation. If the quilter is good at freehand drawing the design may be drawn or traced with a light pencil line. Some quilters prefer chalk or even pinpricks, but these are hard to see, wipe off easily, and take much practice for best use. An iron-on pattern or pencil is available at some shops or catalog services. These come with directions for use, but be sure they are washable. Prominent quilting pattern lines spoil the looks of your quilts and are not acceptable in most quilt shows. There is also a brand of perforated paper and chalk that some quilters find acceptable for transfering patterns.

Yardsticks and other straight edges, cups, saucers, and other objects around the house can be utilized as our foremothers did to make simple geometric designs. Cut paper in snowflakes or other shapes to aid in reproducing the more elaborate patterns.

If a pencil or iron-on pattern is noticeable after the quilting is finished, the top should be washed before it can be shown off to the best effect.

To photograph your finished quilt, be sure the light does not strike directly on the front of the quilt top. The light should hit at an angle, so that it casts small shadows that will show off the quilting as well as the pieced or appliquéd patterns in the photograph. This will reveal the complete beauty of your quilt's design.

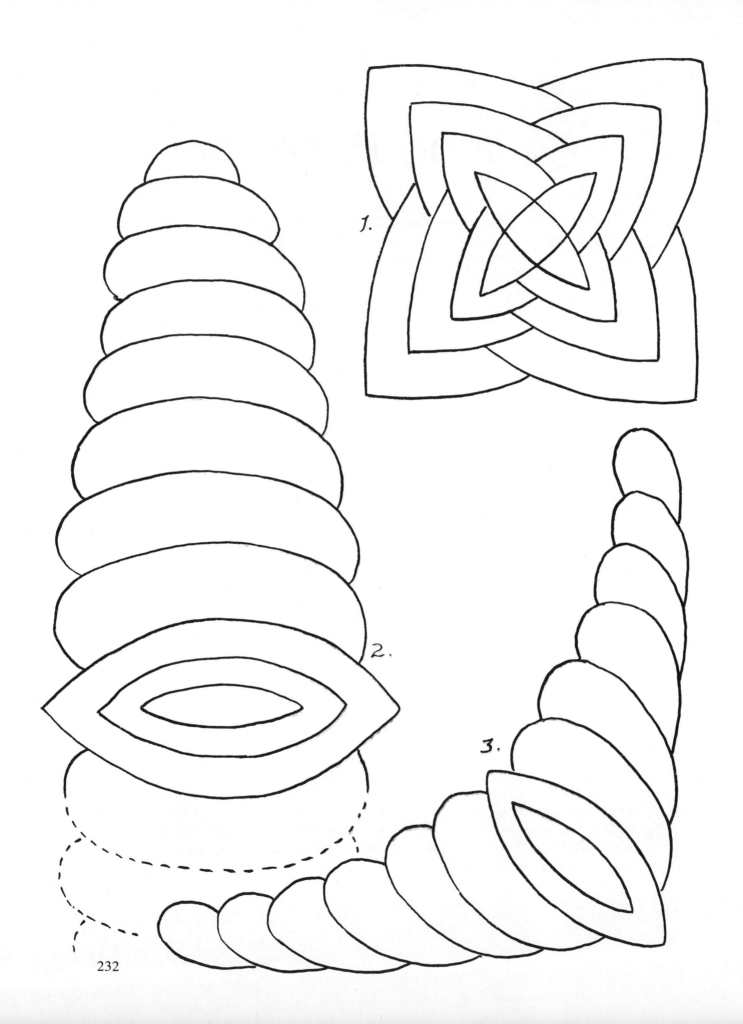

1.

2.

3.

232

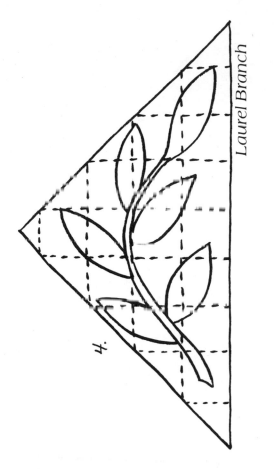

Laurel Branch

4.

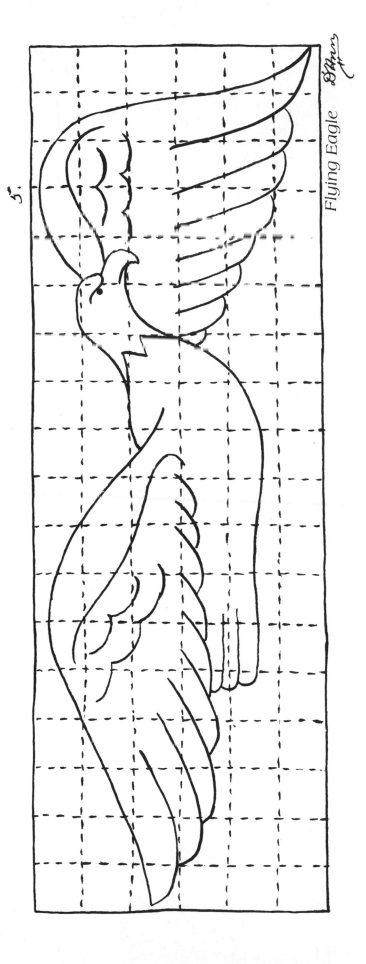

5.

Flying Eagle

Each square equals 2 inches

234

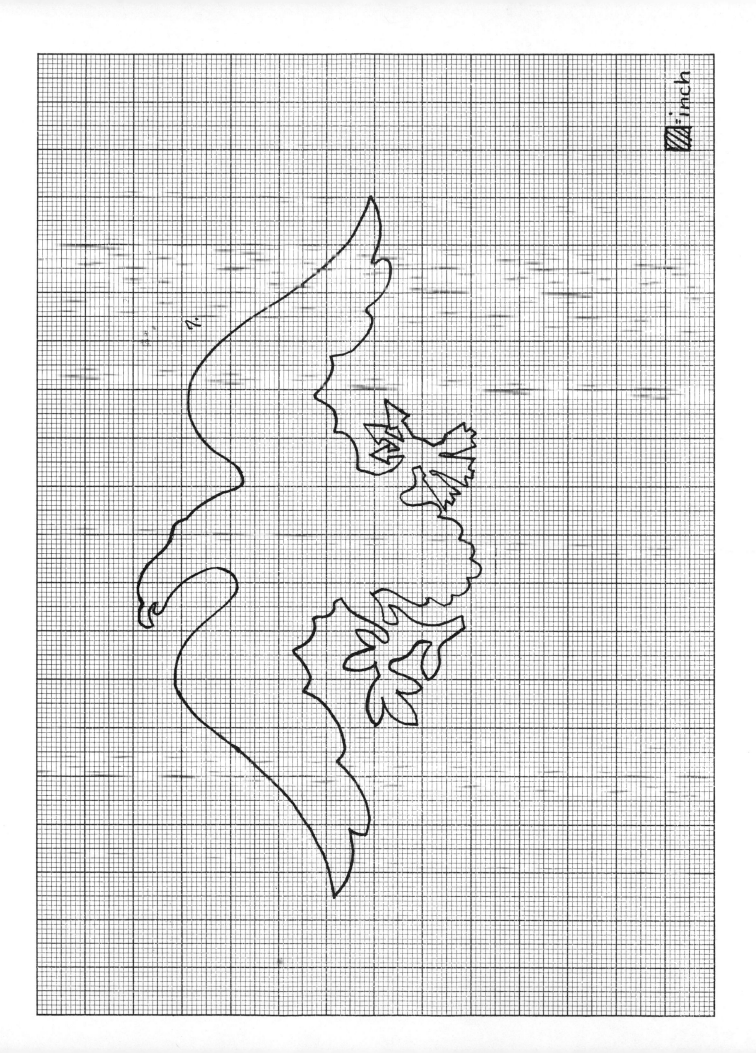

inch

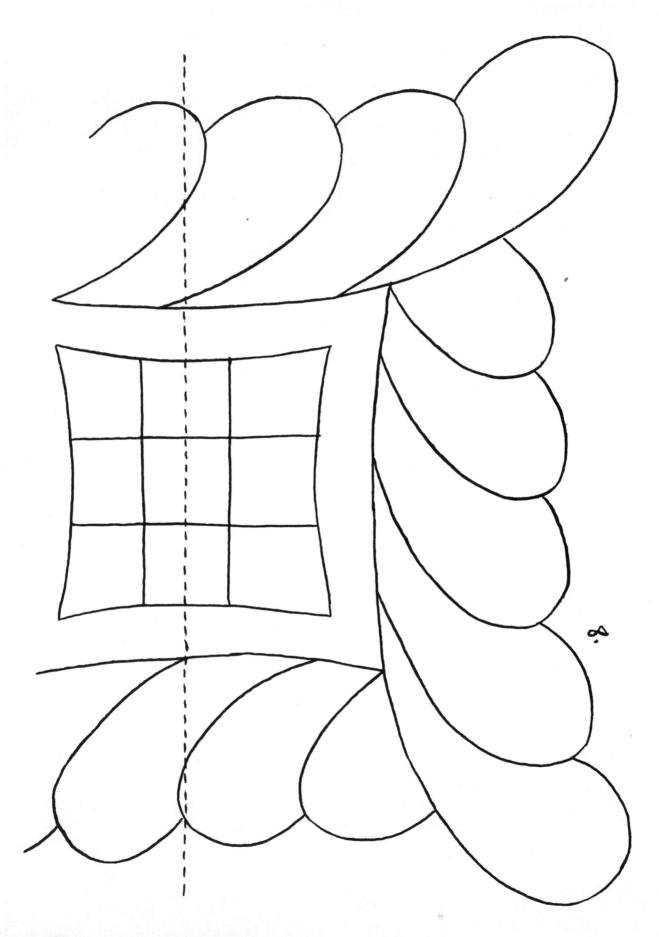

8.

237

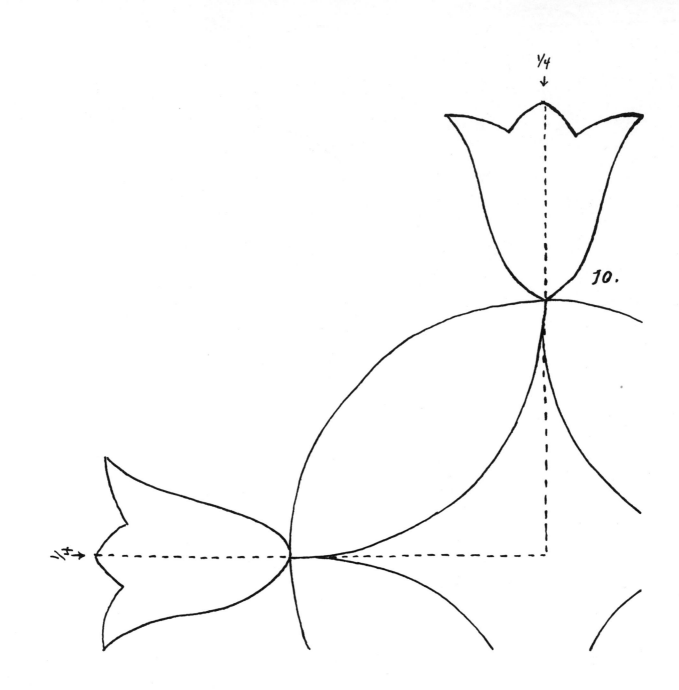

10.

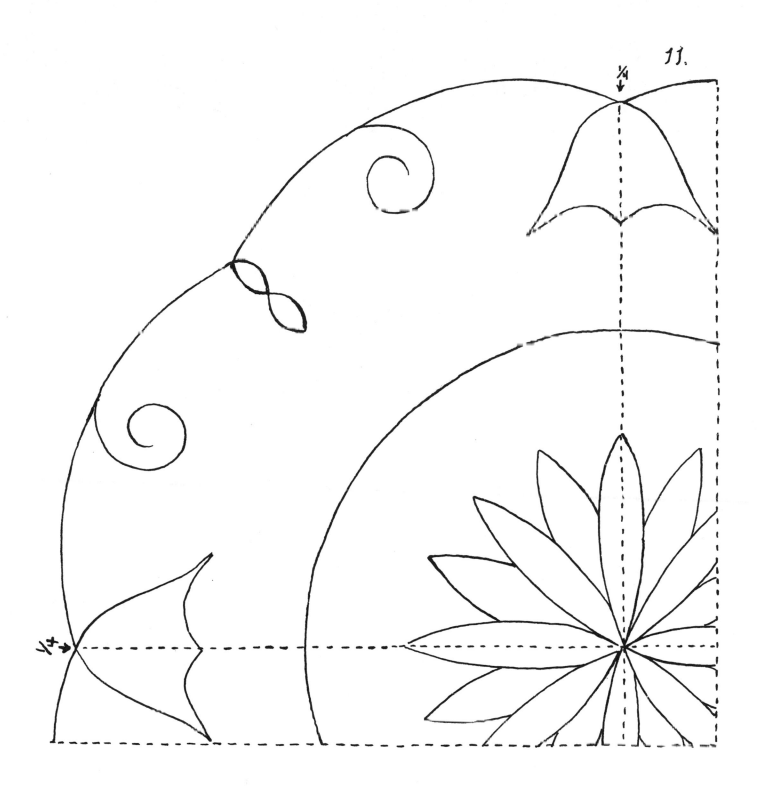

11.

¼

¼

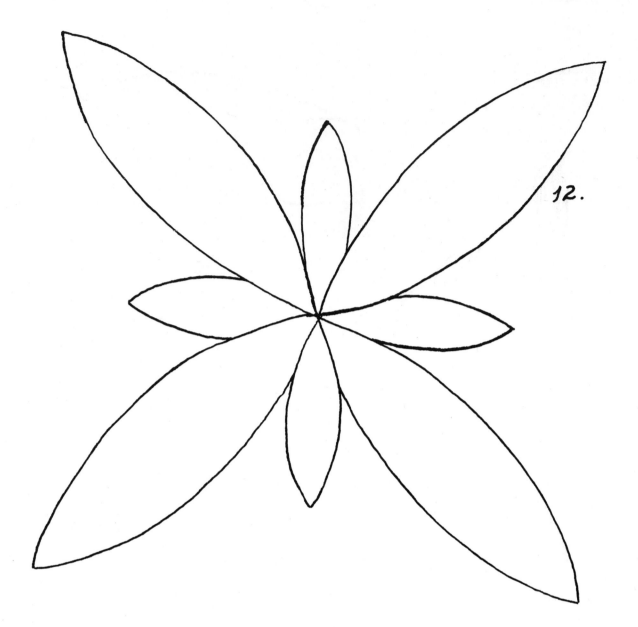

12.

240

13.

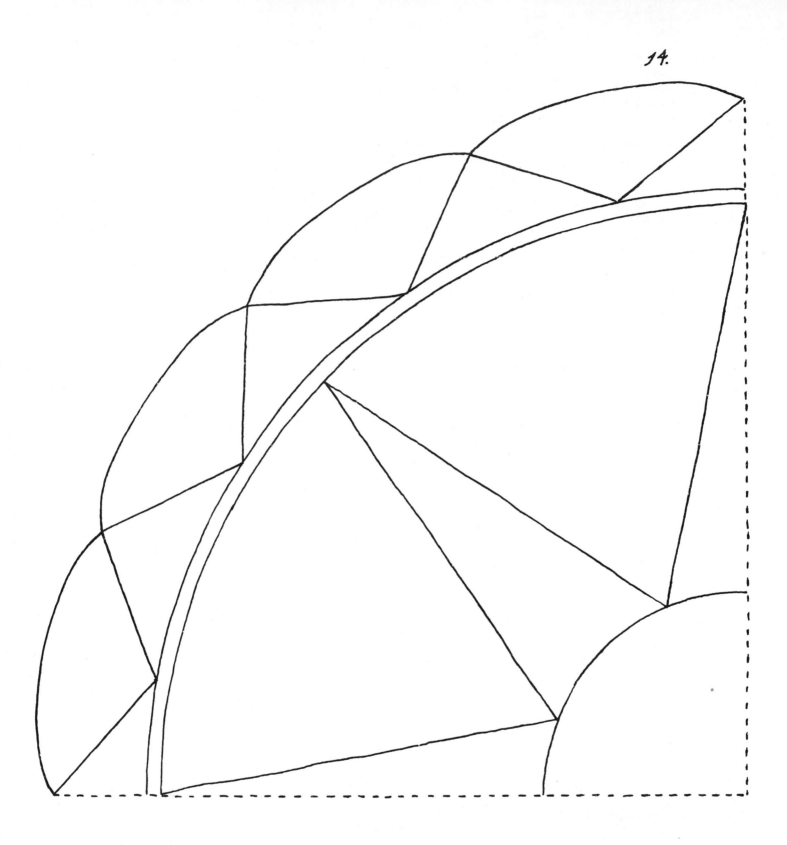

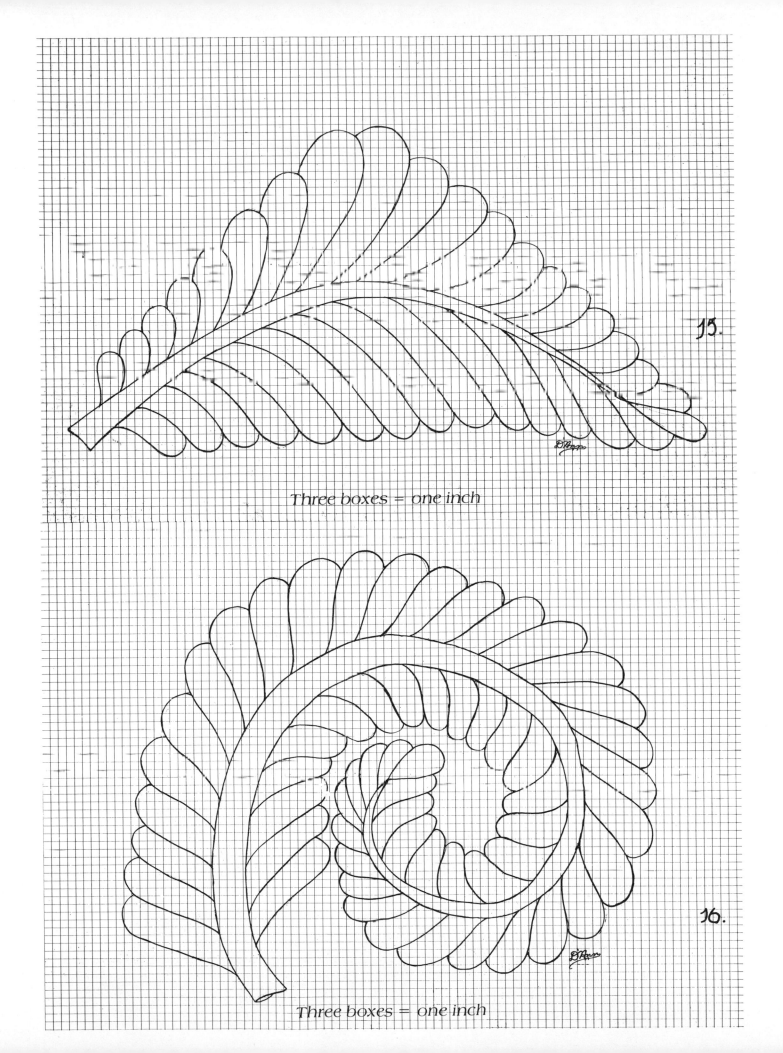

14

15.

Three boxes = one inch

16.

Three boxes = one inch

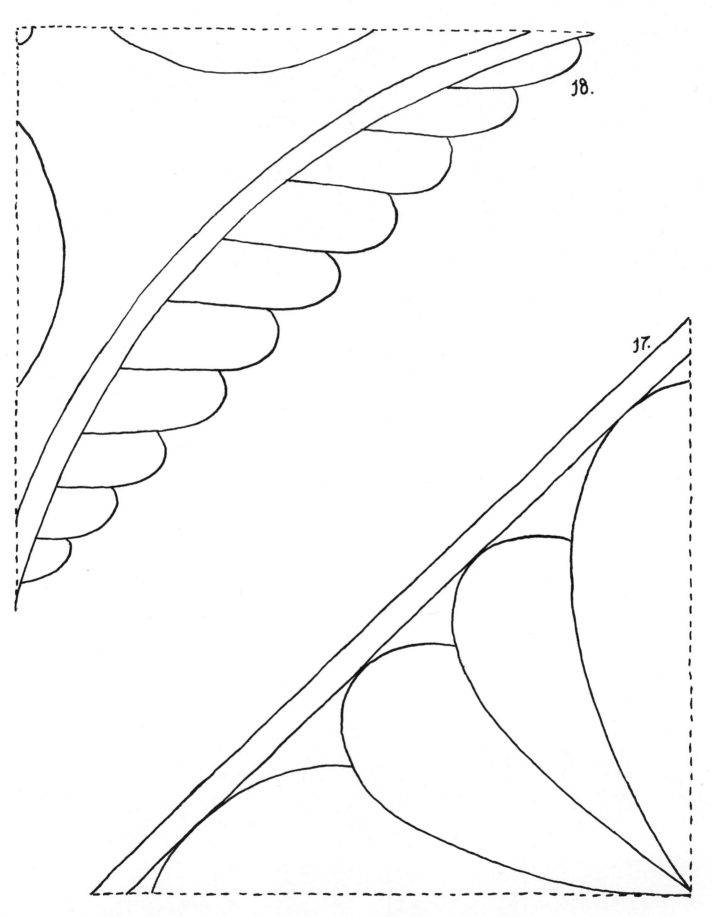

18.

17.

244

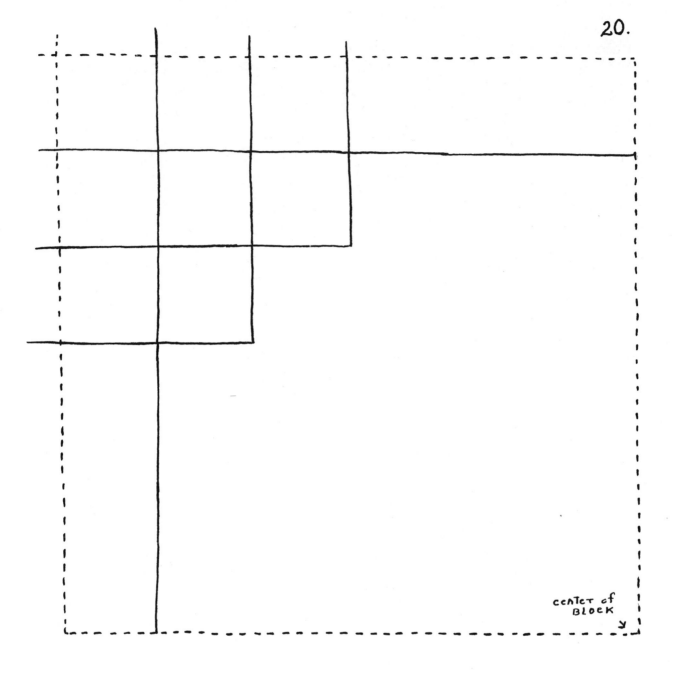

center of
BLOCK

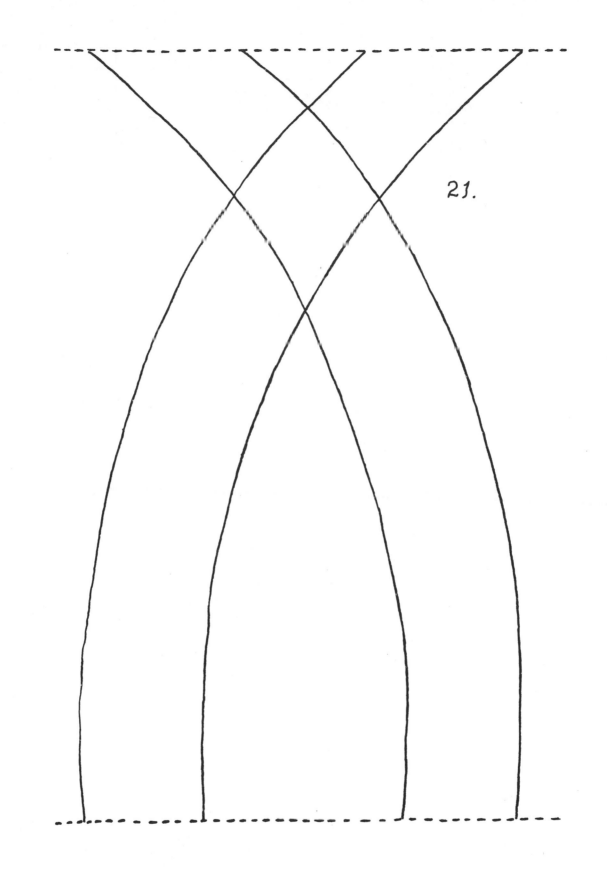

21.

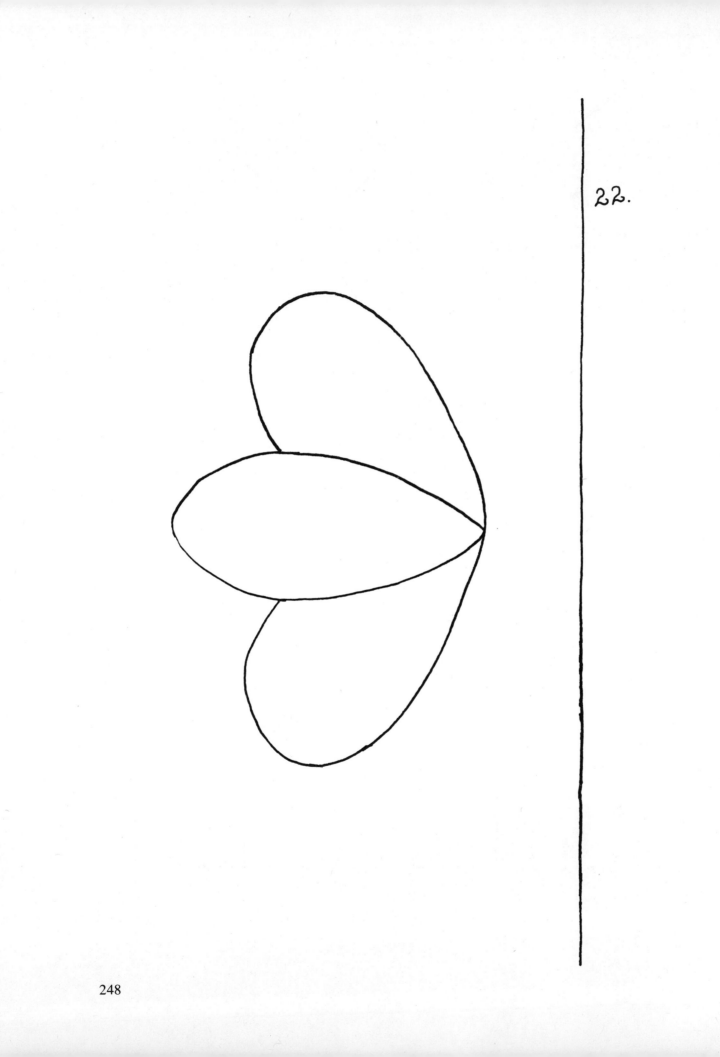

22.

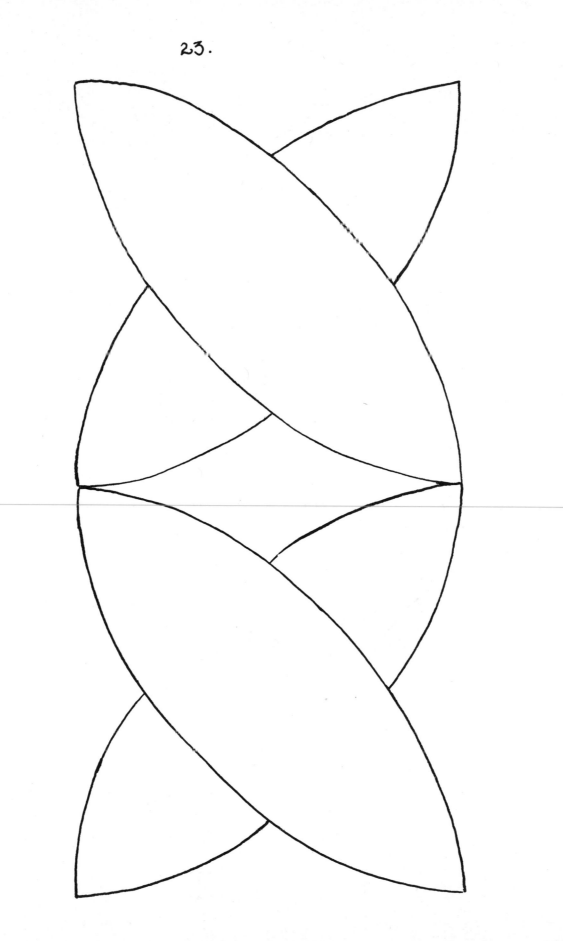

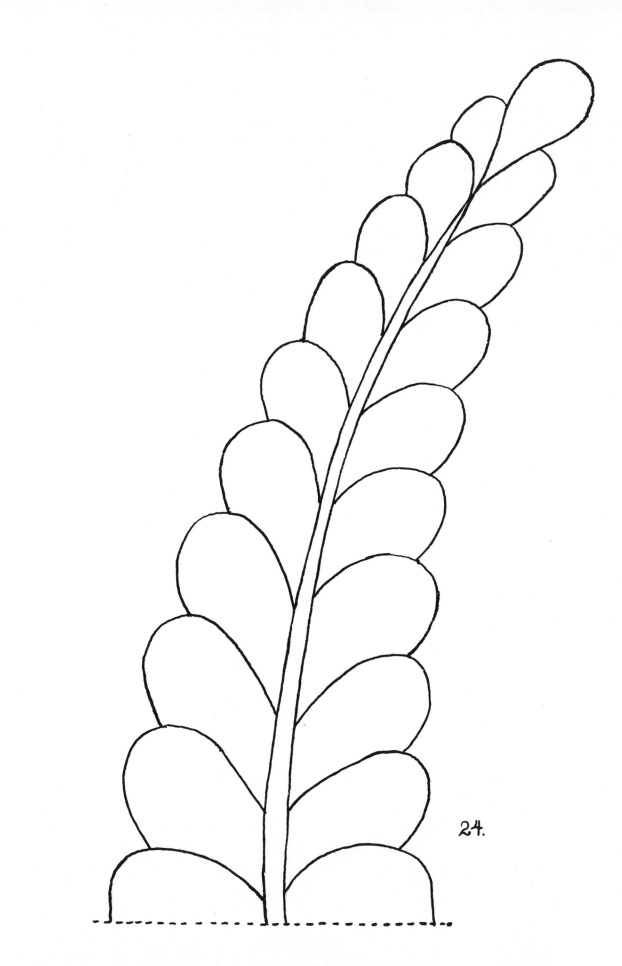

24.

Index

* denotes original pattern by the author.